The Science of Training – Soccer

Physical training is a key part of preparing to play soccer (football) at any level, but organising a genuinely effective training programme requires both an understanding of the physiological principles involved and a practical knowledge of the demands of the game. Bridging theory and practice, this book explains the design of scientifically sound fitness programmes for football.

Includes:

- planning seasonal training to peak at the right time
- training for strength, speed, aerobic and anaerobic fitness
- designing appropriate sessions for training and rehabilitation
- best methods for recovery from exercise and reducing injury risk
- preparation for play in different environmental conditions
- evaluating the effectiveness of training programmes
- diet, sleep, lifestyle, young players and long-term development.

Clear explanations of the physiological concepts and sport science research evidence are given throughout, and the book contains many examples to illustrate the training principles in practice. This is an essential text for students of the game and a valuable resource for coaches, physical trainers and sport scientists working in soccer (football).

Thomas Reilly is Professor of Sports Science and Director of the Research Institute for Sport and Exercise Sciences at Liverpool John Moores University. He is President of the World Commission of Science and Sports, and Chair of the International Steering Group on Science and Football.

The Science of Training – Soccer

A scientific approach to developing strength, speed and endurance

Thomas Reilly

 Routledge
Taylor & Francis Group

LONDON AND NEW YORK

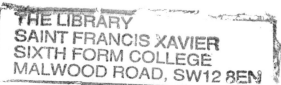

First published 2007
by Routledge
2 Park Square, Milton Park, Abingdon, Oxon OX14 4RN

Simultaneously published in the USA and Canada
by Routledge
270 Madison Ave, New York, NY 10016

*Routledge is an imprint of the Taylor & Francis Group,
an informa business*

© 2007 Thomas Reilly

Typeset in Goudy by
Newgen Imaging Systems (P) Ltd, Chennai, India
Printed and bound in Great Britain by
The Cromwell Press, Trowbridge, Wiltshire

British Library Cataloguing in Publication Data
A catalogue record for this book is available
from the British Library

Library of Congress Cataloging in Publication Data
Reilly, Thomas, 1941–
    Science of training – soccer: a scientific approach to developing
strength, speed and endurance / Thomas Reilly.
        p. cm.
    Includes bibliographical references and index.
    1. Soccer – Traning. 2. Soccer – Physiological aspects. I. Title.

GV943.9.T7R45 2006
613.7′11–dc22   2006009640

ISBN10: 0–415–38446–X (hbk)
ISBN10: 0–415–38447–8 (pbk)
ISBN10: 0–203–96666–X (ebk)

ISBN13: 978–0–415–38446–9 (hbk)
ISBN13: 978–0–415–38447–6 (pbk)
ISBN13: 978–0–203–96666–2 (ebk)

Contents

Figures

Tables

Preface

The importance of training as necessary preparation for playing soccer is now underlined at all levels of the game. The top players gain an edge to their performances as a result of the structured training procedures they undergo. Recreational players too benefit from training, being able to play the game more safely due to their improvements in fitness and game skills. Whilst playing and practising games skills play a large part in preparing for match-play, these are not enough on their own without a formal programme of fitness work. It was the need to provide a theoretical framework for soccer training that motivated the writing of this book.

The application of scientific principles to training for soccer calls for a bridge between theory and practice. The fact that fitness for games embraces many components and many concepts makes the design of training programmes for soccer players quite complex. It is essential that practitioners understand training principles so that they are able to intervene when things go wrong, when plans are disrupted and performances are under par. There are therefore no universal formulae for fitness but rather trainers must have an understanding of the adaptation processes that accompany the various forms of training. Where possible the fitness work can be integrated into games drills to impact directly on practice, ensure validity and economise on players' time.

The fitness training of soccer (football) players is the subject of this text. Its main purpose is to provide a scientific basis for the design of fitness programmes for the game. In the soccer profession there is a need for a scientific approach to training which is currently being recognised by professionals in the field and relevant governing bodies worldwide. Professional development programmes for coaches and physical trainers extend the likely interest beyond the traditional physical education and sports science communities. What is missing up to now is an evidence-based book on which practitioners can rely and which provides readers with a theoretical framework for the correct training practices to be used. This proposed book provides information on how to train, what to do and when to do it, as well as the reasons for doing it in the ways prescribed.

The content of this book should be relevant to all those concerned with closing the gap between theory and practice and effecting a link between science and soccer. There are expanding research programmes within sports science that are focused on soccer, whilst practice can also benefit from the many research investigations that inform the theory of training. More and more, the results of these research findings are being translated by applied sports scientists and are being adopted by practitioners. In some instances practitioners need to be cautious before taking up practices that become fashionable in advance of any scientific evidence for their value.

Physical trainers and coaches should have an interest in the content of the book. Those sports scientists operating in a soccer context will have a primary attraction for the material that is covered. The range of training modes described and the illustration of major practices will be relevant to those working with youths as well as with amateur and professional teams both males and females. The material is also geared towards students of sports science and science and soccer, as well as individuals working towards acquiring coaching qualifications.

In order to cater for this range of readers, the text embraces the training options that are available and outlines their physiological basis. There is a progression from an outline of training principles to their expression in targeting specific fitness components. Specific examples of training sessions are described where appropriate. Environmental factors and lifestyle are also considered and placed in perspective. In these ways a holistic view of the training process and means for its evaluation are presented in a novel and original manner.

An explanation of training principles is provided at the outset. There is guidance on planning the annual programme, conducting the pre-season training, avoiding overtraining at key times in the seasonal calendar, accelerating recovery from strenuous exercise and reducing injury risk. Separate chapters cover different physiological and performance aspects, including strength and power, weight-training, aerobic and anaerobic training, and alternative training methods applicable to a soccer context. Attention is directed also to warming up, cooling down and coping with different environmental conditions. Nutrition, diet, sleep and lifestyle are deemed essential elements in complementing physical conditioning in the systematic preparation of players to perform at their best in competition.

The contents include details of training sessions and the rationale for their design. Evidence from the scientific literature is used to support the sessions that are illustrated. Scientific arguments are presented where appropriate. The readership must have an understanding of the game, an interest in sports science and some knowledge and experience in physical training or coaching to gain optimal benefit from the text.

Acknowledgements

This text is the result of many years of listening to experts, observing training practices, reading relevant literature and conducting research where needed. There are many people to whom I have listened and learnt from in the soccer world and in the sports science community, too numerous to mention. I am indebted to colleagues at the Research Institute for Sport and Exercise Sciences at Liverpool John Moores University who have supported the developments in 'science and football' over the years, culminating in the Science and Football programmes offered at BSc, MSc, MRes, MPhil and PhD levels. Many students and co-workers from outside the institution as well as within it have contributed to the evidence-base on which the book is written. Thanks are due to Zoe Miveld for wordprocessing the contents and manipulating the illustrations in electronic form.

Chapter 1

The training process

Introduction

Everybody concerned with the game of association soccer (football) realises that training is a necessary part of preparing for competition. Playing soccer itself is only one part of that preparation. There is a requirement to be fit to play, to work on correcting physical deficiencies and enhance individual strengths.

The basic purpose of training is to improve human capabilities in all their manifestations. These capabilities are characterised in physical, physiological, psychomotor and psychological attributes. Their maximal expression, for example in fitness assessments, comprises limits to human performance, and training programmes must therefore be designed to raise these functional limits. The player may be deemed to be adequately fit when he or she has the capabilities to meet the demands of match-play in all its aspects (Figure 1.1). Further improvements in fitness will enable the player to operate at an even higher level of performance and match tempo.

The ideal level of fitness is arguably never achieved. Athletes always strive to improve, to push their limits as far upwards as possible. As soccer makes demands on the majority of the body's physiological systems, fitness for the game includes many factors besides competence in game skills and tactical awareness. A key aim in fitness for soccer is to enhance or maintain fitness in areas of strength while correcting weaknesses. In this way the goal of securing an optimal combination of fitness measures can be realised.

The process of training takes place in a dynamic context where short-term goals may change, often on an irregular or unanticipated basis. At the early stages the immediate aim may be to become fit enough to train more intensively, the more strenuous preparation later being orientated towards match-play. This situation may apply after a long recess or absence through injury. During the rehabilitation period a systematic programme of exercise is first needed before the individual can train again with the ball. The recovery process entails recurring cycles in which training is stepped up on a planned basis until the individual is ready to be integrated into team training.

If vigorous exercise is undertaken too early in the normal training process, the player may be unable to cope and might even incur injury. As a result he or

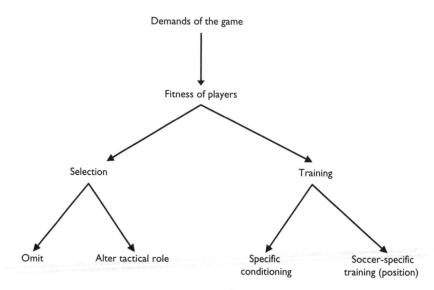

Figure 1.1 How demands of the game and the capabilities of players are related.

Source: Reprinted with permission, from Reilly, 2005 (http://www.tandf.co.uk/journal/titles/02640414. asp).

she regresses rather than improves. Even a well-trained individual may be overloaded too far and eventually succumb to injury if there is insufficient time for recovery between strenuous training sessions. The key to effective training is to experience the appropriate training stimulus at the right time. Some of the principles in doing so are now outlined.

Fundamental concepts

A basic principle of training is that the biological system to be affected is overloaded. The training stimulus or stress presented is greater than that which the individual is normally accustomed to. Otherwise there is no requirement for the body to adapt and force the occurrence of this adaptation process. Adaptation entails functional changes in the skeletal muscles and other tissues that have been engaged in exercise. At molecular level the exercise stimulus switches on signal transduction processes that activate intracellular responses. Genes carry the genetic information encoded in DNA to build proteins and mRNA for several metabolic genes are acutely elevated after a single bout of exercise (Hawley *et al.*, 2006). Alterations in ultrastructure occur concomitantly with recovering from the session inducing overload (see Table 1.1).

As physiological adaptation takes place, the training stimulus is more easily tolerated. For fitness to improve further, the training stimulus must be raised to a new level for a renewal of the overload principle. It is clear therefore that the training process is progressive and goes through a spiral of

Table 1.1 Three key principles of training theory

Overload	The training stimulus presented is greater than the body has been accustomed to handle
Reversibility	Adaptations are gradually lost when training ceases or falls below a maintenance threshold
Specificity	Adaptation occurs only in the tissues and systems that are overloaded during training

Table 1.2 Muscle fibre types and their main characteristics

	Type I	Type IIa	Type IIb
Fibres per motor unit	10–180	300–800	300–800
Diameter of motorneurone	Small	Large	Large
Nerve conduction velocity	Slow	Fast	Fast
Motor unit force	Small	Large	Large
Contraction time (ms)	110	50	50
Type of myosin ATPase	Slow	Fast	Fast
Oxidative capacity	High	Moderate	Low
Glycolytic capacity	Low	High	High

overload – fatigue – recovery – adaptation. If the training is progressed too quickly, 'overtraining' may be the result. This state is one in which performance falls rather than continues to improve. It can also be induced by training too much at any stage.

The concept of progressive overload was accepted from the time of the ancient Olympic Games. The fabled Milo of Croton gained his strength by regularly lifting a growing calf over his head each day. The improvement in fitness over time is not a linear process. The greatest improvements in fitness accrue during the early stages of a fitness training programme. Gains become increasingly difficult to obtain as the tissues approach their theoretical limit of adaptability.

The law of disuse indicates that the fitness of the organism deteriorates if it is not regularly subjected to load. Gains in fitness are reversed if the training stimulus is too low, if the athlete has incurred injury or training is abandoned during the off-season period. Gradually the physiological adaptations acquired through strenuous training are lost as 'detraining' sets in, although the rate of loss may be less than that at which gains were acquired. Without exercise skeletal muscles atrophy and the bones of the skeleton lose mineral content and become weakened. Some physical activity during detraining and recovery from injury helps to reduce the fall in fitness level and eases the later return to fitness training.

The principle of specificity suggests that training effects are limited to the pattern of muscular involvement in the conditioning exercises that are used. Different types of motor units exist within skeletal muscle so that a given type of exercise recruits a specific combination of motor units best suited to the task in hand (see Table 1.2). Training programmes for soccer should, whenever possible, be related to the demands of the game. In some instances training can be designed for players to work 'with the ball'. In other instances, for example in training the strength of the hamstrings or adductor muscle groups, it is necessary to isolate the muscles for specific training.

The principles of overload, reversibility and specificity contain a framework for designing and regulating training programmes. Their operation at a generic level provides an understanding of how continuous adaptation is achieved. At the outset individuals will differ in their capabilities due to genetic factors. They will also vary in the extent to which these capabilities can be improved in training. The trainer's quandary is how to tread the thin line separating optimum physiological accommodation from unwanted harmful overload and a failure to adapt.

The training stimulus

The effects of training depend on the physiological stimulus provided by the exercise undertaken. The dimensions of exercise are its intensity, its duration and its frequency. A consideration relevant to these factors is the type of exercise performed.

The intensity of training is sometimes referred to as its quality. It may be quantified in physiological terms, depending on the type of training. Aerobic training may be expressed as a percent of maximal oxygen uptake or as a percent of maximal heart rate. Alternatively it may be characterised as below, corresponding to, or exceeding the 'anaerobic threshold'. The rating of perceived exertion (see Figure 1.2) is a subjective means of indicating the severity of exercise. The lactate accumulating in the blood provides an index of the intensity of 'speed – endurance' training. For strength training the intensity may be gleaned from the %X-RM, that is the percent of the maximum load (repetition maximum or RM) that can be lifted x times.

The duration of training is expressed in minutes, especially appropriate when the exercise is continuous. Equivalent alternatives would include the overall work done or the distance run. Intermittent exercise is best broken down into exercise to rest ratios and number (and duration) of repetitions. The length of the intermissions between sets of repetitions should also be prescribed. For example, a session of weight-training may include 3 sets of 6 repetitions of 6-RM (100%) with 3 min between sets whilst an interval training session might be 6-times 600 m with 3 min in between each run.

The frequency of training refers to how many separate training sessions are undertaken each week. These may include sessions twice-a-day at certain parts of the competitive season, especially during the pre-season period. Fewer sessions would be expected at times when the competitive calendar is congested with fixtures.

These training dimensions are not entirely independent as they interact with each other. Intensive training cannot be sustained for as long as say skills training at relatively low intensity. Low-intensity work promotes a preferential

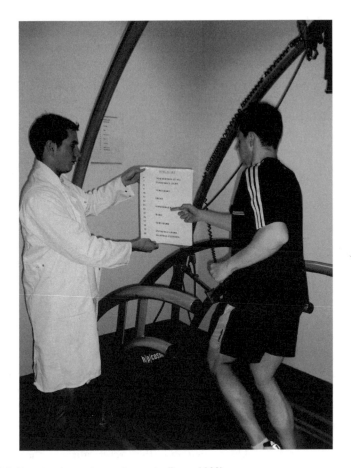

Figure 1.2 Perceived exertion rating scale (Borg, 1982).

use of fat rather than carbohydrate and can therefore have a role to play in implementing a weight-control programme in conjunction with a dietary regimen. High-intensity training can make demands on the body's energy systems and on its connective tissues, and so activity needs to be varied on consecutive days to allow these systems to recover.

Altering the type of exercise can permit the stressed areas of the body to be rested while other areas are overloaded. An example is where speed – endurance running on one day is followed by training in water or deep-water running on the next day. Similarly a morning session may consist of conventional soccer skills and training drills with the ball whilst the afternoon session might engage trunk and upper-body muscles in strength-training. Players with lower-limb injuries may continue to train the upper body, and maintain aerobic fitness by use of cycle ergometry or exercises in water. In these ways a reversal of fitness is prevented while recovery processes are taking place.

Muscles in movements

Movement and actions in soccer are executed by means of the body's musculoskeletal system. The main function of skeletal muscle is to control the motion of body segments by way of a series of contractions and relaxations. These activities are regulated and co-ordinated by the nervous system. Voluntary activity is controlled by the motor cortex in the brain, but information about movement is co-ordinated in the cerebellum whilst neural afferents from within the muscle spindles provide details about changes in the length of skeletal muscle fibres.

Each muscle has its own nerve and blood supply which extends to individual cells that are known as muscle fibres. The muscle is wrapped in an outer layer of connective tissue, the epimysium, but within it there are bundles of fibres organised in fascicles and surrounded by connective tissue referred to as the perimysium. The connective tissue around each muscle fibre is known as the endomysium, beneath which is a thin membrane called the sarcolemna. Each muscle fibre contains several hundred to several thousand myofibrils that consist of long strands of smaller subunits called sarcomeres. The sarcomeres are connected at their ends by Z discs which appear as dark zones on a light microscope. There are two main protein rods or filaments that constitute the contractile machinery of muscle: the thicker filament is made of myosin and is located towards the centre of the sarcomere whereas the thinner actin filament overlays the end portion of myosin and extends to the Z disc on each side of it. The connections between the actin filaments joining at the Z disc are formed by another protein α-actinin. Desmin links the Z-discs of adjacent myofibrils and keeps the Z-discs in register. Other protein molecules that help to maintain the architecture of the sarcomere include titin and nebulin.

There are various ways in which a muscle contracts. Tension is generated by the formation of cross-bridges between the two protein filaments, actin and myosin. The individual muscle sarcomere is shortened by the attachment of actin to myosin, pulling the former towards the centre of the unit, an event which is repeated along the entire length of the muscle fibre. The way contraction occurs is known as the 'sliding filament theory' and is initiated when an action potential is generated in the muscle fibre. The contractile system is activated by the release of calcium from the sarcoplasmic reticulum across the sarcolemna or thin membrane surrounding the muscle fibre. Its entry frees the myosin heads from inhibition by another protein troponin, lifting the protein tropomyosin off the active sites on the actin filament and allowing actin to become attached to the myosin head. The sliding of actin on the thicker myosin rod is likened to successive strokes of an oar on water. The myosin heads contain ATPase, enabling the myosin molecule to bind with adenosine triphosphate (ATP) for muscle contraction to occur. Relaxation occurs with a reversal of these events as calcium is pumped back into the sarcoplasmic reticulum and the deactivation of troponin and tropomyosin once again blocks the connection of myosin heads and actin binding sites. This reversal process also requires use of ATP and is facilitated by magnesium (Figure 1.3).

The myosin molecule plays an important role in force generation. Each molecule contains two globular heads and a long tail: the globular heads contain the key ATPase enzymes and each molecule comprises two heavy chains (HC) and four light chains (LC). The force generated and the power produced by muscle cells depend on the structure and composition of the myosin HC. Different HC and LC isoforms have been identified; these are proteins that share the same basic chemical composition but which display different properties due to a difference in

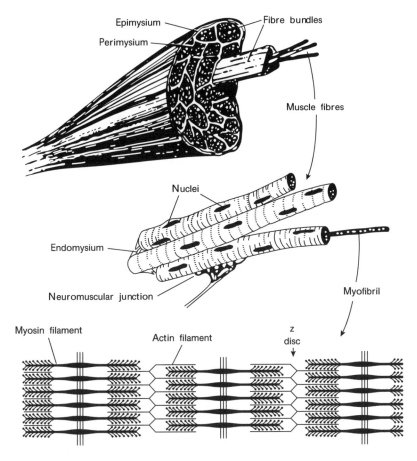

Figure 1.3 The structures involved in muscle contraction (from Reilly, 1981).

the relative positions of atoms within the molecules. Fibres that contain only HC-1 are labelled Type I whereas those that contain only HC-2A or HC-2B are labelled Type IIA and Type IIB, respectively. Fibres may contain a mixture of different heavy chains, frequently observed after training or injury. These isoforms are in rough correspondence to the fibre types summarised in Table 1.2 and classified according to their twitch characteristics (Staron and Pette, 1993).

A muscle acts isometrically when tension is generated but there is no overall change in its length. Examples in soccer include the action of trunk muscles to stabilise the body when making a tackle or the action of the muscles of the standing leg during kicking. A concentric contraction occurs when the muscle shortens, as occurs in the quadriceps when kicking a ball. An eccentric action refers to a stretch of the muscle's length while resisting the tension that is being developed: examples are the action of the hamstrings in slowing down limb movement when a ball is being kicked. The fact that a muscle can be increased in length as well as shorten indicates it has elastic as well as contractile elements, which lie in series and in parallel in the muscle and its musculotendinous unit. Each of these types of contraction must be considered relevant to the design of training programmes.

Another relevant consideration is the force–velocity characteristic of muscle. The force generated is a function of the tension developed within the muscle and is related to its cross-sectional area. Force is greater under isometric conditions than when the muscle acts concentrically and decreases as the velocity of contraction increases. Force increases during eccentric contractions beyond maximum isometric tension until there is no overlap between actin and myosin filaments for active tension to be developed (Figure 1.4). Eccentric contractions are economical in energy utilisation due to the contribution to tension of so-called parallel–elastic components that supplement the series–elastic elements of the actin–myosin complex. The force is greater when concentric action follows an eccentric contraction in a stretch-shortening cycle such as occurs in a semi-squat motion or counter-movement prior to a jump. Energy generated in muscle lengthening is stored in the cell's elastic elements and released in the subsequent shortening of the muscle. The result is a potentiation of the force in the concentric part of the force–velocity curve, reflected in a shift upwards in the right section of the curve shown in Figure 1.4.

Skeletal muscle represents 40–50% of the body's overall weight, and is a greater proportion than this figure in professional male soccer players. Female players have less skeletal muscle mass and relatively more body fat than their male counterparts. With successive years of conditioning and match-play the muscles of the male players undergo hypertrophy and increase in size, the cross-sectional area increasing due to enlargement of muscle fibre diameter rather than an increase in the number of fibres. The sex hormone testosterone has a role to play in the hypertrophy of muscle, accentuating the differences between the sexes. The muscular development of soccer players is reflected in physique or somatotype. The physique of international soccer players is expressed in the

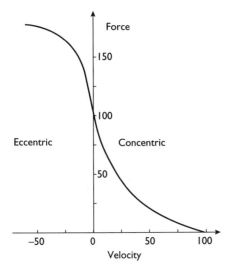

Figure 1.4 The force–velocity relationship of muscle under eccentric, isometric and concentric conditions.

Source: Reprinted with permission, from Klausen, 1990, p. 45.

classical dimensions of endomorphy (roundness), mesomorphy (muscularity) and ectomorphy (linearity). Median values for the classical somatotype were 4.0 for each of the three components. Mean values for Copa America participants were 2.2–5.4–2.2, indicating a tendency towards leanness and a muscular physique in these international players (Rienzi *et al.*, 2000). Given the fitness needs of soccer players for the game, muscular development tends to be more pronounced in the thigh and calf compared to the upper body.

Neuromuscular factors

Skeletal muscle is supplied with nerves, organised within a highly complex system. The central nervous system accommodates sensory information transmitted via afferent pathways from muscles, tendons and joints as well as efferent pathways to the muscles. A single α-motorneurone supplies a number of muscle fibres scattered throughout the muscle, these fibres forming a motor unit. A motorneurone when fired produces a synchronous electrical discharge through all its axonal branches, causing all the muscle fibres innervated to contract. Muscles that are employed in precise control of fine movements tend to have a small number of fibres per motor unit whereas weight-bearing muscles have a relatively large number of motor units and many fibres per unit.

Neurons are the basic units of the nervous system and communicate with each other across synapses. The synaptic connection at which an axon branch of the motorneurone meets the muscle cell is known as the neuromuscular junction. Nerve impulses originating in the motorneurone reach the point of axon termination causing an influx of calcium through voltage sensitive channels. Acetylcholine stored in presynaptic vesicles is released into the postsynaptic membrane, along with the other substances, the release being stimulated by external calcium and depressed by magnesium. The resultant effect is that a muscle action potential is spread through the sarcolemma, causing excitation to be coupled with contraction as the acto-myosin complex is activated. The elctromyographic activity associated with these physiological processes can be registered from surface electrodes placed on the skin overlying the skeletal muscles engaged. In this way insights have been gained into the pattern of muscle engagement in soccer skills such as different styles of kicking the ball (McCrudden and Reilly, 1993).

The motor units that are recruited for exercise are determined by the force demanded rather than the velocity of action. Low-threshold units that are responsive to a minimal amount of stimulation are recruited when the exercise is at a low intensity, these units activating the slow-twitch muscle fibres. More force is generated when more muscle fibres are recruited and so at the more strenuous exercise loads, the fast-twitch fibres are engaged. For a maximal training stimulus as associated with heavy exercise, all motor units must be recruited.

Energy systems

Metabolism refers to the production of energy within the body. Playing soccer raises the metabolic rate according to the pace of the game. Energy can be produced from aerobic or anaerobic sources, and may be fuelled by different substrates. The immediately available substrates within the muscle cells are high energy phosphates. Adenosine triphosphate (ATP) is necessary for the muscles to contract. The splitting of this compound yields the energy for the contraction but its stores are limited to supporting only a short sprint. As these stores would be depleted within a few seconds they must be continually restored for exercise to be maintained.

The next available source of energy is creatine phosphate. Degradation of this substance occurs when sprints are repeated with incomplete recovery in between. The use of creatine as an ergogenic aid is designed to boost this system for repeated bouts of high-intensity exercise.

A minor contribution of anaerobic energy is due to degradation of adenosine diphosphate (ADP) to adenosine monophosphate (AMP). This activity is regulated by the enzyme AMP kinase. The AMP can be further broken down to inosine monophosphate (IMP) and ammonia (NH_3). These reactions occur primarily during very heavy exercise or towards the end of prolonged exercise.

Another source of energy is glycogen, the form in which carbohydrate is stored within the muscles and in the liver. When the exercise intensity is very high and sustained, as in a long sprint forward from defence to attack (or a track back to head off a counter-attack), muscle glycogen is broken down anaerobically. Lactic acid is produced as a by-product of this reaction and gradually diffuses into the blood. When production within the active muscles exceeds its clearance rate, lactate accumulates in the blood and is circulated throughout the body in increased concentration.

During sustained continuous exercise muscle glycogen may be broken down aerobically, that is in the presence of oxygen. Glycogen from liver stores can also contribute, mobilised as glucose in the circulation to enter the muscle cells where it is utilised, facilitated by the action of insulin. A diet high in carbohydrate is useful in boosting glycogen stores in preparation for a match. By combining training and diet in an appropriate manner, both liver and muscle glycogen depots can be increased above normal levels.

Aerobic metabolism is also supported by oxidation of lipids. There are some limited stores within muscle but this substrate is mobilised in the form of free fatty acids. Stores of fat are vast compared to depots of glycogen but the problem is more one of mobilisation rather than availability. It may take 30–45 min for triacyl-glycerol to become available from peripheral adipose tissue stores so that use of lipids increases as exercise is prolonged. Fat is a preferred source of fuel at low-intensity exercise, the high-intensity exercise being demanding on carbohydrate stores. Proteins are also used as an energy source during 90 min of exercise at an average work-rate equivalent to that of match-play, although its magnitude is likely to be only 2–3% of the total energy metabolism (Wagenmakers *et al.*, 1989).

Clearly aerobic metabolism is predominant and aerobic fitness is essential for exercise lasting 90 min. Whilst soccer is largely an aerobic sport, critical events during the game are dependent on anaerobic metabolism, examples including sprinting to win the ball or outrun an opponent and jumping to make contact with the ball in the air. Oxygen must be supplied continuously to the active muscles both during exercise and to aid the recovery process in between the hard bouts of exertion. The oxygen transport system embraces the lungs, the pumping power of the heart and the oxygen carrying capacity of the blood. The ability of the skeletal muscles to utilise the oxygen delivered to them is a function of endurance training, and is a limiting factor in the untrained individual. The adaptive responses of the heart include an increased cardiac output, mediated long-term by altered dimensions of the left ventricle. At the cellular level of skeletal muscle there is increased capillarisation and enlarged activity of aerobic enzymes.

Peaking

The objective in training is to improve the individual's capability to perform within the team. Improvement of individual fitness levels makes it easier for the coach to harmonise the team into an effective competitive unit. In individual sports such as athletics, swimming and cycling it is possible to organise the training programme so that fitness reaches its high point to coincide with major championships. Soccer is more complex in that performance must be maintained for the duration of the prevailing league competitions. It must also be sustained through each round of matches in knock-out competitions.

A soccer player's normal week will have a match at weekend. The week can be broken down into training for recovery from the previous match, strenuous training around mid-week, then tapering in preparation for the match at which a peak performance is anticipated. This cycle is repeated each typical week. The bi-modal shape to energy expenditure in training and match-play is reflected in the daily energy expenditure values illustrated in Figure 1.5.

This pattern is disrupted when players have two matches in one week, that is three in eight days. The more strenuous mid-week training, perhaps over three successive days, is replaced by a day's taper, a match and a recovery day. The quandary then is how to maintain fitness over this period without compromising performance in the games.

In an attempt to reach peak fitness the training load may burden individual players beyond their capabilities to adapt. In such circumstances the performance level of the player may decline rather than further improve. This condition is referred to as under-performance, over-reaching or overtraining syndrome. Overtraining reflects the individual's attempt to compensate for a drop in performance. This decline may be associated with incomplete recovery from illness or from a failure to recover from previous strenuous training. It may also result from inadequate nutrition. The increased effort in training becomes counterproductive and the athlete enters an underperformance spiral shown in Figure 1.6.

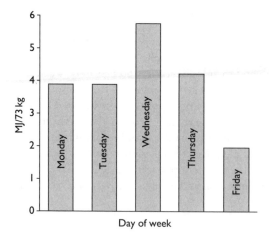

Figure 1.5 Energy expended by professional soccer players during training.

Source: Reprinted with permission, from Reilly and Thomas, 1979 (http://www.tandf.co.uk/journals/titles/00140139. asp).

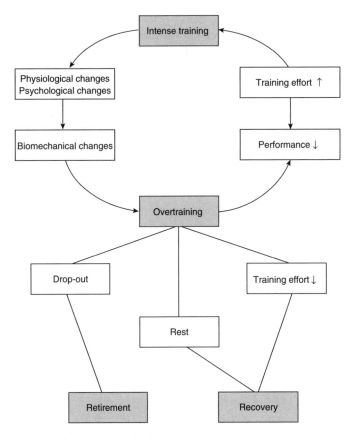

Figure 1.6 The vicious cycle of overtraining.

The process of biological adaptation to overload emphasises anabolic processes. Testosterone and insulin-like growth factor (IGF-1) play important roles in recovery from strenuous exercise and promoting protein synthesis. In the 'over-reaching' state catabolic processes dominate as cortisol levels rise and testosterone falls. The hypothalamic-pituitary-adrenocortical axis is disturbed, causing increased release of cortisol from the adrenal gland. This condition has been observed when matches are played in quick succession and at training camps where the training load has been too heavy. The cortisol–testosterone ratio has been promoted as a putative marker of 'overtraining'.

Reaching a peak requires preservation of an optimal training stimulus balanced by opportunity to recover. An essential step in the training process is the establishment of a firm fitness base upon which the more specific training can be built. An example is the necessity for strength work to precede plyometric training which emphasises stretch-shortening cycles of muscle action. Without the conditioning of muscle fibres and connective tissue, the muscles will be ill-prepared for the high tension levels to be experienced in plyometrics or stretch-shortening cycle exercises. Another example is the need for low-intensity aerobic exercise before the more intensive programme of aerobic-interval training is initiated.

There is no universal formula that prescribes the perfect path to peak fitness. The theory underpinning the alterations in training to engender peak fitness levels is based on empirical observations more than on experimented evidence, due largely to the many factors that must be harmonised and are too difficult to model fully in laboratory investigations.

Training theory

The most comprehensive models of training theory divide the programme into recurring cycles referred to as macrocycles. These are further divided into sub-harmonics, recurring schedules of shorter duration and termed microcycles. Their durations are not linked to any known biological rhythms but they represent a method of organising a training programme on a progressive basis throughout the year. In the original system devised by Matveyev (1981), microcycles were periods of 2 weeks or less, mesocycles varied in length from 2 weeks to 6 months and macrocycles lasted 6 months to 1 year. The training emphasis could be given the appropriate bias according to the need to reach a peak for chosen competitions.

It is assumed that there are overall goals to the competitive calendar to which the training is geared. The expectation is that fitness elements improve with successive macrocycles, each of which has its own intermediate goals. Within each microcycle there is variation between high-intensity and recovery training. Besides, the relative emphasis on fitness aspects changes as the individual makes progress towards the intermediate fitness goals that are set. For example, muscle strength and whole-body endurance may be prioritised early on whilst speed is given increasing emphasis later in the programme.

These rhythmic models are most appropriate for individual training, allowing re-entry of a player at a particular step after injury. They represent a conceptual approach to training rather than a rigidly set design. For soccer training the annual schedule may be divided into periods which differ in length and some of which are not precisely defined. A typical division is pre-season, early season, mid-season, late season and off-season (see Table 1.3). An alternative is that the competitive season is separated into first half and second half, especially in countries where there is a mid-season break.

Training for injury prevention

The effects of training are negated if injury is incurred. The team formation may be adversely affected if key individuals are injured. The fitness level of the injured player regresses although the decline can be reduced if exercise of some

Table 1.3 An outline of the annual phases of the soccer calendar

Phase	Activity	Weeks
Pre-season	General preparation – basic endurance, base conditioning	1–3
	Specific preparation Friendly matches	4–6
Early-season	Competition Extend training	7–20
Mid-season	Competition Consolidate fitness, boost training	21–33
Late-season	Competition Maintain fitness, quality training	34–46
Off-season	Recuperation – detraining, alternative activity	47–49
	Transition – cross-training, base conditioning	50–52

form can be performed. The rehabilitation programme is geared towards restoring the player to full training and eventually to match-play.

The occurrence of injury is attributable to both external and intrinsic factors. The former would include injury from an opponent's tackle, poor surface or colliding with another player. Intrinsic mechanisms might include poor flexibility causing hamstring tears, weak muscles on the left leg leading to injury on that limb or strong extensors relative to the strength of joint flexors. For example, if the eccentric strength of the hamstrings is below that of the quadriceps when they shorten, one of the hamstring muscles may tear when under stress. Some external factors are out of the player's control but targeted training can reduce injury risk due to intrinsic factors.

It has been shown that a systematic programme of flexibility reduced the incidence of injuries in Swedish professional players (Ekstrand, 1982). Similarly, flexibility as part of a systematic warm-up was associated with a reduction in acute injuries in games players (Reilly and Stirling, 1993). It was considered important that the flexibility exercises are specific to actions in the game and the common injuries that are observed.

Weak muscles may also be a cause of injury in the game due to its contact nature. Weaknesses identified in fitness assessments may be targeted for strength training. If players continue to compete without remedying a deficiency in muscle strength, that weakness is likely to let them down eventually.

Injury has also been linked to asymmetry in muscle strength. Both asymmetries between limbs and between flexors and extensors are implicated (Fowler and Reilly, 1993). The weaker of the limbs is the more likely to be injured. The appropriate flexor–extensor ratio varies with the joint concerned, the concentric strength of the agonists and the eccentric strength of the antagonists being relevant. This relationship is known as the dynamic control ratio.

Dvorak and colleagues (2000) considered various possibilities for reducing the rate of injuries in soccer, referring to perspectives of trainers, medical staff and players. The trainers' perspectives included structured training sessions, appropriate warm-up, appropriate ratio of training to games, and reduction of physical overload. The medical perspective included adequate rehabilitation, sufficient recovery time, sufficient regard for complaints and routine taping of ankle joints. The players' perspective embraced performance and lifestyle factors. The former included flexibility, skills, endurance and improvement of reactions. The latter included personal habits such as smoking and alcohol, nutrition and fair play. Other issues were related to implementation of the rules, observance of existing laws and improving them where necessary.

Overview

The training programme is progressive and as far as possible specific to the game. Further gains become increasingly difficult to acquire as fitness levels approach their peak. Fitness for soccer is complex in that it is made up of various components and if one is neglected, overall fitness for the game is adversely affected.

If the attempt to improve fitness is pushed too far, staleness or overtraining may be the undesirable result. A model of how this state may be induced was provided in Selye's (1974) stress theory (see Figure 1.7). It was thought that the body used its 'adaptation energy' in resisting the training stress, improving its capabilities in the process. Irrespective of the nature of the stress the body displays a 'general adaptation syndrome'. At first there is an alarm reaction. If the stress is continued without any abatement, the organism moves from the resistance and adaptation stages towards breakdown. Effectively it has run out of adaptation energy and succumbs to exhaustion. The theory was originally based on experiments with rats exposed to cold stress and offered no specific markers

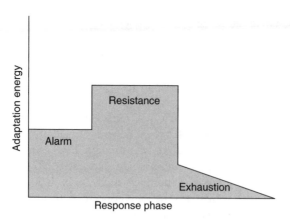

Figure 1.7 The stages of stress response in Selye's (1974) theory.

of overload that would be helpful in practice. Nevertheless, its abstract model appealed to many trainers and coaches whose experiences included observing these processes in players who lose form without obvious explanation.

Intrinsic mechanisms may explain many of the injuries incurred during training. Hard tackling can be limited or even excluded in training games and extra care should be taken in matching shoes worn to the training surfaces. The duration of training can be curtailed on the day after a hard match and on the day before competing in order to avoid fatigue due to 'overtraining'. Alternative forms of training which avoids ground impacts, such as deep-water training, can also be adopted while players recover from bruises and muscle soreness incurred during the game.

Injury-avoidance drills may also be adopted to improve players' agility in situations of high risk. The drills may include exercises over hurdles and around cones, acquisition of falling techniques and zig-zag runs performed at speed. The ability to fall correctly without getting injured is particularly important for the goalkeeper. Exercises that improve balance and aid proprioception, such as those used on the physiotherapist's wobble-board, are also relevant. Co-ordination of neural inputs, from muscle spindles which give information about rate of change in length, from Golgi tendon organs which provide information about the tension being transmitted, from joint receptors and the vestibular apparatus in the ears must be effective for dynamic balance to be controlled.

The annual cycle of training must be outlined at the very beginning, with key stages identified. Some flexibility must be maintained to allow for how all players cope with the training load and to accommodate alterations within the squad. A new player joining the team is unlikely to have the same training background and his/her training may have had a different emphasis to that of the teammates. It is essential to keep records of training activities so that successful elements can be repeated in subsequent years. Any elements that did not work can be analysed and failures avoided in future years. Adherence to fundamental principles rather than being swayed by transient training fads is the likely recipe for acquiring fitness.

References

Borg, G.A.V., 1982, Psychophysical bases of perceived exertion. *Medicine and Science in Sports and Exercise*, **14**, 377–381.

Dvorak, J., Junge, A., Chomiak, J., Graf-Baumann, T., Peterson, L., Rosch, D. and Hodgson, R., 2000, Risk factor analysis for injuries in soccer players: possibilities for a prevention programme. *American Journal of Sports Medicine*, **28**(5), 569–574.

Ekstrand, J., 1982, Soccer injuries and their prevention. Doctoral thesis, Linkoping University.

Fowler, N. and Reilly, T., 1993, Assessment of muscle strength asymmetry in soccer players. In: *Contemporary Ergonomics* (edited by E.J. Lovesey), London: Taylor and Francis, pp. 327–332.

Hawley, J.R., Tipton, K.D. and Millard-Stafford, M.L., 2006, Promoting training adaptations through nutritional interventions. *Journal of Sports Sciences*, **24**, 709–721.

Klausen, K., 1990, Strength and weight-training, In: *Physiology of Sports* (edited by T. Reilly, N. Secher, P. Snell and C. Williams), London: E and F.N. Spon, pp. 41–67.

McCrudden, M. and Reilly, T., 1993, A comparison of the punt and drop-kick. In: *Science and Football II* (edited by T. Reilly, J. Clarys and A. Stibbe), London: E and F.N. Spon, pp. 362–366.

Matveyev, L., 1981, *Fundamentals of Sports Training*. Moscow: Progress Publishers.

Reilly, T., 1981, *Sports Fitness and Sports Injuries*. London: Faber and Faber.

Reilly, T., 2005, An ergonomics model of the soccer training process. *Journal of Sports Sciences*, **23**, 561–572.

Reilly, T. and Stirling, A., 1993, Flexibility, warm-up and injuries in mature games players. In: *Kinanthropometry IV* (edited by W. Duquet and J.A.P. Day), London: E. and F.N. Spon, pp. 119–123.

Reilly, T. and Thomas, V., 1979, Estimated daily energy expenditures of professional association footballers. *Ergonomics*, **22**, 541–548.

Rienzi, E., Drust, B., Reilly, T., Carter, J.E.L. and Martin, A., 2000, Investigation of anthropometric and work-rate profiles of elite South American international soccer players. *Journal of Sports Medicine and Physical Fitness*, **40**, 162–169.

Selye, H., 1974, *Stress without Distress*. London: Corgi Books.

Staron, R.S. and Pette, D., 1993, The continuum of pure and hybrid myosin heavy chain-based fibre types in rat skeletal muscle. *Histochemistry*, **100**, 149–153.

Wagenmakers, A.J., Brooks, J.H., Conley, J.H., Reilly, T. and Edwards, R.H.T., 1989, Exercise-induced activation of the branched-chain 2-oxo acid dehydrogenase in human muscle. *European Journal of Applied Physiology*, **59**, 159–167.

Chapter 2

The soccer context

The measurement of performance

Soccer differs from individual sports in that there is no definitive index of each player's performance. The coach may consider that the individual played well if he/she has contributed to executing the overall game plan. Spectators are swayed by the more spectacular aspects of the performance such as a display of exquisite skill or the scoring of a goal. The players themselves will form their own impressions about how each one of them has done in the game. These are essentially subjective views, in contrast to sports such as track and field athletics, cycling, rowing and swimming. Rank order in finishing, time to complete the distance, and the distance jumped constitute precise measures of competitive performance.

The physical contribution of an individual player to the total team effort may be gauged by the overall distance covered in a game. The energy expended is directly related to the distance covered, irrespective of the speed of movement. The physiological demands over a fixed time period, such as 95 min (to include an allowance for added time), are reflected in the exercise intensities of the many different activities performed within a game. These range from all-out sprinting to casual walking.

The overall distance covered is a global measure of workrate, averaged over a whole game. It may be broken down into the thousand or so discrete actions of each individual player that occur in a match. These actions or activities can be classified according to type of movement, intensity (or quality), duration (or distance) and frequency. The activity may be viewed along a time-base so that exercise-to-rest ratios can be determined. These ratios may then be used in designing various elements of the players' training programmes.

The workrate profiles highlight that the exercise performed in a game varies in intensity and that the activity is intermittent. The player is under pressure when exercise is all-out and when the recovery period between short bursts of intense activity is short. For those reasons it can be useful also to focus on the periods when the intensity of exercise is high, usually when possession of the ball is being contested and the player is directly engaged in play.

Motion analysis provides an objective means of examining the performance of individual players from the viewpoint of workrate. Activities can be coded according to intensity of movement, the main categories being walking, jogging, cruising (hard but sub-maximal), sprinting, whilst other game-related activities include moving backwards or sideways, playing the ball, jumping, tackling and so on. The result is an overall profile detailing the frequent breaks in activity which can be aggregated to provide a comprehensive record of performance.

Motion analysis

The original method of motion analysis entailed a coded commentary on the activity of one player per game (Reilly and Thomas, 1976). The method was validated by comparison with video analysis of the same player over a complete game. The method requires the calibration of each individual's stride length for each intensity of motion. An alternative approach is to track the player's movement on a computerised model of the pitch, using changes in mathematical co-ordinates of the player's location to establish the distance moved and the velocity of motion. A review of methods of motion analysis and their uses has been published elsewhere (Reilly, 2003; Carling *et al.*, 2005).

The most comprehensive method of motion analysis is the multi-camera system now used by many clubs in the top European professional leagues. Six cameras are placed, three on each side of the pitch, usually located at a high vantage point in the stands. They are synchronised by means of a computer link and it is possible to collate behavioural information on all 22 players on the pitch. The data can provide relatively quick feedback for the coach and individual players, usually the day following the game. The feedback can include not only individual workrate profiles but also a collation of game events that explain patterns of play. The commercial service is relatively expensive and generally accessible to only the wealthier professional clubs.

The relative distances covered in different categories of activity for outfield players are illustrated in Figure 2.1. The overall distance covered consists of 24% walking, 36% jogging, 20% cruising or striding, 11% sprinting or all-out activity and 7% moving backwards. About 2% of the total distance covered is in possession of the ball. Moving sideways and diagonally are masked within these broad categories. These figures are fairly representative of contemporary play in the major national leagues in Europe, even though the tempo of the Premier League is now higher than prior to 1992 when it was established (Strudwick and Reilly, 2001).

A review of the distance covered during games (see Table 2.1) indicates that players now cover 10–14 km in a game. This figure varies with positional role, the greatest distance being covered by midfield players and the least among outfield players by the centre-backs. This effect of playing position is consistent over the last three decades (Figure 2.2). Full-backs or wing-backs must be versatile and depending on exact role may exhibit the work-rate profile of midfield players. A midfield player employed in a 'holding' role to protect the defence rather then participate in attack may not cover as much ground as team-mates in other midfield roles but may be more involved in tackling and contesting possession.

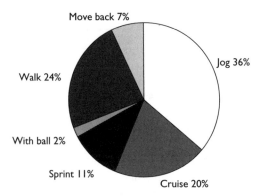

Figure 2.1 The relative distance covered by players in outfield positions according to categories of activity.

Table 2.1 Distance covered in match-play for contemporary top-level players

League	n	Distance (km)	Method	Reference
English Premier League	24	11.26 ± —	Video-film	Strudwick and Reilly (2001)
	6	10.10 ± 0.70	Video-film	Rienzi et al. (2000)
Italian league	18	10.86 ± 0.18	Video-film	Mohr et al. (2003)
Danish league	24	10.33 ± 0.26	Video-film	Mohr et al. (2003)

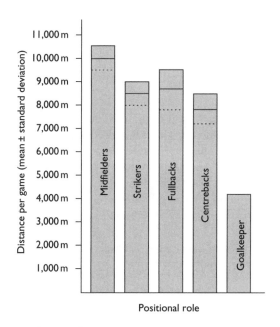

Figure 2.2 The overall distance covered per game according to positional role.

Source: Based on T. Reilly and V. Thomas, 'A motion-analysis of work-rate in different positional roles in professional football match-paly'. *Journal of Human Movement Studies*, **2**: 87–97 (1976).

The overall activity profile indicates that exercise is mostly at a sub-maximal intensity, yet high-intensity bouts of exercise are associated with crucial events in the game. On average players undertake a hard effort – either cruise or sprint – every 30 s but sprint all-out every 90 s. The high-intensity efforts are the most constant feature in the game, even though individual workrate profiles are relatively reproducible from game to game for individual players (Bangsbo, 1994).

The ratio of low-intensity to high-intensity (cruising and sprinting) efforts is about 5:2 in terms of distance covered (Reilly, 2003). When categories of activity are based on time, this ratio is about 7:1, emphasising the predominantly aerobic nature of competitive soccer. On average each outfield player has a short static rest pause of only 3 s every 2 min, though rest periods are longer and occur more frequently at lower levels of play where players are more reluctant to run to support a teammate in possession of the ball. Without the aerobic fitness to do so, a player will be unable to offer continual support for a colleague or keep up with play. Anaerobic fitness is important also, whether in possession of the ball or not, the timing of anaerobic efforts being a crucial factor in tactical ploys.

In women's soccer the game appears to be played at the same relative intensity but the average distance covered in a game is less than that observed for men (see Reilly, 2003). The difference reflects the fact that male athletes tend to have higher aerobic power ($\dot{V}O_{2max}$) values than females and run faster over relevant competitive distances, from 5 km to half-marathons. Nevertheless some international female midfield players cover distances that overlap the workrates of their male counterparts. It seems also that females playing in national teams take longer rest periods than men do, most notably before restarting the game after the ball goes out of play (Miyamura et al., 1997).

Fatigue in soccer

Fatigue may be defined as a decline in performance due to the necessity to continue activity. It is manifest in soccer by a decline in workrate towards the end of a game. Indeed the overall distance covered tends to be about 5% less in the second compared the first half of a game (Reilly, 2003). This drop in performance has been noted in Belgian, Danish, English and Italian players (see Table 2.2).

The fall in work-rate in the second half does not occur to a similar degree in all players. Reilly and Thomas (1976) reported an inverse relationship between

Table 2.2 Distances covered in 1st and 2nd halves

Belgian players	444 m more in 1st half (Van Gool et al., 1988)
English league players	Decline in workrate correlated with $\dot{V}O_{2\,max}$ (Reilly and Thomas, 1976)
Danish players	Distance in 1st half 5% >2nd half (Bangsbo et al., 1991)
Italian players	Distance in 1st half 160 m >2nd half (Mohr et al., 2003)

maximal oxygen uptake ($\dot{V}O_{2\,max}$) and the decrement of work-rate. There is a high correlation between aerobic measures such as $\dot{V}O_{2\,max}$ and the distance covered in a game and those players with a high level of aerobic fitness tend to last the game best. It seems that the benefits of a high aerobic fitness level are especially evident in the later stages of match-play.

Fatigue may also be experienced transiently during a game. Mohr *et al.* (2003) showed that after the 5-min period in which high-intensity running peaked during a game, performance was reduced by 12% for the next 5 min. The temporary fatigue was evident in players in the Danish League as well as in top professionals in the Italian League. Whilst the transient fatigue is produced by successive bouts of anaerobic exercise, the ability to recover quickly from the metabolic consequences relies largely on aerobic fitness.

Whilst training plays an important role in helping to sustain activity throughout a match, the amount of glycogen stored in the thigh muscles before the start of the game has a protective function against fatigue. In Swedish club players the muscle glycogen stores were reduced by training hard on the day preceding a competitive game and their performance was compared with a group that had rested instead of training. The players who had low glycogen content in their vastus lateralis muscle as a result were found to cover 25% less overall distance than the players who had rested (Figure 2.3).

Furthermore, those with low muscle glycogen stores pre-match covered half of the total distance walking and 15% at high intensity compared to 27% walking

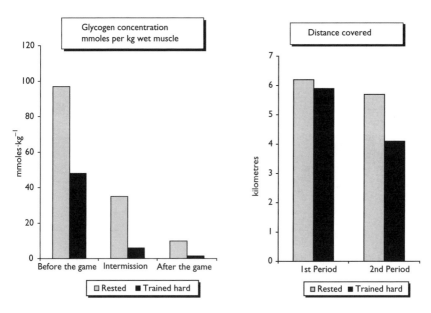

Figure 2.3 Muscle glycogen stores and performance in players who had rested or trained hard in the days prior to playing a match. The illustration is drawn from data reported by Saltin (1973).

and 24% at high intensity for those starting with high concentrations of muscle glycogen (Saltin, 1973). Clearly it is important to avoid draining muscle glycogen as a result of training too severely in the immediate build up to a competitive match. Muscle and liver glycogen depots may be boosted by use of a diet rich in carbohydrate in preparation for the game.

The muscles engaged in game-related activities tend to have lost a portion of their strength by the end of the game. Rahnama *et al.* (2003) employed an intermittent exercise protocol designed to simulate the exercise intensity of playing a match and monitored muscle performance at half-time and after 90 min of exercise. Assessment of muscle strength was done using isokinetic dynamometry in hamstrings and quadriceps at different angular velocities and different modes of contraction. Strength in both muscle groups had declined by an average of 13% by the end of the 90 min (Figure 2.4). In a separate study, there were also changes in electromyographic activity of four lower-limb muscles in response to standard runs conducted pre-exercise, at half-time and post-exercise, that confirmed the occurrence of muscle fatigue (Rahnama *et al.*, 2006). It was suggested that the decline in muscular strength could lead to an increased risk of injury. It is clear

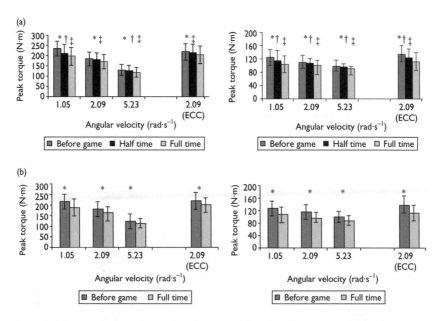

Figure 2.4 Peak torque is shown for dominant (a) and non-dominant (b) leg extensors (left) and flexors (right) at three angular velocities during concentric muscle actions pre-exercise, at half-time and post-exercise. Values for eccentric torque at one angular velocity are also shown.

Source: Reprinted with permission, from Rahnama et al., 2003 (http://www.tandf.co.uk/journals/titles/02640414.asp).

that a substitute coming onto the team in the final quarter of the game would be at an advantage over those playing from the start by having full energy stores and maximal strength capability. Indeed, this advantage was confirmed by Mohr *et al.* (2003) who observed higher workrates in the final 15 min of play in substitutes compared with players who lasted the full game.

In their study of impaired peak torque after 90 min of exercise corresponding to the exercise of a football game, Rahnama *et al.* (2003) reported a reduction in the dynamic control ratio, that is peak eccentric torque of hamstrings relative to peak concentric torque of the quadriceps. This change would leave the hamstring muscle group at increased injury risk in the later stages of the game. Trainers were advised to focus on the eccentric function of the hamstrings as well as the concentric function of the quadriceps in training sessions to ensure a good bilateral muscle balance over a whole range of playing skills. In a separate study, Gleeson *et al.* (1998) reported that after a 90-min simulation of a game by repetitive shuttle running at varying speeds, the electro-mechanical delay of the leg muscles and anterior tibio-femoral displacement (an index of joint laxity) were impaired. They concluded that players may be at increased risk of ligamentous injury towards the end of a game. Such impairments might explain why Hawkins *et al.* (2001) reported an increased injury incidence in the final quarter of a match than at other times.

A decline in performance can also be observed when matches are played in hot conditions. Performance is influenced both by a rise in core body temperature and a loss of body water due to sweating. When relative humidity is high, sweating becomes an ineffective physiological mechanism for losing heat to the environment; players typically cope by reducing the exercise intensity, playing at a slow pace and thereby decreasing the amount of heat generated by muscular activity. In order to reduce the effects of fluid loss, adequate hydration should be implemented before the game and at half-time, with drinks made available by the sideline where stoppages during the game provide an opportunity for fluid ingestion.

Players may lose up to 3 l of water or more in a game or in a lengthy training session. It is possible to schedule stops during training for ingestion of fluids. When training is performed in hot conditions, particularly in the pre-season period, having drinks available is important. In these circumstances players may drink 400–500 ml before starting and smaller amounts of 150 ml every 15 min. Energy drinks can help since inclusion of sodium can hasten absorption of fluid in the small intestine and provision of glucose may safeguard against development of hypoglycaemia.

The style of play can also influence the workrate. Rienzi *et al.* (2000) demonstrated that the distance covered by South American international players was about 1 km less than that by professionals in the English Premier League. The South Americans tended to emphasise controlling the game by retaining possession and raising the pace in a rhythmic fashion in contrast to the sustained higher pace of the English game. Whereas the total distance covered was less, the South American players covered marginally more distance at top speed than the

Premier League players, illustrating the more rhythmic aspect of their game. The team formation and the tactics used also influence workrate. A 'pressing' approach that emphasises attempts to dispossess the opposition is highly demanding of energy reserves. Similarly, a 'direct' strategy that quickly transfers the ball from defence into attack calls for high levels of aerobic capacity in its advocates.

Another way in which tactical factors influence activity in a game is evident when all behavioural events are examined. Rahnama *et al.* (2002) quantified all actions in a game with respect to their potential for causing injury to players. The events with the highest risk of injury were tackling and charging an opponent. These events were more pronounced in the first 15 min and in the last 15 min of the game. The opening period is the time that players seek to register an impression on opponents; in contrast, skills may be deteriorating as fatigue occurs towards the end of the game and tackles may be poorly executed.

'Mental fatigue' is reflected in lapses of concentration as a consequence of sustained physical effort. A consequence may be errors in decision-making that lead to a failure to take goal-scoring opportunities or alternatively open up goal-scoring chances for the opposition. It is often the case that play becomes more urgent as the game nears its closure, despite the decrease in the physical capabilities of the players. The fall in cognitive function may be attenuated by provision of fluid intermittently over 90 min, the best results being obtained when energy is included in the solution (Reilly and Lewis, 1985). Irrespective of the nature of the fatigue process, a team that is physiologically and tactically prepared to last a full 90 min of intense activity is more likely to be an effective unit.

Physiological responses to match-play

The ability to sustain prolonged exercise depends on a high maximal aerobic power ($\dot{V}O_{2\,max}$), but the upper limit at which continuous exercise can be maintained is influenced by the 'anaerobic threshold'. This point represents the relative metabolic load or percent $\dot{V}O_{2\,max}$ at which anaerobic metabolism makes a proportionately increasing contribution to energy expenditure during incremental exercise. It has been estimated that the average exercise intensity during soccer match-play corresponds to 75% $\dot{V}O_{2\,max}$ (Reilly, 1990), a figure that is close to the likely 'anaerobic threshold' of top soccer players. The threshold is typically indicated by the departure from linearity of carbon dioxide production ($\dot{V}CO_2$) or ventilation ($\dot{V}E$) with respect to oxygen consumption ($\dot{V}O_2$) as exercise is increased in an incremental manner. The 'ventilatory threshold' or Tvent refers to the departure of minute ventilation from linearity as oxygen consumption increases, and is close in correspondence to the increase in lactate concentration in the blood (Tlac). Diet and prior exercise can alter the relationship between the ventilatory and lactate thresholds so these two processes may be linked but not causally so. Furthermore, it is often difficult to identify the start of a disproportionate rise in lactate appearance in blood so that it is common practice to express running intensity as corresponding to a fixed lactate concentration, such as V−4 mM.

Both maximal oxygen uptake and 'anaerobic threshold' seem to be significantly correlated with distance covered in a soccer game. Reilly (2003) reviewed evidence of this correlation, confirming the need of a high aerobic fitness level in contemporary players, especially those in a midfield role. Bangsbo and Lindquist (1992) showed that the distance covered was also correlated with the $\dot{V}O_2$ corresponding to a blood lactate concentration of 3 mmol·l^{-1}. Both $\dot{V}O_{2\,max}$ and 'anaerobic threshold' are important to performance in distance running, and seem to be highly relevant also to competitive soccer.

The blood lactate concentration represents a balance between the production of lactate in the muscle, and its clearance by means of oxidation once it appears in the circulatory system. An effect of endurance training is to shift the lactate curve to the right (see Figure 2.5) whereas detraining or injury causes a shift to the left. It is thought that the effect of training is due more to improved clearance of lactate than to a decrease in its production.

The energy expenditure during match-play has been estimated to be about 6.3 MJ or 1,500 kcal (Reilly, 1997). The major metabolic route is aerobic glycolysis, anaerobic glycolysis constituting a relatively minor role. Fat metabolism comes increasingly into play with the duration of exercise. The increase in blood-borne non-esterified fatty acids through the later parts of the game corresponds with elevations in catecholamines which increase the mobilisation of fatty acids from adipose tissue stores. Endurance training improves the capability to utilise fat as a fuel for exercise, thereby sparing muscle glycogen and delaying

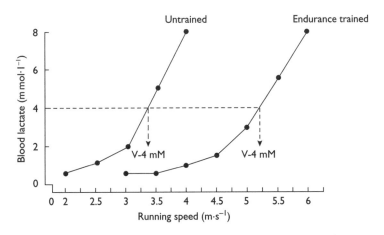

Figure 2.5 The effect of endurance training on the lactate response is illustrated by a shift of the curve to the right.

the onset of fatigue. There is a small contribution to energy production from protein sources, particularly branched chain amino acids, but it amounts to about 2–3% of total metabolism (Wagenmakers *et al.*, 1989).

Anaerobic glycolysis is reflected in an elevation in blood lactate concentration. Values are variable, depending on the activity in the period immediately preceding blood sampling. Ekblom (1986) reported progressively higher values from the fourth to the first division in the Swedish League. Elevated blood lactate values have also been attributed to person-to-person marking compared to a zone-coverage strategy (Gerisch *et al.*, 1988). Values tend to be higher in the first half compared to the second half, or at half-time compared to full-time, reflecting the decline in workrate and the decreased use of carbohydrates as fuel for exercise near to the end of the game (Reilly, 2003).

Game-related activities

The energy expended during a game is greater than that required merely for running the distance covered, largely because the extra demands of game skills add to the overall energy cost. The frequent accelerations and decelerations, angled runs and changes in direction, jumps to contest possession, make and avoid tackles all contribute to the added utilisation of energy. With over 1,000 breaks in activity during a game, there is a change in actions about every 5 s.

Dribbling the ball is an example of a skill that increases energy expenditure over and above that of running at the same speed. Reilly and Ball (1984) compared the physiological responses to dribbling a ball at four different speeds to responses to running at the same speeds. The added cost of dribbling was 5.2 kJ·min^{-1}, irrespective of the speed of movement. The extra energy is partly accounted for by changes in stride length in order to touch the ball, extra muscle activity to make contact with the ball and move it forward and the actions of synergistic and stabilising muscles to maintain balance.

Perceived exertion and blood lactate concentration are also elevated as a consequence of dribbling the ball. The increase in blood lactate becomes disproportionate at the higher running speeds. The 'lactate threshold' was estimated to occur at 10.7 km·h^{-1} while dribbling but not until a speed of 11.7 km·h^{-1} was reached in normal running. One interpretation of this finding is that the training stimulus is elevated for a given speed when exercise is performed with the ball.

Locomotion during a game also entails moving backwards and sideways; indeed these unorthodox movements may amount to 15% of the total distance covered. This percentage is higher in defenders, especially centre-backs who have to back up quickly under high kicks forward, or move sideways in jockeying for position to time a tackle when confronted by an attacking player in possession of the ball. The added physiological costs of these unorthodox directions of motion have been studied by getting subjects to run on a motor-driven treadmill at speeds of 5, 7 and 9 km·h^{-1}. Running normally was more economical than moving backwards or sideways, which were similar to each other (Reilly and Bowen, 1984). The extra energy cost

Table 2.3 Mean (±SD) for energy expended (kJ·min⁻¹) and ratings of exertion at three speeds and three directional modes of motion (*n* = 9)

Speed (km·h⁻¹)	Forwards	Backwards	Sideways
Energy expended			
5	37.0 ± 2.6	44.8 ± 6.1	46.6 ± 3.2
7	42.3 ± 1.7	53.4 ± 3.5	56.3 ± 6.1
9	50.6 ± 4.9	71.4 ± 7.0	71.0 ± 7.5
Perceived exertion			
5	6.7 ± 0.1	8.6 ± 2.0	8.7 ± 2.0
7	8.0 ± 1.4	11.2 ± 2.9	11.3 ± 3.2
9	10.2 ± 2.1	14.0 ± 2.0	13.8 ± 2.5

Source: Reproduced with permission of publisher from Reilly, T. and Bowen, T. Exertional costs of changes in directional modes of running. *Perceptual and Motor Skills*, 1984, **58**, 149–150. © Perceptual and Motor Skills 1984.

of the unorthodox modes of running increased disproportionately with the speed of running. Since moving backwards and sideways are not natural means of locomotion in humans, these activities must be trained if soccer players are to become effective in their use (Table 2.3).

Implications for training

The demands of match-play place a variety of physiological stresses on performance. In order to cope with these demands players must undertake training programmes which will improve their ability to meet the challenge posed by competition. The programme must include the appropriate combination of fitness factors and should be organised so that these factors are complementary.

The first characteristic of soccer is that exercise is intermittent with high-intensity, all-out efforts being called for on an unpredictable basis. A second characteristic is that the exercise pattern must be sustained over the full game. These factors mean that both anaerobic and aerobic training are relevant. The game includes rapid changes in direction and short quick movements which mean that agility training is also important.

Soccer players need to be strong to deal with the physical aspects of play. These include executing game skills such as tackling, holding off opponents and coping with their physical challenges. Muscular power is required for the more explosive actions such as jumping or accelerating past a marker. Strength training is also relevant for protection against injury as well as for coping with the more physical aspects of the game. Flexibility work must be included both as a warm-up in preparation for the more vigorous training later in the session and as an end in itself to facilitate range of joint motion.

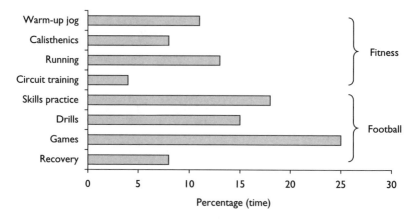

Figure 2.6 The relative time distribution of training according to different fitness components (data are derived from Reilly, 1979).

Many of these elements can sometimes be integrated within the training session which includes practice of game skills, rehearsal of tactical drills and games. A scheme for distributing training components across the training session is shown in Figure 2.6. The relative time allocated to each element is based on observations at a professional club in the top English League (Reilly, 1979) that are still relevant to contemporary play. It includes individual training which could be done as a group or separately and at an alternative time of the day.

Overview

Workrate during competitive soccer may be expressed as distance covered, which can be further broken down according to categories of activity. Players at a professional level cover 10–14 km in a game, typically with a fall-off in intensity towards the end. Aerobic metabolism is the main source of muscle activity and fatigue late in the game may be attributed to reduced stores of muscle glycogen. Aerobic fitness helps players to recover from the short bouts of intense activity when anaerobic metabolism predominates. Anaerobic activity is emphasised when there is direct involvement in the play, either when in possession of the ball or contesting possession. Training must therefore include aerobic and anaerobic components and due to the physical contact associated with the game strength training is also relevant. As movement is not always linear, players must be agile as well as fast, capable of reacting to game events and changing direction quickly. All-round fitness for the game requires that a variety of elements are included in the training programmes of players.

References

Bangsbo, J., 1994, The physiology of soccer: with special reference to intense intermittent exercise. *Acta Physiologica Scandinavica*, **150**, Suppl. 619.

Bangsbo, J. and Lindquist, F., 1992, Comparison of various exercise tests with endurance performance during soccer in professional players. *International Journal of Sports Medicine*, **13**, 125–132.

Bangsbo, J., Norregaard, L. and Thorso, F., 1991, Activity profile of competitive soccer. *Canadian Journal of Sport Sciences*, **16**, 110–116.

Carling, C., Williams, A.M. and Reilly, T., 2005, *A Handbook of Soccer Match Analysis*. London: Routledge.

Ekblom, B., 1986, Applied physiology of soccer. *Sports Medicine*, **3**, 50–60.

Gerisch, G., Rutemoller, E. and Weber, K., 1988, Sports medical measurements of performance in soccer. In: *Science and Football* (edited by T. Reilly, A. Lees, K. Davids and W.J. Murphy), London: E. and F.N. Spon, pp. 60–67.

Gleeson, N.P., Reilly, T., Mercer, T.H., Radowski, S. and Rees, D., 1998, Influence of acute endurance activity on leg neuromuscular and musculoskeletal performance. *Medicine and Science in Sports and Exercise*, **30**, 596–608.

Hawkins, R.D., Hulse, M.A., Wilkinson, C., Hodson, A. and Gibson, M., 2001, The association football medical research programme: an audit of injuries in professional football. *British Journal of Sports Medicine*, **35**, 43–47.

Miyamura, S., Seto, S. and Kobayashi, H., 1997, A time analysis of men's and women's soccer. In: *Science and Football III* (edited by T. Reilly, J. Bangsbo and M. Hughes), London: E. and F.N. Spon, pp. 251–257.

Mohr, M., Krustrup, P. and Bangsbo, J., 2003, Match performance of high-standard soccer players with special reference to development of fatigue. *Journal of Sports Sciences*, **21**, 519–528.

Rahnama, N., Reilly, T. and Lees, A., 2002, Injury risk associated with playing actions during competitive soccer. *British Journal of Sports Medicine*, **36**, 354–359.

Rahnama, N., Reilly, T., Lees, A. and Graham-Smith, P., 2003, Muscle fatigue induced by exercise simulating the work-rate of competitive soccer. *Journal of Sports Sciences*, **21**, 933–942.

Rahnama, N., Lees, A. and Reilly, T., 2006, Electromyography of selected lower-limb muscles fatigued by exercise at the intensity of soccer match-play. *Journal of Electromyography and Kinesiology*, **16**, 257–263.

Reilly, T., 1979, *What Research Tells the Coach about Soccer*. Reston, VA: AAHPERD.

Reilly, T., 1997, Energetics of high intensity exercise (soccer) with particular reference to fatigue. *Journal of Sports Sciences*, **15**, 257–263.

Reilly, T., 2003, Motion analysis and physiological demands. In: *Science and Soccer, 2nd edition* (edited by T. Reilly and A.M. Williams), London: Routledge, pp. 59–72.

Reilly, T. and Ball, D., 1984, The net physiological cost of dribbling a soccer ball. *Research Quarterly for Exercise and Sport*, **55**, 267–271.

Reilly, T. and Bowen, T., 1984, Exertional costs of changes in directional modes of running. *Perceptual and Motor Skills*, **58**, 49–50.

Reilly, T. and Lewis, W., 1985, Effects of carbohydrate feeding on mental functions during sustained exercise, In: *Ergonomics International '85* (edited by I.D. Brown, R. Goldsmith, K. Coombes and M.A. Sinclair), London: Taylor and Francis, pp. 700–702.

Reilly, T. and Thomas, V., 1976, A motion analysis of work-rate in different positional roles in professional football match-play. *Journal of Human Movement Studies*, **2**, 87–97.

Rienzi, E., Drust, B., Reilly, T., Carter, J.E.L. and Martin, A., 2000, Investigation of anthropometric and work-rate profiles of elite South American international players. *Journal of Sports Medicine and Physical Fitness*, **40**, 162–169.

Saltin, B., 1973, Metabolic fundamentals in exercise. *Medicine and Science in Sports*, **5**, 137–146.

Strudwick, T. and Reilly, T., 2001, Work-rate profiles of elite Premier League football players. *Insight: the F.A. Coaches Association Journal*, **4**(2), 28–29.

Van Gool, D., Van Gerven, D. and Boutmans, J., 1988, The physiological load imposed on soccer players during real match-play. In: *Science and Football* (edited by T. Reilly, A. Lees, K. Davids and W.J. Murphy), London: E and F.N. Spon, pp. 51–59.

Wagenmakers, A.J.M., Brookes, J.H., Conley, J.H., Reilly, T. and Edwards, R.H.T., 1989, Exercise-induced activities of the branched-chain 2-oxo acid dehydrogenase in human muscle. *European Journal of Applied Physiology*, **59**, 159–167.

Chapter 3

Warming up and warming down

The physiology of warming up

A formal warm up has not been a tradition in the soccer community. The practice of warming up prior to playing matches was introduced into English soccer once it was evident how opposing European teams organised themselves in the hour before kick-off. Their appearance in the pitch for 'callisthenics' and a 'kick-about' was a source of amusement at first, until it was realised that there was a distinct purpose to their behaviour. It seems strange now that a practice which had a long history in other sports, most notably in track and field athletics, took such a long time to become accepted into the culture of soccer. Nowadays all professional teams in the English Leagues and in the major footballing nations have a warm-up ritual prior to their matches. They also place importance in the conduct of warm-up exercises before undertaking the more strenuous parts of their training sessions.

Besides, there is a sound physiological rationale for warming up before exercise. Some of the main reasons for it are listed in Table 3.1. First, the term itself signifies that the objective is to raise body temperature so that performance potential is enhanced. As muscles use up energy in contracting, less than a quarter of the energy goes towards producing mechanical work, the remainder generating heat within the muscle cells. Muscle performance is improved as temperature rises, but only up to a point. An increase in body temperature of one degree [Celcius] is sufficient to get the maximum ergogenic effect on the active muscles (see Reilly and Waterhouse, 2005). The easiest means of generating the necessary internal heat is by running.

There is also a role for injury prevention within the warm-up regimen (Shellock and Prentice, 1985). In this respect the type of activity is important. Stretching the main muscles due to be active later, that is by producing so-called eccentric contractions, gains a transient increase in flexibility. This enhanced range of motion improves the capability of the muscle to yield under the antici-pated strain. Stretching the main thigh muscles is especially important before evening matches and in cold winter conditions. Particular attention is directed towards the hamstrings and hip adductor muscles. Tightness in these muscle

Table 3.1 Main reasons for warming up before a game

- Elevate body temperature
- Increase muscle temperature
- Reduce muscle tightness
- Decrease risk of injury
- 'Potentiate' neuromotor performance
- Rehearse game skills
- Raise arousal levels
- Familiarise with the environment

groups is often found in soccer players and is associated with a predisposition to injury (Ekstrand, 1994).

Injury prevention strategies are most effective when the warm-up is specific to the sport (Reilly and Stirling, 1993). This principle implies that the warm-up routines should include unorthodox running (backwards, sideways, agility runs with sharp turns) and game-specific motions such as jumping.

There are specific effects of the warm-up on the neuromotor system. Among the more obvious consequences are the likely psychological benefits of rehearsing well-practised skills such as controlling and passing the ball. There is also the 'potentiating effect' of stimulating the nervous system by means of brief but highly intense muscular efforts prior to competition. Post-tetanic potentiation refers to the phenomenon whereby the size and shape of a muscle twitch are affected by previous contractile activity: the effect is thought to decay after 10–15 min. This practice has come from track and field athletics, most notably the 'explosive events', whereby maximal stimulation of skeletal muscle about 15 min or so prior to the main event seems to benefit performance in the subsequent anaerobic exercise. Only a small number of such pre-event efforts is advocated; for example, 2–3 all-out 15–20 m sprints included in the body of the warm-up should be sufficient. The so-called 'fast-feet' drills do not provide the necessary forceful stimulus as these routines emphasise speed rather than force but they are nevertheless useful for preparation purposes.

It is important that the warm-up should be neither too long nor too intense overall. Otherwise, the regimen itself begins to draw on the body's energy stores rather than prime it for action. Unnecessarily reducing the body's glycogen reserves would start to negate the best laid training and nutritional preparations of the previous week. There is a balance to be struck between the 'arousal' and 'activation' benefits on the one hand and the induction of 'fatigue' on the other. It is feasible that all the requirements of a good warm-up can be incorporated into 20–25 min without being hurried.

The intensity and duration of the warm-up should be reduced when the weather is hot. Even at a temperature of 21.5°C, a 15-min warm-up run at 70% $\dot{V}O_{2\,max}$ for 15 min that raised rectal temperature to 38°C caused impairment in exercise performance. The performance measure was time to exhaustion on an intermittent exercise protocol that consisted of repeated runs at 90% $\dot{V}O_{2\,max}$ for 30 s separated by 30 s of static recovery. A passive heating procedure that produced a similar elevation in core temperature led to a more premature exhaustion (Gregson *et al.*, 2005).

A further benefit of warming up is the opportunity it offers to do work with the ball. In conjunction with this effect is the graded alert given to the nervous system by means of a smooth elevation in the arousing hormones adrenaline and noradrenaline. There is also a chance to get a feel for the playing surface and the likely competitive 'atmosphere'.

A final consideration is the timing of the warm-up so that its benefits are not lost before the game starts. Muscle and body temperature will remain elevated for some minutes after exercise is finished; body temperature might even continue to rise for 3–5 min or so since warm blood is still being circulated throughout the body. Players at this stage will gain advantage from the short recovery and the private respite for their final mental preparations.

Irrespective of the level of play, the warm-up routine has relevance (Figure 3.1). The routines of two different Premier League sides are illustrated in Tables 3.2 and 3.3. This protocol must be modified to suit the needs and capabilities of the amateur. Both physiotherapist and fitness trainer can be involved in planning the details and accommodating any individual requirements.

Figure 3.1 Professional teams warm-up using the width of the playing pitch.

Table 3.2 Example of a warm-up routine used at Premier League level

	Activities	Duration (minutes) or Distance (metres)
1	Ball-work in pairs (medium-length passing)	5 min
2	Jog easy across pitch Stretching	4 × 50 m
3	Jog (cruise) across pitch First – orthodox run 2nd – backwards (during return) 3rd – sideways/shuffle 4th – cross-steps (during return) Stretching	4 × 50 m
4	Jog (cruise) across pitch First – orthodox run 2nd – agility run back 3rd – orthodox run 4th – high knee pick-up on return Stretching	4 × 50 m
5	First – cruise across pitch 2nd – faster return 3rd – cruise across pitch 4th – all-out for middle 20 m Stretching	4 × 50 m
6	Ball-work in pairs (15–25 ball contacts per player per minute) Return to dressing room	5 min

The concept of flexibility

Flexibility exercises form an essential component of the warm-up, although the order in which exercises are done is a matter of choice. The manner in which flexibility exercises and game-related practices are integrated can be observed in the warm-up practices of professional clubs (Tables 3.2 and 3.3). Special attention should be given to exercises for the hamstrings, calf muscles, hip adductors, quadriceps, back and abdominal muscles. In the example in Table 3.3, flexibility exercises are done at the outset rather than distributed between the breaks from running in the other example. 'Flexibility' is also referred to as 'mobility', a term which usually applies more to a rehabilitation context. In such instances the range of motion is restricted due to the injury incurred and there is a focus on restoring the normal range.

In North America exercises used to improve flexibility were traditionally known as 'callisthenics'. This term refers more to a loosely structured programme of whole-body exercises than a targeted series of drills for specific local effects.

Table 3.3 Alternative warm-up routine used at Premier League
level

Activities	Duration (minutes) or Distance (metres)
1 Stretching exercise (knee-joint, trunk, hamstrings etc.)	5 min
2 Fast-feet drills 'on the spot' Stretching – individually (groin, lateral trunk flexion) Stretching – partner-assisted	3 min
3 Jog (2 × 5-m accelerations on return) Walk and stretch	2 × 50 m
4 Ball-work in pairs – one touch (or ball-work in small groups)	2 min
5 Speed drills – 10-m course (i) Run 3 m, decelerate and back, then run hard for ~6m (short quick strides)	
(ii) Sideways run along start line, then sprint forward	3 min
(iii) Players walk in line, peel off in turn for 10-m sprint back to start	
(iv) Jump twice at start, then sprint ~10 m	2 min
6 Formal ball-work Pass in triangles, pairs or juggle individually	2 min

Flexibility is joint-specific and this function is highly amenable to training effects. Some individuals may have inherited ligamentous laxity, which means that all of their joints are more supple than the norm. Possession of lax ligaments would facilitate a greater range of motion but constitute an increased risk of injury. This function therefore would be a disadvantage in soccer, although such laxity might be useful in sports such as gymnastics and ballet.

Flexibility for injury prevention

Muscles respond to strength training by means of adaptations in their contractile apparatus and in their connective tissue. The consequence can be overall stronger and more powerful muscles but with a loss of flexibility at the joint concerned due to muscle tightness. In particular, soccer players are susceptible to tightness in the hamstrings and adductor muscle groups, unless stretching these muscles is regularly practised.

Ekstrand (1994) provided evidence that muscle tightness in hamstrings and adductors led to an increased incidence of injury in these muscle groups

Table 3.4 Causes of injury in the Swedish leagues (% of total)

Player factors	
Joint instability	12
Muscle tightness	11
Inadequate rehabilitation	17
Non-training	2
Total	42
Non-player factors	
Equipment	17
Surface	24
Rules	12
Other factors	5
Total	100

Source: From Ekstrand, 1994.

(see Table 3.4). In a remarkable study that entailed an intervention into the training of the League clubs in Sweden, he showed that the problem of muscle tightness could be overcome. The teams that added a regimen of flexibility training to their typical programme were effective in reducing injuries to the hip extensors and adductors. The message was clear: attention to flexibility of hamstrings and adductors can help to reduce muscle injury.

The effect of the flexibility training used by the Swedish teams was a chronic adaptation to the habitual training regimen. The tissues as a whole are strengthened and stiffness at the joint is reduced. Proprioceptive mechanisms are also enhanced so there is a greater protection against sudden imbalance or strain.

There are also acute effects on flexibility, which explain the value of warming up. The effects observed within a single warm-up may persist for more than one day. Persistent effects require 3–4 weeks of regular training.

The importance of the right kind of warm-up was emphasised in a study by Reilly and Stirling (1993) of a variety of games players. The injury-prone players spent less time on technique work and on lower body exercises in warming up compared to the non-injured. The rehearsal of game actions within the pre-exercise regimen for mobilising the joints most at risk does seem to be important in protecting against injury.

Training methods

Methods of training flexibility can range from active exercises, static stretching, passive exercises, passive mobility methods (such as heat treatment and cycloid vibration massage) to dynamic exercise. Each can have a role depending on the particular purpose to hand, whether as part of the warm-up or for increasing the range of motion at particular joints. The choice of method will vary between the physiotherapist who is focused on rehabilitation and the trainer who is concerned with enhancement of performance capability. A fuller consideration of training methods is produced in other texts (e.g. Reilly, 1981; Williams *et al.*, 1997; McAtee and Charland, 1999).

Passive exercises can incorporate the principle of proprioceptive neuromuscular facilitation (PNF). There are various PNF procedures, most notably contract–relax, and contract–relax agonist–contract. The belief is that voluntary action of the agonist muscle provides neural activation that causes reciprocal inhibition of its antagonist counterpart. The result is that an increased range of motion is achieved.

Proprioceptive neuromuscular facilitation (PNF) stretching is one aspect of training that refers to a highly complex and effective form of physical therapy. An isometric contraction prior to the stretch achieves greater gains than are obtained from stretching alone. This form of stretching is generally done passively, the physical therapist doing the stretching for the patient or the physical trainer doing it for the athlete. The neuromuscular mechanisms incorporated in facilitated stretching include muscle reflexes. The myotatic or stretch reflex refers to activity within the muscle spindles whereby their gamma motor neurons respond to an increasing muscle length by stimulating the alpha motor neurons of the muscle fibres to shorten. This action is offset by the trainer's resistance. The Golgi sensory organs detect the level of tension within the muscle's tendon and respond by inhibiting the force production of the agonist and exciting the antagonist muscle, thereby acting as a safety measure to avoid forceful overstretching. Normally when an agonist muscle is stimulated to contract, its antagonist is switched off to allow the desired motion to occur, a process that is known as reciprocal inhibition.

Including PNF stretching in a dynamic warm-up with recreational soccer players has produced positive results. The stretches were selected in a specific movement order in which one stretch leads smoothly onto another. The warm-up included activities that gradually become more demanding and sports specific. This gradual increase in intensity facilitates the activation of more motor units and prepares the player physiologically for the demands of the subsequent training session or game (Arnheim and Prentice, 2000).

A training effect on flexibility is reflected in a greater movement at the joint in question. Increased range of motion must be linked with strength training within the newly acquired range. To achieve this end, use of isometric training exercises within this limited additional range can be effective.

Dynamic flexibility refers to the ability to move part or parts of the body quickly. The concern here is in overcoming stiffness or the forces opposing motion over any range, rather than the magnitude of the motion itself. Such exercises will be relevant in pre-match warm-ups. An example would be the inclusion of 'high kicks' as part of the warm-up, both legs being used individually in turn.

Allied to dynamic flexibility is the notion of functional stability. It refers to the ability to correct functional imbalance and is more a measure of postural control. In a dynamic context, the training for improved flexibility and balance needs to be combined.

Measuring flexibility

Range of motion at each joint can be measured using a variety of techniques. The posture is controlled from start to completion of the motion and the measurement protocol follows standard procedures. In performance-oriented assessments of flexibility, complex three-dimensional motion patterns may be analysed in a broad field of view (Borms and Van Roy, 2001). Such measurements are useful in technical sports events and are more relevant to clinical applications in soccer. Gross motions of body segments and coupled motions might be analysed for diagnostic purposes.

As outlined in more detail in Chapter 10, equipment used in assessing flexibility may be simple or highly sophisticated. The simplest forms of devices are portable goniometers, hygrometers or conventional flexometers. These are used to measure the angle through which the joint has moved. Three-dimensional electrogoniometers are both complex to interpret and expensive to use and are restricted mainly to dynamic movements and research purposes. The uses and limitations of a range of devices for assessing flexibility were reviewed elsewhere by Borms and Van Roy (2001).

Probably the best-known field test is the sit-and-reach method of measuring flexibility. It incorporates a number of muscle groups, but can identify hamstring tightness as well as stiffness in the lower back. Nevertheless, it is a crude indication of flexibility and results require more specific follow-up. A variation of this test is the stand-and-reach in which the athlete stands on a raised platform and slowly stretches down to move a marker with the fingertips. The marker is moved over a scale graded in cm, and the score is based on where the marker finally rests.

The stage of the season and the overall fitness of the player should be taken into consideration when the individual's flexibility data are evaluated. The time of day at which measurements are made is also relevant, since there is a clear diurnal variation in flexibility (Reilly et al., 1997). Activity during the day can impair flexibility later on, so prior to evening matches a complete rest is useful in recovering from residual stiffness (see Figure 3.2). The diurnal variation means also that stretching exercises are especially important for preparing the body for training when sessions are conducted in the morning.

The physiology of warming down

There is little question that warming up before training and competing is relevant to soccer players. This acceptance is in sharp contrast with what happens at the end of a game when a warm-down (or cool down) would be beneficial both

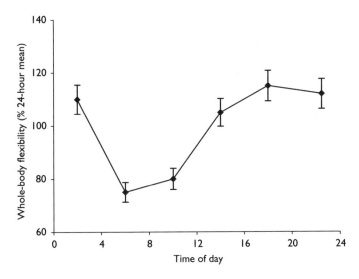

Figure 3.2 Whole-body flexibility as a function of time of day (from Reilly *et al.*, 1997).

in accelerating recovery and easing subsequent discomfort but is rarely practised. The faster recovery would be especially useful in the event of a succession of matches within a short period.

Warming (or 'cooling') down after strenuous exercise is regarded as essential in sports such as running, swimming and cycling. It is ingrained in the routines of participants in these sports, following both training and competing in races. It has never been seen as a part of the culture of soccer. Whereas coaches may accept their physiotherapist's advice about warming down after training, they are more reluctant to advocate a 'team warm-down' after a game. All engaged in the match are trapped by the emotions that linger on from the game's incidents and the communal mindset is not yet focused on the recovery process.

Nevertheless, to a limited extent warming down has been adopted and practised within the professional soccer game. The outstanding German international side of the 1970s and 1980s used to warm down as a squad after matches in the World Cup and European Nation's tournaments. The warm-down was done soon after the game finished but away from the public glare. In England, Football Academy youth teams began the practice of warming down on the pitch as a unit, ending the customary rush to the dressing room. Individual players within many of the Premier League teams nowadays warm down on the pitch, the ground being emptied relatively quickly once the game is over. Although warming down no longer has to be a furtive activity and is unlikely to become the habit among recreational players, it has a role to play in the habitual activity of the player who is seriously committed to performance in the game.

Physiological basis of warming down

Active warm-down plays an important role in restoring physiological equilibrium following strenuous exercise. Gentle exercise, such as jogging, promotes venous return of blood and accelerates the clearance of biological waste products. Blood lactate is elevated at the end of matches and an active warm-down helps in clearing lactate from the circulation. Above about 50% $\dot{V}O_{2\,max}$, more lactate is produced than is dispersed and warm-down is less effective. Consequently, there should be no high-intensity exercise attempted in the warm-down.

Body temperature is elevated after exercise, often by over 2°C at the end of a game. The heart rate may also be close to its maximal value, especially if the contest has been a hard one. Even in cold winter conditions, heat production will exceed heat loss to the environment [except for low-level recreational play], so that an overall heat gain is evident. The temperature will continue to rise for a few minutes after exercise stops since the blood being circulated is still warm. As there is no longer a heat load induced by exercising muscle, the transport of blood to the skin for convective heat loss is decreased and the sweat glands discontinue their secretions. This process of thermoregulatory adjustment is more smoothly achieved by the graded reduction in exercise that is associated with a warm-down.

Free fatty acids and catecholamines [adrenaline and noradrenaline] are elevated at the end of a match. The greater the competitive stress, the higher are the catecholamine levels afterwards. Insulin and the catecholamines produce rapid and pronounced effects on lipolysis in human adipose tissue, causing free fatty acids to be released into the circulation after the breakdown of triacylglycerols in adipose tissue cells. El Sayed et al. (1996) addressed the potential pathological effects of the rise in free fatty acids post-exercise. Warming down after 90 min submaximal exercise compatible with the intensity of match-play (70% $\dot{V}O_{2\,max}$) failed to reduce the elevations in free fatty acids during recovery. In contrast, ingesting a carbohydrate drink 15 min pre-exercise and after 45 min of exercise attenuated the elevations in free fatty acids (see Figure 3.3). These observations do not negate the benefits of warming down as it can help in restoring arousal levels within the nervous system towards normal. The result is likely to be an improved quality of sleep in the immediate night to follow.

Warm-down represents good hygiene and partly offsets a temporary depression of the immune system. There is a j-shaped relationship between exercise and the immune response. Strenuous exercise has a depressant effect on immune system function whereas light exercise has a beneficial influence. The 'open window' theory proposes that the body is more vulnerable than normal to infection, particularly upper respiratory tract infections, for a 4–6 h period after exercise. Finishing off the session with a light warm-down could help to offset the detrimental effects of the preceding intensive exercise on the immune system. It could also help to avoid a sudden change in thermal state that appears to be implicated in picking up a common cold. The warm-down may be especially

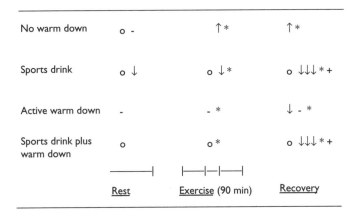

	Rest	Exercise (90 min)	Recovery
No warm down	o -	↑*	↑*
Sports drink	o ↓	o ↓*	o ↓↓↓*+
Active warm down	-	- *	↓ - *
Sports drink plus warm down	o	o*	o ↓↓↓*+

Figure 3.3 Plasma FFA concentrations (mean ± SE) at rest (0 min), during exercise (45 and 90 min), and into recovery (10, 20 and 30 min). AWD = active warm-down; C = carbohydrate. * Significantly ($p < 0.05$) higher mean value than that observed at rest and 45 min during exercise in both trials. + Significantly ($p < 0.05$) lower mean value than that found during AWD trial. ↓↑ change compared to control (from El Sayed et al., 1996).

important after a match in periods where the fixture list is congested and it is essential to remain free of infection for the next game.

There is evidence that a warm-down does accelerate the recovery of sprinting ability in the subsequent days. It is also effective in reducing the soreness known as 'delayed onset muscle soreness' or DOMS (Reilly and Rigby, 2002). This discomfort is linked with eccentric contractions of muscle such as in plyometric training. This form of exercise causes microtrauma to the thin membranes within the active muscles when they are forcibly stretched and subsequent leakage of substances through the small tears incurred. The warm-down activity lasted for 12 min, and consisted of three phases (i) jogging for 5 min; (ii) stretching (5 min); (iii) lying prone with legs raised and 'shaken down' by another player. Compared to a control group that returned to the dressing room and rested for 12 min, the players who warmed down showed a lower reduction in jumping and sprinting in the subsequent days and a faster recovery of performance to normal values.

Warming down: the practice

There can be a short break after finishing a game and before starting the warm-down. After exercise stops, hot blood is still being re-circulated around the body. Sweating continues whilst skin, muscle and core temperatures remain elevated for about 5 min or so, as are blood pressure and heart rate. The lactate concentration in the blood is also likely to be elevated above resting levels. This period can be used for any emotional purpose, but it is important to drink some fluid to start the rehydration process. Soccer boots may be discarded for training shoes, depending on the pitch surface. The best form of warm-down is jogging. The duration is somewhat arbitrary rather than scientifically based, but 10–20 min are adequate. The intensity should not exceed about half that of match play. It may be shorter after a game than after training. The fundamental activity may be interspersed with gentle stretching exercise for calves, hamstrings and adductors. Circumstances permitting, exercises can include 'shaking down' the legs from a lying position to aid venous return.

Clothing may be changed before the warm-down routine is commenced. If it is windy, appropriate head-gear should be worn to prevent large losses of heat through the head. A waterproof top is advised if it is raining. It is especially important not to become quickly overcooled in wet–windy conditions. For this reason, hanging around to talk or chat is not recommended when the weather is cold and interruptions to the warm-down should be avoided.

It is not necessary to use the ball in warming down after a game. However, various low-intensity drills in small groups could be devised as warm-down practices towards the end of normal training. The training context may also be the more appropriate for targeting specific flexibility exercises. Including some dynamic flexibility exercises into the warm-down routine can help in alleviating feelings of stiffness. The stretching exercises can engage calves, hamstrings, quadriceps, adductors, gluteals and lower-back muscles.

Overview

Warming up is important both for reducing injury risk and preparing for impending competition. It should be structured so that it provides specificity for soccer. Flexibility exercises form a relevant component of any warm-up practices. There is a physiological basis for the desirability of warming down, yet it is only rarely practiced. Its main benefit may lie in the acceleration of recovery processes. The main resistance to its universal adoption is likely to be the psychological state of those involved in the game who may be bound up in the emotional aftermath of the game's events.

The warm-down allows the players a few moments of reflection after the day's match or training. It may be a group activity after training or more individualistic after a game. In the latter case, thoughts can revolve around things done well or focus on aspects that were less successful. Emotions can be held in check whilst composure is regained should there have been any critical incidents in the game. By the time the player returns to the dressing room the arousal level is restored towards normality and the activities of the day can be evaluated in a balanced manner. In this way the warm-down draws the professional aspects of the day's work to a close.

References

Arnheim, D. and Prentice, W., 2000, Proprioceptive neuromuscular facilitation techniques. In: *Principles of Athletic Training (10th Edition)*, Boston, MA: WCB McGraw Hill, pp. 394–397.

Borms, J. and Van Roy, P., 2001, Flexibility. In: *Kinanthropometry and Exercise Physiology Laboratory Manual: Tests, Procedures and Data (2nd Edition), Vol. I: Anthropometry* (edited by R. Eston and T. Reilly), London: Routledge, pp. 117–147.

Ekstrand, J., 1994, Injuries. In: *Football (Soccer)* (edited by B. Ekblom), London: Blackwell Scientific Publications, pp. 175–194.

El-Sayed, M.S., Rattu, A.J.M., Lin, X. and Reilly, T., 1996, Effects of active warm-down and carbohydrate feeding on free fatty acid concentrations after prolonged submaximal exercise. *International Journal of Sport Nutrition*, **6**, 337–347.

Gregson, W.A., Batterham, A., Drust, B. and Cable, N.T., 2005, The influence of pre-warming on the physiological responses to prolonged intermittent exercise. *Journal of Sports Sciences*, **23**, 455–464.

McAtee, R.E. and Charland, J., 1999, *Facilitated Stretching*. Champaign, IL: Human Kinetics.

Reilly, T. (ed.), 1981, *Sports Fitness and Sports Injuries*. London: Faber and Faber.

Reilly, T. and Rigby, M., 2002, Effect of an active warm-down following competitive soccer. In: *Science and Football IV* (edited by W. Spinks, T. Reilly and A. Murphy), London: Routledge, pp. 226–229.

Reilly, T. and Stirling, A., 1993, Flexibility, warm-up and injuries in mature games players. In: *Kinanthropometry IV* (edited by W. Duquet and J.A.P. Day), London: E. and F.N. Spon, pp. 119–123.

Reilly, T. and Waterhouse, J., 2005, *Sport, Exercise and Environmental Physiology*. Edinburgh: Elsevier.

Reilly, T., Atkinson, G. and Waterhouse, J., 1997, *Biological Rhythms and Exercise*. Oxford University Press.

Shellock, F.G. and Prentice, W.E., 1985, Warming-up and stretching for improved physical performance and prevention of sports related injuries. *Sports Medicine*, **2**, 267–278.

Williams, M., Borrie, A., Cable, T., Gilbourne, D., Lees, A., MacLaren, D. and Reilly, T., 1997, *Umbro Conditioning for Football*. London: Ebury Press.

Chapter 4

Strength and power training

Introduction

Training for muscle strength entails use of the overload principle and progressive resistance exercise offers a means by which the training stimulus can be upgraded on a regular basis. The intensity can be regulated by use of the RM principle, which can be determined from a single maximum effort (1-RM) or a number of repeated efforts (e.g. 10-RM). The training programme may be designed on the basis of the number of repetitions of each specific exercise, the number of sets of these repetitions and the rest periods in between.

The intensity of the exercise or the level of force demanded by the active muscle determines the type and number of motor units that are recruited. This concept applies irrespective of the velocity of the action. Only a few motor units are activated when low force is required and these tend to be associated with slow-twitch muscle fibres. At moderate intensities the FTa (Type IIa) fibres are recruited whilst in efforts of maximal strength the FTb (Type IIb) fibres are called into play. Therefore strenuous efforts for brief repetitions (e.g. 6×6-RM) represent a good means of activating the majority of the muscle fibres. When all of the motor units are recruited, the muscle can exert its greatest possible force.

Training for power must exploit the force–velocity characteristic of muscle. This requirement reflects the trade-off due to the velocity-specific effects of training. Perrin (1993) concluded that concentric exercise performed at slow velocities improves force production only at the training velocity whereas exercise at high velocities is not so specific to the exact velocity used. The football player requires both great force production for muscle development and fast actions for game-related movements.

Muscle strength can be increased by a more effective recruitment of muscle fibres contributing to the generation of force and a reduction of neural inhibitory influences. Neural adaptations resulting in increased voluntary activation of muscle may account for improvements in strength over the initial weeks of a resistance-training programme (Staron *et al.*, 1994). After about 8 weeks longer-term effects are generally associated with increases in cross-sectional area of the muscle.

Muscle hypertrophy indicates an increase in the size of existing muscle fibres as opposed to an increase of the number of fibres (hyperplasia). Hypertrophy reflects the balance between protein synthesis and degradation. Positive regulators of protein synthesis include testosterone and IGF-1 whereas myostatin acts as a negative regulator. Calpain is the main substance regulating protein degradation. Resistance exercise can knock out the myostatin brake on muscle growth and so promote a positive protein balance necessary for hypertrophy. It seems the fast-twitch muscle fibres are more prone to hypertrophy and hence to high-intensity training than are the slow-twitch muscle fibres.

Neuromuscular mechanisms of strength training can embrace higher level supraspinal controls known as 'central command' and including afferent feedback. They may also include lower-level controls mediated at a spinal level. With strength training there is an increase in muscle activation, reflected in the percentage of the motorneurone pool that is engaged in the action. With 'explosive' type activity more motor units are recruited early, the rate of force development increases and the time to reach peak torque is decreased.

In this chapter various exercises that are used in training for strength and power are described. A selection of these is shown in Figure 4.1. An emphasis is placed on the correct execution of the exercises, both for performance enhancement and safety reasons. The biological rationale for their incorporation into the training programmes is mentioned where appropriate.

Resistance training

Muscle strength is improved by working against resistance. Suitable exercises can be divided according to the amount of skeletal muscle engaged. Exercises involving the arm and the shoulder joint may be described as light muscle group work whereas large muscle group work employs the muscles of the thigh and those of the trunk. Training these muscle groups in particular is relevant to soccer.

It is important that the exercises are executed correctly, especially when loose weights are handled. The most common injuries in weight-training are to the wrists, back and knee. Mostly they occur when heavy weights are being lifted or when the technique is faulty (Reilly, 1981). Injuries to the back tend to occur when spinal flexion is permitted. Safety should override all other factors when heavy lifts are being attempted.

Many soccer clubs have strength training facilities on their premises. They are often designed for players to use during rehabilitation programmes. Few clubs would have facilities on the scale available to American football players at a top University in the United States. Nevertheless the equipment available at a commercial gymnasium with a specialised facility for strength and conditioning work would accommodate a whole range of exercises for implementing a comprehensive training programme.

Figure 4.1 Various exercises used for strength training including half-squats (a), bench press (b), overhead pull (c), dead-lift (d), rowing (e) and leg press (f).

Large muscle group work

Squats

The squat thrust is one of the most favoured exercises for games players. It does seem to be relevant to soccer. Wisløff *et al.* (2004) showed that maximal squat strength was correlated with sprint performance and vertical jumping in elite Norwegian players. The muscles involved are the plantar flexors of the ankle which act eccentrically to permit the closing of the ankle between the tibia and the foot, the extensors of the knee and hip, and the extensors of the spine and elevators of the scapula working isometrically.

In a full squat a loaded barbell is supported on the back of the neck. A piece of foam rubber or a towel is sometimes used to alleviate pressure on the cervical vertebrae. The body is lowered from a standing to a squat position, from which its weight plus the loaded barbell must be lifted by powerful contraction of the knee extensors. This exercise has been criticised because of the risk of incurring knee joint degeneration from strain on the patellar bursae. During deep knee bending without attendant weights, the patello-tendon force has been calculated to reach 7.6 times bodyweight (Reilly, 1981).

In the full squat position with posterior aspects of thigh and calf in contact, the knee ligaments are overstretched and long-term ligamentous damage may be caused. In this position the lateral meniscus may also suffer from being caught between the femoral condyle and the tibial plateau (O'Donoghue, 1970). For these reasons performance of partial squats is advised, though full squats may be permitted at much less frequent intervals to provide maximum overload and maintain the joint's range of movement.

Maintaining stability during this exercise may present a problem for some individuals. Initially the player takes up a starting position with feet apart underneath the hips to provide best support for bodyweight. Stability is achieved by keeping the line of gravity within the base of support. This aim is effected by pushing the hips back slowly as the bodyweight is lowered. By retaining heel contact with the ground the base of support is kept relatively large and stability is facilitated.

Balance may be assisted by elevating the heels by means of an inclined board or by performing the exercise with a board placed underneath the heels. A more satisfactory procedure is to use a steel rack which arrests movement of the bar in the fore and aft direction and which incorporates obvious additional safety factors. These racks are installed in all well-equipped gymnasia.

More weight can be lowered than lifted, as the muscles work eccentrically when lowering a load compared to contracting concentrically when lifting it. Therefore, a useful modification of the half-squat is to overload the individual beyond maximal lifting capacity and to allow him/her to lower the weight slowly under eccentric muscular control. A weight about 120% of lifting capacity can easily be handled for six repetitions. If the stretching force is 130 to 140% of one concentric repetition maximum (1 RM), it is not possible to slow the lowering sufficiently in a free movement resisting gravity to permit the involved muscles to develop maximal tension. For safety purposes the load should be supported by pins at the end of the eccentric movement.

Power cleans

This exercise involves approximately the same energy demands as a full squat (Reilly, 1983). The weight is lifted from the floor to above head height in one complete movement. Special attention to technique is needed in the initial lifting movement. The knee-lift, with the back straight to prevent the turning of the spine into a cantilever with consequent spinal strain, is preferable to the back-lift with knees straight. Correct placement of the feet is essential prior to attempting the lift. The player should become accustomed to performing the action with the head erect and looking directly ahead in order to avoid the natural temptation to look down at the weight as he/she attempts to overcome its inertia. As the forces on the spine are a function of the distance the weight is away from it, it is recommended to keep the weight close to the body as it is being lifted.

It is important not to suspend breathing when heavy weights are held overhead. When the breath is held and the epiglottis closed, intrathoracic pressure is increased to a point that precipitates the Valsalva manouvre. This action results in a reduced venous return to the heart and consequent rapid drop in blood pressure with possible loss of consciousness. International weightlifters have been known to faint and lose consciousness during competition as a result of failure to time their breathing correctly.

High pulls

This exercise involves the same gross muscular action and equivalent energy expenditure as power cleans (Reilly, 1983). The barbell is taken from the floor to a height roughly in line with the clavicles. The player may increase the work done by coming up on to his or her toes to complete the lift, good co-ordination being demanded for this action. The elbows are raised above the bar at its high-point, which does not go overhead. Again it is important to keep the back straight during the lift as jerking into back extension, particularly during the early phase of the action, can lead to injury. The major muscles engaged in this exercise are the ankle plantar flexors, the extensors of the spine working isometrically, the shoulder abductors, elbow flexors and the elevators of the scapula.

Bench step-ups

Bodyweight plus a weighted barbell provide the resistance as the individual steps repeatedly on to a bench with load supported on the shoulders. Ideally the bench should be matched to the stature of the individual, otherwise there is a risk of a quadriceps muscle tear where the smaller players operate with a high bench. When the weight used is too heavy, the rhythm of stepping may be disrupted with consequent danger of losing balance and incurring injury.

Leg press

This exercise entails knee extension and can be done from different postures (Figure 4.1). It is usual to start from a sitting position with the knees and hips flexed. Peak torque is generated at about 120° of knee extension and if the hip is flexed too much the angle of the knee will not allow enough force to be developed to move heavy weights. An alternative starting posture is a recumbent supine position from which the weights are pushed upwards and vertically. It is recommended that the lowering of the weights to the starting position is performed under careful control.

Leg curls

In order to maintain the correct balance between flexion and extension, the hamstrings should be trained as well as the quadriceps. An appropriate exercise is knee flexion with the subject in a prone position. This activity is best performed using a fixed training station. The muscles are engaged eccentrically as the load is returned to its starting position.

Trunk exercises

Sit-ups (trunk curls or crunches)

The resistance is normally provided by approximately half the body mass which the abdominal muscles must move against gravity. The load on the abdominals in a sit-up action from supine lying can be increased by holding a loaded barbell on the chest. This exercise is preferable on comfort criteria alone to holding a disc behind the neck. A partner may hold the ankles of the athlete to facilitate the action. Another variation is to sit-up with a twist, arms behind the ears, to touch each knee alternately with contra-lateral elbows.

Exercise for the abdominal muscles is commonly known as performing 'the crunch' and there are several commercially available devices with claims of enhancing the training stimulus. Robinson et al. (2005) used electromyography of lower rectus abdominis, upper rectus abdominis and obliquus externus abdominis muscles to investigate the effectiveness of five different abdominal exercises; these included a sit-up (crunch) with a 5-kg weight held behind the head and a sit-up with a commercial roller-crunch device. The highest stimulus to all three muscles was provided by a crunch whilst sitting on a 'gym ball', and a crunch with legs raised. The greater muscle activity in these exercises was attributed to the unstable surface and the need to support the legs off the ground. The commercial aid was no different from a standard sit-up in the muscle activity it induced.

Back extension

A basic exercise for the spinal muscles is to assume a prone position on the ground with the arms extended over the head and touching the floor. The head, arms and legs are then raised off the floor and this position is held for about 6 s. After a 5-s rest the exercise is performed up to 12 times.

An alternative is to take up a standing position, crouched at the hips with a barbell on the shoulders. The back is kept straight whilst the weight is lifted upwards, then lowered in a controlled manner to the starting point. This exercise must be done carefully and unduly heavy weights avoided.

Light muscle group work

Bench press

The player lies supine on the bench with feet apart and supported on the ground on either side. Two spotters are used for precautionary reasons. The bar is taken from supporting stands by the spotters and handed to the athlete on his/her upper chest (Figure 4.2). This exercise is very popular with all athletes that use weight-training programmes.

Taking the bar in too high near the throat is to be avoided on safety considerations. Normally a wide knuckles-up grip is adopted. A wider hand hold is used to handle greater weights, though this defeats the purpose of imposing greatest resistance on anterior deltoids and triceps. The wider grip promotes strength in the pectoral area, the narrower grip favouring a contribution from the triceps muscles (Gilbert and Lees, 2003). However, care must be taken that the grip is sufficiently wide not to jeopardise security and continual concentration is required of the spotters as 40 kg is sufficient to lacerate the facial bone from a fall of half a metre. The weight is pushed vertically from the chest. Prior to the movement it is necessary to have the chest full of air to provide a rigid base from which the weight is moved. The performer exhales after the weight ascends. The bar should be lowered slowly so as to permit complete control of the weight throughout. Altering the hand spacing affects the pattern of muscular involvement. Dumb-bells may be used to replace the barbell and, though this change means a lower resistance, it allows movement through a greater range.

An alternative procedure is to have the assistants lift the barbell, the player's task being to control its lowering by eccentric muscle contractions. In this way, the limitation of performing only unidirectional work is overcome. Whilst heavier loads can be handled than in concentric work, the benefits of the training programme are enhanced when both concentric and eccentric actions are employed.

Bench pressing is ubiquitous in the weight-training programmes of athletes. It has been widely accepted by runners, jumpers and games players. It would seem appropriate for soccer players attempting to improve upper-body strength, making it more difficult for opponents to master them in physical challenges. The main muscles involved are the protractors of the shoulder girdle, the abductors of the scapula and the elbow extensors.

Overhead press

Overhead press can be performed standing upright or sitting on a bench. The starting position can be from the chest but usually the weight is pressed vertically

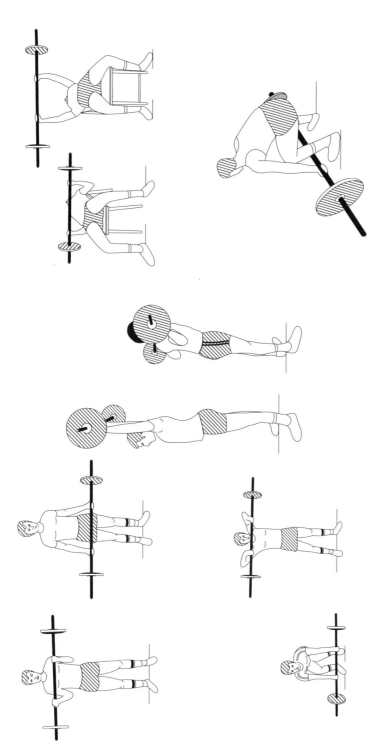

Figure 4.2 Exercise for light muscle groups (top and centre) and large muscle groups (bottom).

from behind the neck until the arms are at full stretch overhead, an inflated chest acting as a platform from which the action takes place. In the standing posture heavy weights may produce compensating movements in the legs or trunk to allow the action to be completed. In younger individuals acquiring the technique, an assistant can apply light pressure at the scapulae to prevent swaying (Figure 4.2).

Alternatively, it may help if the action is performed with immediate visual feedback from a mirror. If dumb-bells are used the line of action of the specific competitive performance can be employed. Goalkeepers, for example, may use one or both arms alternately or simultaneously at an angle of release in the sagittal plane of approximately 30°.

Pull downs

This exercise is best performed using a pulley system. The bar to which the weighted pulley is attached is held overhead but to the front of the body. The task is to pull it down in front of the head to approximately chest level. It can be released under control and the exercise repeated. The exercise is sometimes described as a 'lat pull' due to the engagement of the latissimus dorsi muscle.

Rowing

A rowing action may be performed from an upright or a bent-forward posture. Activity should be restricted to the arms and shoulders, with careful attention given to the exclusion of movement in the back and trunk. In both forms, the downward movement of the bar should be controlled. An observer can ensure the posture does not get progressively higher with each succeeding effort in bent-forward rowing. This deviation can indicate the performer is tiring and when fatigued the player is most likely to handle weights incorrectly. Again, the use of a mirror in learning the technique is recommended. A partner may be used to exert light pressure on the upper back to prevent accentuation of the lordotic curve.

If performed in a quick jerky manner with the knees locked, damage to the intervertebral discs can occur with pressure on the disc forcing its fluid-like centre, the nucleus pulposus, to project posteriorly causing medical complications. This possibility can be avoided either by resting the forehead on a padded table while the lift is performed or bending the knees to about 15° flexion. This posture releases tension from the muscles of the posterior thigh and back and allows the lumbar spine to retain a normal curvature. The muscles isolated in this exercise are the latissimus dorsi, teres major and rhomboids.

In upright rowing a narrow grip is used with the elbows pointing upwards. In bent-forward rowing the elbows assume a more lateral orientation. Both procedures are widely used by individuals seeking an increase in upper-body strength.

Overarm-pulls

This exercise may be performed with the individual lying supine on a bench and feet supported on the ground. The arms may be held straight or flexed. A mild flexion is recommended to reduce strain on the shoulder joint. The weights lifted should not be unduly heavy, otherwise they will be difficult to control at the outer ranges of movement. The barbell may be taken from a position on the ground in a circular motion forward to a position over the chest or continued further to rest on the thighs. The serratus anterior muscle is stretched as the weight is lowered to recommence the movement. Correct timing of breathing is important, inhalation occurring as the weight descends towards the ground and exhalation as the load is taken back up.

Bicep curls

Curls implicate elbow flexion and may be performed with barbells or with one or two dumb-bells (Figure 4.2). It is difficult to operate at maximal loads in standing without other muscle groups being introduced to assist fatiguing elbow flexors. Again, care should be taken so that loads are not so heavy as to accentuate lordosis of the spine. The elbow flexors may be isolated by supporting the limb being exercised on a bench or table. The other limb should then be exercised to ensure symmetrical strength development.

Tricep curls

Tricep curls may be done with dumb-bells. These are held with the arms overhead, elbows pointed forward. From a position with the elbow flexed, the weights are brought forward as the joint is extended. This action has some similarity to the throw-in if two light dumb-bells are used together.

Isometric exercise

Whilst actions in soccer are mostly dynamic, muscles may be employed isometrically to stabilise body parts whilst other muscles are active. Examples are the muscles in the standing leg during kicking or the muscles of the trunk. In these instances isometric training of these muscles is relevant. It can also be used to target areas of weakness within the range of motion at a particular joint.

Various forms of resistance can be used for facilitating isometric training. A partner may provide an opposing force to limb or whole-body motion. The individual may attempt to move a load that is too heavy, for example pushing against a loaded leg press machine. Typically the effort can be held for 6–10 s with a longer period of recovery before a further attempt. Up to 20 repetitions may be performed for large muscle group work, 10–12 for light muscle groups.

Electrical stimulation has been used in experimental conditions to elicit maximal contraction and the force generated may exceed that produced voluntarily. Its main use is in rehabilitation. Since the central neural input is bypassed when the muscle is stimulated electrically, this form of increasing strength is not advocated for soccer players.

Core stability

Core stability refers to the balance between stabilising and mobilising muscle actions. Most emphasis is placed on the muscles directly engaged in movement at a joint, the agonists, and the antagonists which relax to permit the desired movement to occur. These muscles are located superficially towards the surface of the body. The stabilisers secure the integrity of the joint and are located deeper than the mobilising muscles.

Core strength provides a base from which soccer-specific actions can be developed. The trunk stabilisers are the transversus abdominus and the lumbar multifidus. An example of an exercise for core stability is where the player assumes a press-up position but with the lower leg supported on a large inflated gymnasium (Swiss) ball. In this posture the abdominal stabilisers work isometrically to keep the body stationary.

Eccentric (Plyometric) training

Stretch-shortening cycles

When a muscle is stretched prior to a concentric action, the tension within the muscle is potentiated during the shortening phase. The elastic elements within the muscle store energy which is then released once the muscle begins to shorten. In activities such as jumping, the performance is enhanced when a counter-movement precedes the jump. Exercises which employ such stretch–shortening cycles of muscle action are referred to as plyometric training. A range of different exercises for plyometric work is listed in Chu (1998).

Hopping, on one leg or on both legs together (bunny hops), is a basic form of plyometric training. In this activity the hips should not sink below the level where the femur is parallel with the ground in order to avoid placing undue strain on the knee joint. The hops may be performed over a series of hurdles or can include diagonal movements over a low bench. Lateral movements can be designed so that the adductor muscles are activated.

It is important that the muscles have experienced some conditioning work before formal plyometric training is attempted. Stretch–shortening exercises induce soreness which peaks about 48–72 h post-exercise. The soreness is linked to micro-trauma within the muscle's ultrastructure causing disarrangement of the Z discs within the myofibrils. There is local inflammation and damage to the sarcolemma through which creatine kinase leaks into the bloodstream. This enzyme has been used as a marker of muscle damage caused by eccentric contractions. With training the damage is reduced, a phenomenon known as the 'repeated bouts effect'.

Delayed onset muscle soreness is therefore not a lasting problem, but players carrying an injury should be excused from intensive plyometrics. Bounding, hopping and jumping exercises can be included within any training system but formal plyometrics at high intensities can be restricted to twice a week. Skipping, lunging and footwork drills all entail plyometric activity at low intensity. Other means of inducing stretch–shortening cycles may be incorporated in the high-intensity sessions.

Depth jumping

Drop jumping or depth jumping utilises the individual's body weight and gravity to exert force against the ground. The individual steps out from a box, drops to the ground and immediately drives the body upwards as quickly as possible. The eccentric part of the action where the lowering of the body is controlled is known as the amortisation phase, before the body is directed vertically. Learning to co-ordinate the whole movement into a smooth performance is essential for this exercise to be fully effective (Figure 4.3).

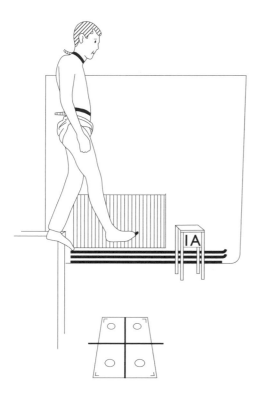

Figure 4.3 Depth jumping is performed from a box.

Depth jumping has been adopted with success by high jumpers and triple jumpers. It is relevant in soccer where the lower-limb muscles generate high power output in fast 'explosive' actions. It was originally prescribed by Verhoshanski (1969) who recommended a box height of 0.8 m for achieving maximum speed and 1.1 m for developing maximal dynamic strength. He recommended no more than 40 jumps in a single work-out. In later studies a box height of 20–40 cm was thought to be sufficient (Boocock et al., 1990).

Squat jumps

Here the athlete jumps high into the air from a squat or partial squat with a loaded barbell supported on the shoulders. Good co-ordination is essential to prevent overbalancing on landing. Frequently a towel is used underneath the bar to cushion its jarring effect. When ascending it is necessary to pull down hard on the bar to avoid its bouncing against the back of the neck. It is particularly beneficial to athletes such as soccer players who during performances move the body explosively against gravity.

An alternative exercise is to dispense with any equipment and perform a split squat with a cycling action in mid-air. After jumping upwards, the front leg kicks to the rear position and the back leg comes flexed to the front. The individual lands in the split-squat position to jump again immediately.

Pendulum training

The pendulum method of training was developed in eastern Europe as a means of inducing stretch-shortening cycle exercises without the accompanying delayed-onset muscle soreness. The individual is located on a set-up as in a child's swing and pushes towards a wall, absorbs the 'shock' and immediately pushes off again (see Figure 4.4). The desired muscle actions are produced whilst body weight is supported on the seat.

In experimental studies a force platform was built into the wall to record the forces generated when training using the pendulum method. Fowler et al. (1997) established that the system was effective as a training method and reduced both the acute load on the skeleton and the degree of transient muscle damage. Its use is limited to one individual at a time and it has been adopted more for laboratory work rather than as a specific useable training tool.

Complex training

Different forms of training at high intensities may be combined into a single session. This integration is referred to as complex training. It might include jumping actions with overload in formal arrangements such as 3–4 sets of

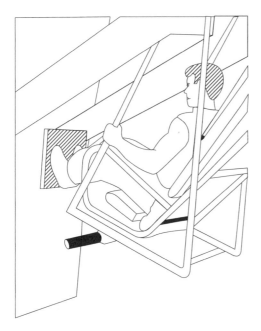

Figure 4.4 The pendulum device used for plyometric training.

6 repetitions. These may be performed alongside repetitive bounding, for example for 30 s, and exercises with loose weights. The regimen includes concentric as well as eccentric actions and exploits the force–velocity characteristic of muscle, most of the exercises being performed towards the faster end of the curve.

Isokinetics

Isokinetics describes the form of exercise permitted by machinery with the facility to adapt resistance to the force exerted. Normally when weights are lifted through a range of movement the maximum load is limited to that sustainable by the muscles involved at the weakest point in the range. Consequently other points within the range undergo sub-maximal training stimuli. With isokinetic machines this problem is overcome as the speed of contraction is pre-set, a speed governor in the apparatus allowing the resistance to adapt to the force applied. In this way, the greater the effort exerted the greater the resistance, and maximal effort can be performed throughout the complete range of movement. Where comparisons have been made, training programmes using isokinetic machines have proved superior to isometric and typical progressive resistance programmes with high speeds producing best results.

These results may reflect the fact that the training programmes are mostly evaluated using isokinetic equipment.

Modern isokinetic equipment permits eccentric as well as concentric actions. Typically, the top angular velocities available on the equipment tend to be higher under concentric than in eccentric modes of action. Nevertheless the angular velocities that are possible are well below the maximal velocities achieved in playing actions such as kicking a ball.

Training at high velocities is likely to assist slow movements whereas training using slow movements is likely to be velocity specific in its effects. The velocity-specific adaptations are linked with the pattern of motor unit recruitment. Improvements in muscle strength are to be expected from training at slow angular velocities, due to the recruitment of a large population of motor units. Such actions close to maximal efforts can induce muscle hypertrophy, provided repetitions are sufficient and the programme of training is sustained for some months. In order to avoid muscle hypertrophy whilst at the same time improve strength (due to neuromotor factors), no more than 3 sets of 6–8 repetitions are recommended.

Isokinetic facilities are expensive and so are not normally available for team training. Their main benefit is in training muscle strength during rehabilitation. In this instance it can be allied with physical therapy in a comprehensive progressive programme.

A limitation of isokinetic exercise is that it may interfere with the natural pattern of acceleration employed in competitive actions. Furthermore, movements are linear and so do not correspond to musculoskeletal function in the game. Nevertheless isokinetic apparatus is very effective in identifying deficiencies at individual joints. The appropriate muscle groups can then be isolated for remedial training.

Multi-station equipment

Use of weights is implemented in circuit-weight training in which a series of separate exercises is organised for sequential performance in a circle. The individuals rotate in a circle as they make progress through the training session. The circuit should allow variation of muscle groups involved between work stations to avoid cessation of work due to local muscular fatigue. In theory this method is ideal for team training provided the number in the group does not exceed the number of work stations laid out. In practice, group organisation invariably presents some problems as do inter-individual differences. Where weight-training is included in the circuit, a fixed load may not be suitable for all or many of the group while altering the loads slows up the performance and allows untimely recovery. Ideally a homogeneous group, a thoroughly well organised routine and repetition of the circuit or supplementary training are necessary to achieve objectives.

Multi-station exercise machines overcome the organisational problems of circuit-training and the injury risks of weight training using traditional resistance modes. The machine illustrated in Figure 4.5 was one of the first to be designed on ergonomic principles to provide the training stimulus requirements for strength, power, local and general endurance. Resistance is alternately supplied by bodyweight, weighted stacks and isokinetic machines. Muscle groups are rotated from station to station and use of the machine involves abdominals, leg, shoulder, arm and back muscle work. Physiological studies have shown the training stimulus to the circulatory system is significantly greater than conventional circuit-training routines (Reilly and Thomas, 1978). However, as delay in altering loads at any one station is minimal, the circuit of 12 stations can be repeated to perform two or more sets in a training session.

The advantage of stationary equipment for resistance training is that safety is secured compared to the risk of accidents in using free weights. The arrangement at each station can be changed quickly to accommodate different physiques and capabilities. This type of equipment is available at most fitness centres and sports training complexes.

Technological aids

Mechanical devices

Various devices have been developed over the years for facilitating strength and power training. In some instances the commercial claims have not been supported by laboratory studies. Some of the most positive constructions are now described.

Pulley systems incorporate both concentric and eccentric actions for back and thigh muscles. The best devices regulate the magnitude of the eccentric phase by reference to the concentric actions.

Exercise machines with the arc of motion dictated by a cam device have been in use for some decades. The cam design allows the resistance to be increased at parts of the joint's range of motion where force is decreased. In this way the resistance accommodates to the force exerted throughout the range of movement, conforming to the force–angle curves for the joint in question.

Vibration plates

Vibration platforms have been utilised for strength training in some of the top European soccer clubs. These systems have also been used by professional Rugby Union players as part of their conditioning programme. There have been some positive results but it seems that these apply to specific vibration frequencies. Devices like the Galileo Sport machine (Novotec, Germany) have a tilting

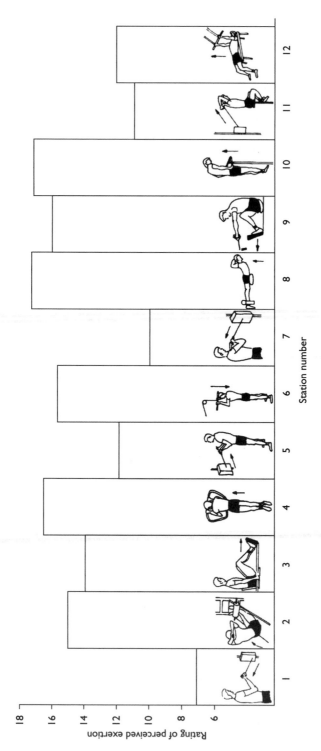

Figure 4.5 The original multi-station equipment validated by Reilly and Thomas (1978).

Source: Reprinted from Reilly and Thomas, 1978, with permission from Elsevier.

platform that delivers oscillatory movements to the body at frequencies from 0–30 Hz around a horizontal axle. The individual is largely passive, merely standing on the platform whilst it vibrates at a pre-set frequency.

For many years ergonomists have recognised the potential adverse effects of vibrations delivered to the human body by hand-held tools such as pneumatic drills and chain saws. More recently exercise devices that include whole-body vibrations have been promoted as training aids. Vibration of soft tissue is a natural phenomenon; the tissues in the lower limbs vibrate at their natural frequencies with the shock impact of landing as the heel strikes the ground on each footstrike. Ideally the frequency of stimulation should be tuned to the resonant frequency of the individual to induce training effects. Results of studies have been mixed, negative results being attributed to amplitudes that were too low, incorrect frequencies or durations that were too long (Cardinale and Wakeling, 2005).

Benefits to performance have generally been observed with sinusoidal vibrations at frequencies of 26 Hz and amplitudes of 4–6 mm. Acute applications of whole-body vibration for 5 min at 26 Hz and 10 mm amplitude were reported to shift the force–velocity curve of well-trained subjects to the right (Bosco *et al.*, 1999). Other positive effects have been observed on skeletal health and on flexibility (Cardinale and Wakeling, 2005). Acute enhancement of flexibility and muscle power has been attributed to stimulation of the muscle spindles and recruitment of additional motor units via activation of multiple nerve synapses (Cochrane and Stannard, 2005).

Issurin (2005) distinguished whole-body vibration from vibratory stimulation of local tissues combined with strength-training exercises and static stretching. In these instances vibratory stimulation is superimposed on muscle contraction or stretch. The balance of research evidence indicated positive effects with short-term use but suppressive effects on muscle force when stimulation was prolonged (6–30 min). Greater effects were observed in dynamic than in isometric muscle actions and were most pronounced in fast movements. The main benefit of this method may be in physical therapy for individual muscles.

Functional overload

Various forms of natural resistance may be provided to overload the active muscles. These include running uphill, on sand dunes or ankle deep in water. Traditionally soccer coaches used stadium terrace steps in the pre-season training of their players.

Activities related to the game may also be set up with overload in mind. Jumping with ankle weights or jackets weighted with lead are examples. Graham-Smith *et al.* (2001) examined the use of an additional load of 10% body weight in the form of a Power Vest© during a typical plyometric training session of 5 sets of 10 repetitions of vertical jumping with 3 min recovery between sets. The unique load distribution around the shoulders, lumbar region and waist led

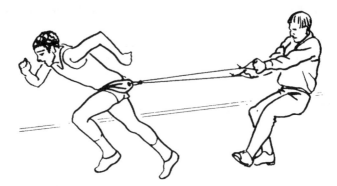

Figure 4.6 Functional overload may be provided by means of a running harness.

them to conclude that this model was a safe device for resistance training. Improvement in performance can be pronounced: Bosco (1985) reported an average increase in vertical jump performance of 10 cm after wearing a vest (11% of body weight) for only 3 weeks.

Running harnesses may be employed to create resistance against the athlete attempting to accelerate from a standing start. The amount of resistance can be controlled by a partner or trainer (see Figure 4.6). Alternative means are attachment to a sled or similar load by means of an abdominal belt. For optimal effects the normal vigorous running action should not be unduly modified. Parachutes have been advocated to increase air resistance when running but their efficacy has not been seriously addressed.

Functional resistance to locomotion may slow the individual too much for the resultant training effects to be of benefit to the football player. Murray *et al.* (2005) showed that speed was generally reduced over 10–20 m as players towed weights ranging from 0–30% body mass, using a waist harness and a 5-m rope. Loads up to 10% body mass are favoured and the procedure seems to promote peak anaerobic power rather than maximal running velocity.

Medicine balls may be utilised for improving sports-specific skills such as throw-ins. Throwing distance can be increased with a dedicated strength training programme for pull-over strength and trunk flexion (Togari and Asami, 1972). These balls can also be used for one-handed exercises in the case of the goalkeeper for whom the skill of throwing the ball long distances is directly relevant.

Overview

Strength and power training should be integral parts of preparation for competitive soccer. The basic foundation may be laid for strength work in the off-season and in the early pre-season. Emphasis can be shifted towards more training for power as the pre-season conditioning is developed. Within each session muscle groups can be altered sequentially to target the different joints: this strategy differs from that used by bodybuilders who might focus on a narrow range of muscle groups in one session. Strength training can be performed 3–4 times each week in the build up and during the season may be reduced to twice a week for maintenance purposes. Some aspects of power training can be incorporated into regular training, for example elements of plyometric exercise. Such inclusions inject variety into the daily training routine.

References

Boocock, M.G., Garbutt, G., Linge, K., Reilly, T. and Troup, J.D.G., 1990, Changes in stature following drop jumping and post exercise gravity inversion. *Medicine and Science in Sports and Exercise*, **22**, 385–390.

Bosco, C., 1985, Adaptive response of human skeletal muscle to simulated hypergravity. *Acta Physiologica Scandinavica*, **124**, 507–513.

Bosco, C., Cardinale, M. and Tsarpela, O., 1999, Influence of vibration on mechanical power and electromyogram activity in human arm flexor muscles. *European Journal of Applied Physiology*, **79**, 306–311.

Cardinale, M. and Wakeling, J., 2005, Whole body vibration exercise: are vibrations good for you? *British Journal of Sports Medicine*, **39**, 585–589.

Chu, D., 1998, *Jumping into Plyometrics, 2nd edition*. Champaign, IL: Human Kinetics.

Cochrane, D.J. and Stannard, S.R., 2005, Acute whole body vibration training increases vertical jump and flexibility performance in elite female field hockey players. *British Journal of Sports Medicine*, **39**, 860–865.

Fowler, N.E., Lees, A. and Reilly, T., 1997, Changes in stature following plyometric deep jump and pendulum exercise. *Ergonomics*, **40**, 1279–1286.

Gilbert, G. and Lees, A., 2003, Maximum grip width regulations in powerlifting discriminate against larger athletes. In: *Kinanthropometry VIII* (edited by T. Reilly and M. Marfell-Jones), London: Routledge, pp. 175–180.

Graham-Smith, P., Fell, N., Gilbert, G., Burke, J. and Reilly, T., 2001, Ergonomic evaluation of a weighted vest for power training. In: *Contemporary Ergonomics 2001* (edited by M.A. Hanson), London: Taylor and Francis, pp. 493–497.

Issurin, V.B., 2005, Vibrations and their application in sport. A review. *Journal of Sports Medicine and Physical Fitness*, **45**, 324–336.

Murray, A., Aitchinson, T.C., Ross, G., Sutherland, K., Watt, I., McLean, D. and Grant, S., 2005, The effect of towing a range of relative resistances on sprint performance. *Journal of Sports Sciences*, **23**, 927–935.

O'Donoghue, D.H., 1970, *Treatment of Injuries to Athletes*. Philadelphia: W.B. Saunders.

Perrin, D.H., 1993, *Isokinetic Exercise and Assessment*. Champaign, IL: Human Kinetics.

Reilly, T., 1981, *Sports Fitness and Sports Injuries*. London: Faber and Faber.

Reilly, T., 1983, The energy cost and mechanical efficiency of circuit weight-training. *Journal of Human Movement Studies*, **9**, 39–45.

Reilly, T. and Thomas, V., 1978, Multi-station equipment for physical training: design and validation of a prototype. *Applied Ergonomics*, **9**, 201–206.

Robinson, M., Lees, A. and Barton, G., 2005, An electromyographic investigation of abdominal exercises and the effects of fatigue. *Ergonomics*, **48**, 1604–1612.

Staron, R.S., Karapondo, D.L., Kraemer, W.J., Fry, A.C., Gordon, S.E., Falkel, J.E., Hagerman, F.C. and Hikida, R.S., 1994, Skeletal muscle adaptations during early phase of heavy-resistance training in men and women. *Journal of Applied Physiology*, **76**, 1247–1255.

Togari, H. and Asami, T., 1972, A study of throw-in training in soccer. *Proceedings of the Department of Physical Education, College of General Education, University of Tokyo*, **6**, 33–38.

Verhoshanski, V., 1969, Perspectives in the improvement of speed–strength for jumpers. *Review of Soviet Physical Education and Sports*, **4(2)**, 28–29.

Wisløff, U., Castagna, C., Helgerud, J., Jones, R. and Hoff, J., 2004, Strong correlation of maximal squat strength with sprint performance and vertical jump height in elite soccer players. *British Journal of Sports Medicine*, **38**, 285–288.

Chapter 5

Aerobic training

Introduction

Aerobic training implies that the training programme is designed to improve the oxygen transport system. It is imperative during soccer match-play and training sessions that there is a good supply of oxygen to the active muscles and that these tissues have the capability to use the oxygen that is provided by the circulatory system. Aerobic training therefore has central and peripheral aspects, an effect on the cardiac output and the circulation of blood on one hand and an increased ability of the muscle to take up and utilise the oxygen that is offered.

The dimensions of the training stimulus are its duration, intensity and frequency. The effect can be highly specific to the mode of exercise. Improvements in aerobic fitness are reflected in the capability to sustain exercise at a given intensity for longer than was previously possible. Endurance suggests an ability to maintain exercise for a prolonged period and can be improved by focusing either on the duration or the intensity of training. Training at high intensity can entail intermittent exercise, with recovery periods intervening between the strenuous efforts. Aerobic training enhances the ability to recover quickly from strenuous activity as well as improve the capability to sustain exercise (Tomlin and Wenger, 2001).

In a soccer context the major need to raise the level of aerobic fitness applies in the pre-season period. The game itself may improve the oxygen transport system but not at a rate to achieve optimal physiological changes. For this reason the training prior to the competitive season is likely to have more formal fitness and conditioning work than at other times during the season. Gains accrued from aerobic training are likely to be less pronounced within the competitive season.

The duration of exercise that is sustainable is inversely related to the intensity at which it is performed. The longer that exercise is continued, the lower is the exercise intensity or work-rate that can be tolerated. All-out short-term exercise is fuelled mainly by anaerobic sources whereas sustained endurance exercise is almost entirely supported by aerobic metabolism (Table 5.1). An understanding of the biochemical processes involved is provided by considering the means of energy production.

Table 5.1 Relative contributions of anaerobic and aerobic processes to total energy output, during maximal exercise of different durations

Energy output (kJ)				Relative contribution (%)	
Work time maximal exercise	Anaerobic processes	Aerobic processes	Total	Anaerobic processes	Aerobic processes
10 s	84	16	100	83	17
1 min	126	84	210	60	40
2 min	126	189	315	40	60
5 min	126	504	630	20	80
10 min	105	1,025	1,130	9	91
30 min	84	2,825	2,909	3	97
60 min	63	5,023	5,086	1	99

Source: Reproduced from Reilly, 1981, *Sports Fitness and Sports Injuries*, London: Faber and Faber Ltd.

Aerobic energy production

Aerobic energy is produced within the muscle mitochondria by use of oxygen, which is taken up from the blood. The substrate for this reaction may be formed through glycolysis, which refers to utilisation of carbohydrates. Substrates may also be derived by catabolism of fat and, to a lesser extent, amino acids.

The net reaction of carbohydrate utilisation is:

$$\text{Glycogen (glucose)} + 39(38) \text{ ADP} + 39(38) \text{ P}_i + 39(38) \text{ H}^+ + 6 \text{ O}_2$$
$$\rightarrow 39(38) \text{ ATP} + 6 \text{ CO}_2 + 6 \text{ H}_2\text{O}.$$

Three of the 39 ATP molecules produced are formed anaerobically. Glycogen stored within the exercising muscles is the primary form of carbohydrate used for glycolysis, but glucose taken up in the blood from the liver also can be used. Glucose is formed in the liver from the breakdown of glycogen (glycogenolysis). It may also be formed from precursors such as glycerol, pyruvate, lactate and amino acids by means of a process known as gluconeogenesis.

The net reactions of utilising a representative free fatty acid (such as palmitate) are:

$$\text{Palmitate} + 129 \text{ ATP} + 129 \text{ P}_i + 23 \text{ O}_2 \rightarrow 129 \text{ ATP} + 16 \text{ H}_2\text{O} + 16 \text{ CO}_2$$

Triglycerides (triacylglycerol) stored in the body's adipose tissue cells and also within the muscles form the substrates for fat oxidation. Triglycerides are broken down by lipase enzymes through a process known as lipolysis into glycerol and free fatty acids. The basic unit is one molecule of glycerol and three molecules of free fatty acids. The free fatty acids are mobilised in the bloodstream and enter the muscle fibres by diffusion where they are catabolised by the mitochondria.

Fat provides about twice as much energy per gram as does carbohydrate, and so is a good means of storing energy reserves. Oxidation of carbohydrate requires less energy than does fat and consequently the latter is the preferred fuel when exercise is at high intensity.

Fat is the preferred substrate for exercise during long training sessions and when exercise intensity is relatively low. This form of exercise is useful for weight-control purposes due to the so-called fat-burning effect. The relative contribution to the energy production from oxidation of carbohydrates is increased with increasing exercise intensities. Glycolysis leading to formation of lactate contributes significantly to energy production only when exercise intensities exceed about 60% of maximum oxygen uptake ($\dot{V}O_{2\,max}$). As exercise continues, the glycogen concentration in the exercising muscles becomes progressively reduced, which leads to increases in uptake of glucose from the blood and a greater reliance on fat oxidation.

In the initial phase of exercise the production of energy by aerobic metabolism is limited due to a delay in increasing oxygen supply to the exercising muscles. Direct sources of O_2 which can be used at the start of exercise comprise O_2 bound to myoglobin (Mb) and haemoglobin (Hb) in blood within the muscle, and further O_2 dissolved in the muscles. This local oxygen store represents only about 5% of the total energy turnover during the first 6 s of maximal exercise. The anaerobic energy production for a 30-s exercise bout contributes about 11% of the total energy turnover (Bangsbo, 1994a).

The duration as well as the intensity of the exercise bouts in an intermittent exercise programme determines the amount of lactate that accumulates both in the muscle and in the blood. Saltin and Essén (1971) kept the ratio between exercise and recovery constant at 1:2. The muscle and blood lactate concentrations were only slightly higher than at rest when the exercise time was 10 and 20 s, whereas the concentrations were considerably increased with exercise bouts of 30 and 60 s duration.

The duration of the rest periods in between the exercise bouts also affects metabolic responses during intense exercise. In a study by Margaria et al. (1969), the subjects exercised repeatedly for 10 s at an intensity that led to exhaustion after 30–40 s, when performed continuously. Blood lactate concentration increased progressively when the periods of exercise were separated by 10 s of rest, while it was only slightly elevated with 30 s of rest in between the exercise bouts.

A marked difference in muscle fibre type recruitment has been observed between continuous and intermittent exercise protocols. While it was mainly the slow twitch (ST) fibres that were activated during the continuous exercise, both ST and fast-twitch (FT) fibres were involved in the intermittent exercise (Essén, 1978). The different pattern of fibre type recruitment between continuous and intermittent exercise has important implications for training. By performing the training intermittently it is possible to train some muscle fibres (FT fibres) that would have been recruited only after hours of sub-maximal continuous exercise. This fact is particularly relevant for sports such as soccer in which high-intensity exercise frequently occurs. Intermittent exercise also allows a prolonged high metabolic stress without fatiguing the fibres that are recruited. Essén (1978) compared intermittent exercise with continuous exercise performed at the same power output (corresponding to $\dot{V}O_{2\ max}$). The continuous exercise led to exhaustion within a few minutes, whereas the intermittent exercise could be sustained for 1 hour without inducing fatigue. The rate of glycogen utilisation and lactate accumulation during continuous exercise at the high intensity was greater and the rate of fat oxidation was much lower than during the intermittent exercise. The intermittent protocol was a much more effective means of sparing energy reserves and extending the duration of exercise than was the continuous exercise format.

Oxygen transport

The oxygen transport system comprises an integrated involvement of lungs, heart, oxygen carriage in the blood and utilisation in muscle cells. The take up at cellular level is influenced by the blood supply, the network of capillaries around muscle fibres, the mitochondrial number and content and the type of muscle fibres. Central factors, incorporating pulmonary and cardiac parameters as well as blood volume and content, determine the amount of oxygen that is delivered to the active tissues. Peripheral or local factors refer to the ability of skeletal muscles to use the oxygen that is offered to them by means of the circulation (Figure 5.1). These factors are influenced both by heredity and by training.

The process by which ambient air is brought into the lungs and exchanged with air passing through them is known as pulmonary ventilation. At rest

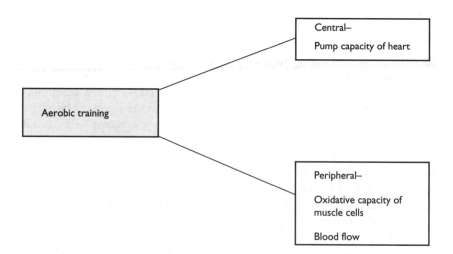

Figure 5.1 The effects of aerobic training are both central and peripheral.

approximately 250 ml of oxygen leaves the *alveoli* and enters the blood for each breath, whereas about 200 ml of CO_2 diffuses in the reverse direction to be exhaled during breathing. Over 20 times this amount of oxygen may be transferred across the alveolar membrane during heavy exercise and pulmonary ventilation may increase from $6 \, l \cdot min^{-1}$ at rest to about $200 \, l \cdot min^{-1}$ in top class athletes. The main purpose of ventilation during aerobic exercise is to maintain a constant and favourable concentration of O_2 and CO_2 in the alveolar chambers. An effective exchange of gases is thereby ensured before the oxygenated blood leaves the lungs for transport throughout the body.

The performance of aerobic exercise is not normally limited by lung capacity except under certain circumstances. Lung function may be restricted in asthmatic individuals. This restriction is usually indicated by a subnormal value for the forced expiratory volume (FEV_1) which is measured in a single breath of forceful exhalation and reflects the power of the lungs. Values are reduced in players suffering from asthma or exercise-induced bronchospasm. Exercise-induced asthma is generally triggered post-exercise and recovery may take 30–50 min unless bronchodilators are employed to ease breathing difficulties.

Ventilatory responses to exercise may be altered as a consequence of aerobic training. As maximal oxygen uptake ($\dot{V}O_{2 \, max}$) is elevated with training, there is an increase in the corresponding minute ventilation ($\dot{V}E_{max}$). There is a reduction in the ventilation equivalent of oxygen ($\dot{V}E/\dot{V}O_2$) at sub-maximal exercise so that less air is inhaled at a given oxygen consumption (Rasmussen *et al.*, 1975). The expired air of trained athletes contains less oxygen than that of untrained individuals for a given $\dot{V}O_2$ (Tzankoff *et al.*, 1972). This reduction reflects the capacity of trained muscle to extract more of the oxygen passing through the tissues in the local circulation. Endurance training also results in an elevation in the ventilation threshold (Tvent) which represents the exercise intensity at which $\dot{V}E$ starts to rise disproportionately to $\dot{V}O_2$ in response to a progressive exercise test. This effect may be related to metabolic alterations but is specific to the exercise modality used in training (Reilly and Bangsbo, 1998).

The cardiac output, which indicates the amount of blood pumped from the heart, is a function of the stroke volume and the heart rate. Cardiac output may increase from $5 \, l \cdot min^{-1}$ at rest to $30 \, l \cdot min^{-1}$ at maximal oxygen consumption, depending on the capacity of the individual. The cardiac output of Olympic endurance athletes may exceed this upper level. With endurance training there is an increase in left ventricular chamber size and a consequent decrease in resting and sub-maximal heart rate, an increase in maximal cardiac output, a rise in maximal oxygen uptake and an increase in total blood volume. The maximal ability to consume oxygen tends to be limited by central factors (cardiac output) rather than peripheral factors (including oxidative capacity of skeletal muscle) in elite athletes who are adapted physiologically to endurance training. Both of these limitations may apply to soccer players.

The improved endurance capacity of trained muscle is partly due to an increase in its capillary density. In athletes, values 20% greater than normal have been reported for the number of capillaries per muscle and in a given cross section (Brodal et al., 1976). A corresponding difference in $\dot{V}O_{2\,max}$ was observed between endurance athletes and an untrained group. There are also metabolic adaptations in muscle that enhance oxidative capacity. There is, for example, an increase in both number and size of the mitochondria with enhancement of enzymes of the Krebs cycle and electron transport system (Holloszy and Coyle, 1984).

Elite endurance athletes tend to be endowed with a muscle fibre type composition that is appropriate to the demands of the sport (Bergh et al., 1978). For example, whilst the twitch characteristics of muscle fibres seem to be unaffected by endurance training, their histochemical properties are altered. Endurance runners have a predominance of ST muscle fibres as do cross-country skiers. The abundance of myoglobin gives rise to the naming of these fibres as red and they also possess high levels of mitochondria. Furthermore with endurance training the so-called intermediate FTa (Type IIa) fibres assume more of the biochemical make-up of ST (Type I) fibres, showing increased oxidative enzymes and elevated myoglobin levels. Muscle biopsies from soccer players demonstrate a balanced combination of fibre types, variability within a team reflecting the specialised roles of different playing positions (see Reilly and Doran, 2003).

Endurance training

General endurance is an important component of fitness for games or prolonged exercise, since individuals are more likely to commit errors and adopt techniques that may lead to injury as fatigue sets in and co-ordination declines. Endurance fitness is chiefly a function of the oxygen transport system and its consumption by the working tissues. It is particularly relevant where a high percentage of maximal oxygen consumption has to be utilised for a prolonged period, such as in elite professional soccer. All endurance training schedules are designed to improve aerobic capacity, the most pronounced effects being shared between the heart and the involved skeletal muscles. In general, central and peripheral factors account approximately equally for the overall improvement. An increase of 25% in $\dot{V}O_{2\,max}$ is regarded as a good training effect but improvements in endurance performance may be much more pronounced than this value. As the variability between individuals in $\dot{V}O_{2\,max}$ exceeds the typical training effects on the parameter, the conclusion is that genetic factors have a greater influence on the determination of top endurance athletes than does physical training. Nevertheless a small improvement in $\dot{V}O_{2\,max}$ can have more emphatic effects on exercise at a proportional utilisation of the maximal value. It can also benefit the soccer player by enabling more activity off-the-ball to be performed and a more speedy recovery from high-intensity activity.

Endurance training protocols fall into one of two categories, namely continuous or intermittent exercise. Regular high-intensity work leads to a significant increase of the respiratory capacity of the active muscles. Because exercise is intense, risk of soft-tissue damage is prevalent, particularly in the muscles and tendons of the lower limbs in running. Long, slow distance work at moderate intensity is used by athletes specialising in prolonged duration events or as background conditioning for events like middle-distance running. Enhancement of respiratory proteins involved in aerobic metabolism and located within the muscle mitochondria is related to the duration of exercise and so this type of training is particularly effective. As a result of the high energy expenditure per workout, fat depots are trimmed and risk of muscle and tendon injury associated with repeatedly lifting 'excess dead-weight' against gravity is reduced. This form of training is demanding in time commitment so that its main use by soccer players is during the off-season and pre-season and then only sparingly.

The exercise intensity during training may be regulated by monitoring the heart rate of players (see Table 5.2). Such a facility is now available by means of short-range radio telemetry. It may be employed in either continuous or intermittent exercise. The heart rate may be maintained within a designated range according to the aims of the session, depending on whether it is a recovery day or an intense day.

A large volume of work is performed in long-duration training and it is not surprising that over-use syndromes may occur. The more common injuries are observed in runners more than in soccer players and include march fractures, lower fibular stress fractures, anterior tibial compartmental problems, chondromalacia patellae and trochanteric bursitis. All too frequently inadequate footwear, hard surfaces and large ground reaction forces are implicated. Such unyielding surfaces may be encountered if soccer training is conducted on sun-baked pitches in the summer's pre-season period.

The duration of a typical long-duration session may be reduced if soccer practice is separated from the fitness work and included later in the day. The exercise intensity is usually around 60–65% of the maximal oxygen uptake with heart rates around 140–150 beats.min^{-1}. Five sessions per week have been recommended as maximum (Pollock and Wilmore, 1990) but this frequency may

Table 5.2 Principles of aerobic training

	Heart rate				Oxygen uptake	
	% of HR$_{max}$		Beats/min		% of $\dot{V}O_{2max}$	
	Mean	Range	Mean[a]	Range[a]	Mean	Range
Recovery training	65	40–80	130	80–160	55	20–70
Low-intensity training	80	65–90	160	130–180	70	55–85
High-intensity	90	80–100	180	160–200	85	70–100

Source: Reprinted with permission, from Bangsbo, 2003, p. 50.

Note
a assumes HR$_{max}$ is 200 beats.min^{-1}.

be too much for soccer players when two matches are scheduled within one week. It is preferable to vary the format of training, in terms of its intensity and type as well as duration.

Interval training

In interval training, repeated work bouts 0.5–5 min in duration are interspersed with recovery periods of somewhat similar lengths. These schedules are used extensively by swimmers, cyclists, rowers and runners and can be adapted for soccer players. High muscle lactate levels may be induced by the exercise bouts and lactate levels in blood may rise progressively with each repeated effort. There is some evidence that recovery from the intense efforts is improved as a result of aerobic training (Tomlin and Wenger, 2001). This ability may be trained by maintaining an activity level at about 60% of the maximal heart rate in between the more strenuous efforts. Active recovery between the successive exercise bouts enhances the removal of lactate from the blood. There is a linear relation between the intensity of the active recovery, and blood lactate disappearance up to an exercise intensity of about 60% $\dot{V}O_{2\,max}$ (Gollnick and Hermansen, 1973).

The coach can vary the number of repetitions, the duration of the effort, the exercise intensity and the recovery time between the efforts. Altering the duration of the efforts between days introduces variety into the training stimulus. The number of repetitions can be increased systematically as fitness is developed whilst the pace can then be quickened. Finally, the recovery periods can be shortened; anaerobic endurance is also stressed when these periods are inadequate to allow full recovery.

In 'interval training' as originally developed, the optimum exercise intensity was deemed to be that which elicited heart rates of about 180 beats·min^{-1} while recovery was terminated when the rate fell to about 120 beats·min^{-1}. These rates were thought to provide the optimum stimulus for the heart. This method of training is more likely to increase maximum oxygen uptake than is continuous sub-maximal exercise performance (Rusko, 1987). Placing an emphasis on high-intensity exercise promotes the recruitment of FT muscle fibres and so enhances training of peripheral as well as central factors.

Variations of interval training

Fartlek, pyramid training and parlauf are forms of interval training that are not so rigid. Fartlek or 'speed play' originated in the running trails of the Swedish forests and entails sustained exercise in which the tempo is frequently altered, usually to coincide with the type of terrain. The intensity may be varied spontaneously from hard efforts to light exercise according to the individual's disposition. This relative freedom makes fartlek enjoyable when players train on their own. The flexibility in applying this training stimulus ensures that all the major metabolic pathways are stressed at some time. Incorporating a fartlek session 3 times a week into the training programme has proved to be more effective than 20 min at so-called 'anaerobic threshold' in improving 10-km time of runners. Both programmes decreased the blood lactate response during sub-maximal exercise without increasing $\dot{V}O_{2\,max}$ (Acavedo and Goldfarb, 1989).

Pyramid training provides a formal means of varying the duration and intensity of exercise and the recovery intermission. Sessions may involve, for example, consecutive runs of 100, 200, 400, 800 and 1,200 m with a short time in between allowed for recovery. The individual then returns down the distances to finish with a sprint before warming down. This programme is suitable for application in small groups. A soccer squad, for example, may be broken down into 3–4 separate groups compatible with their running abilities.

Parlauf or continuous relays can be introduced into training routines to stimulate team spirit for games players. This form of training can engage two, three or four members per team for a period pre-determined by the coaching staff. In the two-per-team format, rest periods do not permit complete recovery so that performance may inevitably deteriorate. This type of regimen promotes competition between pairs and is suited for training by games players when variety is needed.

Aerobics training

The demand for exercise as a means of acquiring health-related fitness spawned the form of exercise known as 'aerobics'. Its popularity developed alongside 'sport for all' campaigns and health-promotion drives to participate in physical training for recreational purposes. It was recognised that exercise programmes, especially when combined with dietary regimens, reduce the risk of cardiovascular disorders and aid recovery from circulatory problems.

Exercise training should engage major muscle groups in continuous activity for 20–30 min a day, 3 days a week for positive physiological benefits to be induced. The intensity of exercise should be within 50–80% $\dot{V}O_{2\,max}$ or in excess of 60% of the maximal heart rate. In calculating the exercise heart rate that elicits a training stimulus to the circulatory system, the formula of Karvonen (1959) has been adapted. This specifies that the exercise heart rate should be above 60% of the estimated heart-rate range (maximum minus resting heart rate). Thus for an individual with a maximum heart rate of 180 and a resting rate of 60 beats·min^{-1} the training threshold is 132 beats·min^{-1}. Where the maximum heart rate is not known, it is estimated by the formula 220–age in years, although in a minority of cases this formula overestimates the ageing effect on the maximal heart rate. The heart rate response to exercise programmes has been used to assess their suitability for training the oxygen transport system in so-called 'aerobics' programmes.

The original form of aerobics consisted of a long sequence of exercises performed to music. High-impact exercises induced injuries and are generally avoided in programmes tailored to individuals of low initial fitness levels. Commercially available videos provide exercise regimens for participants to follow in their own homes. Many of these programmes are not designed on ergonomic principles and do not match the capabilities of those using them (Reilly, 1992).

Circuit weight-training has also been promoted as a means of improving the capacity of the oxygen transport system (Garbutt et al., 1994). The individual rotates around a series of exercises set out in a circle, usually 8 to 12 separate exercises being involved. Muscle groups engaged are varied between work stations, the purpose being that local muscular fatigue is avoided whilst stress is maintained on the cardiovascular system. A suitably designed programme can have relevance for soccer players (see Chapters 4 and 7).

Various exercise modes have been employed over the last decade for 'aerobics' training. These types of exercise include cycling, jogging, swim-aerobics, deep-water running, ladder-climbing and stepping (see Chapter 7). These activities have been supplemented by use of sports equipment such as rowing ergometers and ski-simulators. Their effectiveness depends on product design and flexibility for the individual to raise the exercise intensity. Recreational and amateur players may benefit most from these forms of 'aerobics training' although they can have value at all levels on 'recovery' days.

Combined and cross-training

Soccer makes particular demands on anaerobic pathways and on muscular strength as well as on the oxygen transport mechanisms. Whilst aerobic metabolism provides the main energy sources during soccer matches, the critical aspects of performance may depend on anaerobic efforts (Bangsbo, 1994b). Consequently aerobic training must be used in conjunction with other components of fitness in the preparation of such players for performance. For this reason intermittent regimens, especially if they are related to games drills, are relevant in a soccer context.

There may be unwanted interactions between endurance and muscle strength. When endurance training gets complete emphasis in pre-season conditioning periods, muscle strength may be adversely affected (Hickson, 1980). If muscle strength programmes predominate for a prolonged period, the ensuing hypertrophy of fibres may lead to a lowered capillary to muscle fibre ratio. In this case oxygen supply to active fibres may be compromised. It is, therefore, important that the training programme is balanced according to the needs of the players. It is essential also that the design of training should take into account the stage of the season and the competitive schedule. Rigorous and exhaustive training in the days leading up to competition will adversely affect performance. This is because of a reduction in muscle glycogen to below normal levels at the start of play and an earlier onset of fatigue during the game (Saltin, 1973).

Small-sided games

Soccer players are more attracted to drills performed with the ball than to formal fitness work such as repetitive runs. In one study of the energy cost of dribbling

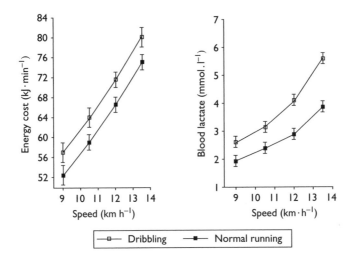

Figure 5.2 The energy cost of dribbling a soccer ball at various speeds of running. The blood lactate responses are shown on the right (from Reilly and Ball, 1984).

Source: Reprinted with permission from *Research Quarterly for Exercise and Sport*, **55**, 269–270, Copyright 1984 by the American Alliance for Health, Physical Education, Recreation and Dance, 1900 Association Drive, Reston, VA 20191 USA.

a ball, Reilly and Ball (1984) showed that oxygen consumption, heart rate, blood lactate and perceived exertion were elevated by the task of dribbling compared to normal running (Figure 5.2). At a particular running speed, the training stimulus was raised when the ball was employed. Their recommendation was to utilise training drills with the ball where possible.

Small-sided games may be used to increase individual player involvement in play. In 9 vs 9 or 7 vs 7, play may resemble behaviour in a full-blown game. It is possible to enhance participation of individual players by imposing conditions on play in smaller-sided games (e.g. 5 vs 5) by setting limits in the number of touches allowed (one-touch, two-touch) and by restricting play to certain areas of the field. The size of the area should be carefully matched to suit the standard of play. The intensity of play may be maintained by vocal support from the coach.

Games of 5 vs 5 are especially suited to indoor gymnasia. MacLaren *et al.* (1988) demonstrated that average heart rates of 170 beats·min^{-1} are sustained during indoor 5-a-side matches. Later, Miles *et al.* (1993) found similar results for female players.

In young players it is important to engage them directly in play as often as possible in order to enhance their learning opportunities. Platt *et al.* (2001) combined a physiological and technical analysis of under-age soccer in the course of a comparison of 3 vs 3 and 5 vs 5 matches. The players studied were all under 12 years of age.

Compared to the 5 vs 5 youth matches, 3 vs 3 games resulted in:

1 more high-intensity activity such as sprinting and cruising;
2 longer periods of time and distances travelled in possession of the ball;
3 more short and medium range passes, more successful passes, forward passes, dribbles and attempts at goal.

Mean heart rates were 184 beats·min^{-1} for the 3 vs 3 compared with 172 beats·min^{-1} for the 5 vs 5 matches. After 10 min of a 15-min game, the difference between groups narrowed (Figure 5.3). The observations as a whole were interpreted as evidence that the smaller-sided condition was more appropriate for development of technical skills as well as providing the higher physiological stimulus.

Classical interval-training stimuli may be mimicked in drills with the ball. Reilly and White (2005) showed that players engaged in work with the ball exercised as hard as players doing repetition runs in 6 times 4-min efforts with 3-min rest. Over a 6-week period supplementary training 3 times per week helped youth players to maintain aerobic fitness equally as well as did interval training over the same period.

In a study of top professional players, Sassi et al. (2005) showed that drills with the ball were as effective as interval training, (e.g. 4 × 1,000 m runs) in eliciting aerobic training stimuli. Pressing players on the ball and small-sided games without a goalkeeper were the most effective models. In contrast technical–tactical work induced lighter loads, more appropriate for recovery days (see Table 5.3).

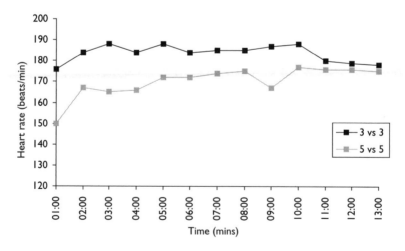

Figure 5.3 Heart rate responses to small-sided games in under-12 year old boys in a 15-min game.

Source: From Platt et al., 2001.

Table 5.3 Mean ± SD heart rate (beats·min⁻¹) and blood lactate (mmol·l⁻¹) during different training drills

	$4 \times 100\ m$	4 vs 4		8 vs 8 (1/2 pitch)		Technical-tactical drills
		Without goalkeeper	With goalkeeper	Free touch	Free touch (pressing)	
Heart rate	167 ± 4	178 ± 7	174 ± 7	160 ± 3	175 ± 4	140 ± 5
Blood lactate	7.9 ± 3.4	6.4 ± 2.7	6.2 ± 1.4	3.3 ± 1.2	—	2.9 ± 0.8

Source: Reprinted with permission, from Sassi *et al.*, 2005, p. 342.

Impellizeri and co-workers (2006) compared generic (running) to specific (small-sided games) training in 40 junior Italian players. The training consisted of 4 bouts of 4 min at 90–95% of maximum heart rate with 3-min active rest periods in between. The sessions were added to normal training twice each week for 4 weeks in the pre-season period and continued for 8 weeks into the competitive season. The most pronounced effects were in sub-maximal lactate responses, but also $\dot{V}O_{2\,max}$ improved. With the elevation in aerobic fitness, there was an accompanying increase in the distance covered in a game of 6% (571 m). The heart rate during matches was in excess of 90% of maximum for longer towards the end of the training period than it was in the pre-season period. This observation highlights how an improvement in fitness is reflected in the increased ability to handle higher training loads as the programme is continued.

In utilising on-field training, the day of the week is highly relevant. Low-intensity recovery training is appropriate the day following a game. Typically, the energy expenditure during training is higher in mid-week in preparation for the week-end's competitive match. Mid-week training often entails a full rehearsal for the impending contest with the first team playing the reserves (Reilly and Thomas, 1979). There is then a gradual taper in training in order to be fresh for match-play.

There is also a need to place training in a seasonal context. During times of frequent matches, for example two matches each week for consecutive weeks, training has mainly a maintenance purpose. At these times tackling can be eliminated in order to reduce the risk of incurring injury. When the fixture calendar becomes congested, the games themselves constitute a strong training stimulus.

A variety of soccer-specific drills is available within coaching manuals which can be modified to provide the desired training stimulus. One of the examples provided by Bangsbo (1994b) was that the pitch may be divided into three zones, players contesting possession in the peripheral zone. At a signal from the coach (or on reaching the intermediate objective), the play is directed across the mid-zone and recommences in the adjacent peripheral zone. The regular switching of activity across the mid-zone (where no play occurs) forces the players to engage in high-intensity locomotion.

An alternative is where goals are placed in the middle of each half. The possession may be contested in this middle area, but touches of the ball are limited to six successive possessions after which an attack must be commenced. The attack must be from behind the goal (in order to score into the back of the goal) and there should be at least three attackers in these areas. Theses rules are designed to maintain the interest of the players and the intensity of the game.

The exercise to rest ratio may be manipulated to form a high-intensity aerobic training session. Examples are alternation of groups of 1 min, 2 min, 3 min or 4 min, with one group actively recovering whilst the other is exercising, in for example a 4 vs 4 set-up. In another high-intensity session, players alternate in a 2 vs 2 set-up and an exercise to rest ratio of 1:1 (Bangsbo, 1994b). There is a progressive rise in heart rate and in blood lactate, sampled in the 1-min recovery after each 1-min training.

Recommendations

The following are advocated:

1 Coaching drills may be modified in order to represent physiological as well as technical training effects; the coach and trainer should agree to the modifications being implemented.
2 Training intensity may be regulated by means of determining exercise to rest ratios and durations of the exercise bouts. It may be monitored by means of physiological responses such as heart rate.
3 The training should be periodised so that the time of the week and the stage of the season are important criteria.

Overview

Aerobic training programmes must place demands on the metabolic pathways stressed in competition. The activity must be matched to that of the game, since training effects are specific to the mode of exercise. Aerobic training must take into account the duration and the frequency of the intense efforts during competition. Adaptations to game intensity may be achieved by using drills with the ball.

Aerobic training engages central and peripheral factors linked with oxygen transport and utilisation by the active muscles. Physiological alterations provoked by endurance training depend on the intensity of exercise, the duration of training, the exercise mode and the training frequency. Adaptations to sub-maximal intensities may be more important than are maximal responses in determining endurance performance. So-called 'aerobics' training has relevance for health-related, rather than elite, performance but may be used on 'recovery' days. Irrespective of the standard of the individual, environmental factors (such as time of day, temperature and pressure) will have an impact on the performance. They must be taken into consideration when the overall training schedules of the team are planned.

References

Acavedo, E.D. and Goldfarb, A.N., 1989, Increasing training intensity effects on plasma lactate, ventilatory threshold and endurance. *Medicine and Science in Sports and Exercise*, **21**, 563–568.

Bangsbo, J., 1994a, The physiology of soccer with special reference to intense intermittent exercise. *Acta Physiologica Scandinavica*, **151**, Suppl. 619, 1–155.

Bangsbo, J., 1994b, *Fitness Training for Soccer*. Storm: Copenhagen.

Bangsbo, J., 2003, Physiology of training: In: *Science and Soccer* (edited by T. Reilly and A.M. Williams), London: Routledge, pp. 47–58.

Bergh, U., Thorstensson, A., Sjodin, B., Hulten, B., Piehl, K. and Karlsson, J., 1978, Maximal oxygen uptake and muscle fibre types in trained and untrained humans. *Medicine and Science in Sport*, **10**, 151–154.

Brodal, P., Inger, F. and Hermansen, L., 1976, Capillary supply of skeletal fibres in untrained and endurance trained men. *Acta Physiologica Scandinavica*, Suppl. 440.

Essén, B., 1978, Studies on the regulation of metabolism in human skeletal muscle using intermittent exercise as an experimental model. *Acta Physiologica Scandinavica*, Suppl. **454**, 1–32.

Garbutt, G., Boocock, M.G., Reilly, T. and Troup, J.D.G., 1994, Physiological and spinal responses to circuit weight-training. *Ergonomics*, **37**, 117–125.

Gollnick, P.D. and Hermansen, L., 1973, Biochemical adaptations to exercise: anaerobic metabolism. In: *Exercise and Sports Sciences Reviews* (edited by J.H. Wilmore), Vol. 1, Academic Press: New York.

Hickson, R.C., 1980, Interference of strength development by simultaneously training for strength and endurance. *European Journal of Applied Physiology*, **42**, 372–376.

Holloszy, J.O. and Coyle, E.F., 1984, Adaptations of skeletal muscle to endurance training and their metabolic consequences. *Journal of Applied Physiology*, **56**, 831–838.

Impellizeri, F.M., Marcora, S.M., Iaia, F.M., Rampinini, E. and Reilly, T., 2006, Physiological and performance effects of generic versus specific aerobic training in soccer players. *International Journal of Sports Medicine*, **27**, 483–492.

Karvonen, M.J., 1959, Problems of training the cardiovascular system. *Ergonomics*, **2**, 207–215.

MacLaren, D., Davids, K., Isokawa, M. and Reilly, T., 1988, Physiological strain in 4-a-side soccer. In: *Science and Football* (edited by T. Reilly, A. Lees, K. Davids and W.J. Murphy), London: E. & F.N. Spon, pp. 230–236.

Margaria, R., Olivia, R.D., Di Prampero, P.E. and Cerretelli, P., 1969, Energy utilisation in intermittent exercise of supramaximal intensity. *Journal of Applied Physiology*, **26**, 752–756.

Miles, A., MacLaren, D., Reilly, T. and Yamanaka, K., 1993, An analysis of physiological strain in four-a-side women's soccer. In: *Science and Football II* (edited by T. Reilly, J. Clarys and A. Stibbe), London: E. & F.N. Spon, pp. 140–145.

Platt, D., Maxwell, A., Horn, R., Williams, M. and Reilly, T., 2001, Physiological and technical analysis of 3 vs 3 and 5 vs 5 youth football matches. *Insight: The Football Association's Coaching Association Journal*, **4**(4), 23–24.

Pollock, M.L. and Wilmore, J.H., 1990, *Exercise in Health and Disease: Evaluation and Prescription for Prevention and Rehabilitation*, 2nd edn, Philadelphia, PA: W.B. Saunders.

Rasmusseon, R., Klausen, B., Clausen, J.P. and Trap-Jensen, J., 1975, Pulmonary ventilation, blood gases and blood pH after training of the arms and legs. *Journal of Applied Physiology*, **38**, 250–256.

Reilly, T., 1981, *Sports Fitness and Sports Injuries*. London: Faber and Faber.

Reilly, T., 1992, Physical fitness: for whom and for what? In: *Sport for All* (edited by P. Oja and R. Telama), Amsterdam: Elsevier, pp. 81–88.

Reilly, T. and Ball, D., 1984, The net physiological cost of dribbling a soccer ball. *Research Quarterly for Exercise and Sport*, **55**, 267–271.

Reilly, T. and Bangsbo, J., 1998, Anaerobic and aerobic training. In *Training in Sport: Applying Sport Science* (edited by B. Elliott), Chichester: John Wiley & Sons Ltd., pp. 351–409.

Reilly, T. and Doran, D., 2003, Fitness assessment. In: *Science and Soccer, 2nd edition* (edited by T. Reilly and A.M. Williams), London: Routledge, pp. 21–46.

Reilly, T. and Thomas, V., 1978, Multi-station equipment for physical training: design and validation of a prototype. *Applied Ergonomics*, **9**, 201–206.

Reilly, T. and Thomas, V., 1979, Estimated daily energy expenditure of professional association football players. *Ergonomics*, **22**, 541–548.

Reilly, T. and White, C., 2005, Small-sided games as an alternative to interval training for soccer players. In: *Science and Football V* (edited by T. Reilly, J. Cabri and D. Araujo), London: Routledge, pp. 344–347.

Rusko, H., 1987, The effect of training on aerobic power characteristics of young cross-country skiers. *Journal of Sports Sciences*, **5**, 273–286.

Saltin, B., 1973, Metabolic fundamentals in exercise. *Medicine and Science in Sports*, **5**, 137–146.

Saltin, B. and Essén, B., 1971, Muscle glycogen, lactate, ATP and CP in intermittent exercise. In: *Muscle Metabolism During Exercise: Advances in Experimental Medicine and Biology* (edited by B. Saltin and B. Pernow), Vol. II, New York: Plenum Press, pp. 419–424.

Sassi, R., Reilly, T. and Impellizeri, F., 2005, A comparison of small-sided games and interval training in elite professional soccer players. In: *Science and Football V* (edited by T. Reilly, J. Cabri and D. Araujo), London: Routledge, pp. 341–343.

Tomlin, D.L. and Wenger, H.A., 2001, The relationship between aerobic fitness and recovery from high intensity intermittent exercise. *Sports Medicine*, **31**, 1–11.

Tzankoff, S.P., Robinson, S., Pyke, F.S. and Brawn, C.A., 1972, Physiological adjustments to work in older men as affected by physical training. *Journal of Applied Physiology*, **33**, 346–350.

Chapter 6

Anaerobic training

Introduction

The energy for rapid development of muscle force is provided through anaerobic pathways. Activities such as jumping, striking the ball or sprinting short distances are largely anaerobic. On average, an outfield player must undertake a high-intensity effort every 30 s and an all-out sprint every 90 s, and there is a change in the level of activity once every 4–5 s. Whilst anaerobic activities occur less frequently than do bouts of aerobic exercise at lower intensity, they often contribute to the winning or losing of a game. Their superior speed over short distances was found to distinguish professional soccer players from other games players more than aerobic measures (Strudwick *et al.*, 2002). It is essential therefore that anaerobic energy systems are trained in conjunction with aerobic mechanisms.

The ATP stored within muscle is the primary source of energy for muscle contractions during very short bouts of exercise performed at high intensity. The available supply of this chemical is limited to about 3 s and so if strenuous exercise is to continue the ATP must be reformed. Phosphocreatine (PCr) also stored within the muscle is broken down by creatine kinase, allowing ATP to be regenerated and muscle activity to be continued:

$$PCr + ADP + H^+ \rightarrow ATP + Cr(creatine)$$

This reaction takes place in the absence of oxygen and so is termed anaerobic. As ATP is the substrate that muscle uses directly, its stores are not depleted whereas those of creatine phosphate can be reduced considerably. In certain activities, such as repeated bouts of high-intensity exercise, increasing PCr stores by means of 'creatine loading' can benefit performance, notably in the later efforts in the sequence. Its benefit in soccer match-play is less likely, but creatine loading may be of value in certain training contexts by permitting more work to be performed at high intensity.

When the recovery period between high-intensity activities is too short or if successive sprints are performed, the PCr stores may be reduced to very low levels. The next available source of energy is from the anaerobic breakdown of glycogen stored within the muscle. Glycolysis is the major means of anaerobic energy production but its capacity too is limited to 30–40 s. Anaerobic degradation of glycogen causes lactic acid to increase within muscle which slowly diffuses into the circulation. Hydrogen ions increase, lowering the pH levels within muscle and subsequently in the blood. The level of performance drops, an effect that has been linked with the elevation in muscle lactate. Other explanations of fatigue have included increased concentrations of potassium in the interstitium, reduced neural activation of the muscle fibres, or a failure of the excitation–contraction coupling process. Either a reduced rate of calcium release from the sarcoplasmic reticulum or a decreased rate of calcium re-uptake to the sarcoplasmic reticulum could also be implicated (Reilly and Bangsbo, 1998).

Irrespective of the causes of fatigue during all-out exercise, it is clear that high-intensity activity cannot be sustained for long without a respite for recovery before commencing the next bout of heavy exercise. During a match the fatigue experienced can be transient, the player recovering when the pause is sufficiently long. Further pressure on this individual whilst temporarily fatigued will place him/her at a disadvantage. The player will be much better able to cope after following a regimen of anaerobic training.

Anaerobic training has multiple effects, the most important of which are enhancement of neural activation of muscles, increased activity of creatine kinase and the enzymes in the glycolytic pathway. Anaerobic training can also increase the amount of glycogen stored within the active muscles and enhance their capacity to neutralise the effects of hydrogen ions, thereby delaying or offsetting fatigue. The aims of anaerobic training can be expressed as:

1 to improve the rate of force development and the peak force achieved during brief, fast movements;
2 to improve speed over short distances;
3 to enhance the provision of anaerobic energy so that an all-out sprint can be sustained for longer without training;
4 to improve the capability of performing repeated sprints by enabling the player to recover quickly from strenuous efforts.

These aims refer to power and acceleration, speed and speed endurance (production and repetition) respectively. These components of physical conditioning for soccer must be complemented by other attributes that form unique requirements of the game. These include agility, reactions, timing of movements and implementation of games skills accurately and often at speed. There is a wealth of practices for training these characteristics, adapted from training theory rather than based on experimental evidence.

Speed training

Stride rate and stride length

It is possible to separate the 'top speed' component of running from the initial acceleration that is dependent on muscle strength and power. Pure speed is

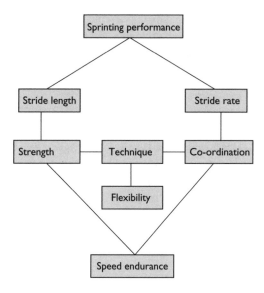

Figure 6.1 Factors limiting performance in sprinting.

Source: Reproduced with permission, from N. Stein (1998) 'Speed training in sport' in *Training in Sport: Applying Sport Science*, edited by B. Elliott. © John Wiley & Sons Limited.

independent of the capability to sustain a sprint or repeat short all-out efforts, a faculty that is loosely referred to as speed–endurance.

Speed in running is a function of stride rate or cadence and stride length. Normally the self-chosen combination of stride length and cadence is optimal and any attempt to alter one or the other spontaneously leads to an increase in energy cost (Cavanagh and Williams, 1982). Stronger muscles and more flexible joints are needed to support an increased stride length, whilst achievement of a faster stride rate must entail altering neuromuscular control mechanisms. When the factors that limit sprinting capability are considered, it is obvious that strength is also a relevant influence on anaerobic performance (see Figure 6.1).

The principle of assistance

Whereas strength training is based on resistance work to increase the load against which the active muscles exert force, speed training can be viewed as 'assistance' work. Providing opportunities for the limbs to move faster than they are accustomed to constitutes a training stimulus for the nervous system. The principle of assistance work was recognised in the sports science regimens in the East European bloc in the 1970s and 1980s. Top sprinters utilised training that entailed being towed at a marginally supranormal speed behind a motorised vehicle, for example. Other 'pull–support' aids include elastic ropes and special pulling systems. Experimental work that allowed athletes to run for repetitions of only 3 to 4 s at a time on a motor-driven treadmill (where there is no air resistance to movement) demonstrated that an improvement in top running speed followed. Such manoeuvres are hardly feasible in a soccer squad, but there are a few simple practices that can be adopted.

Assistance drills

Run with the wind

The coach may take advantage of prevailing weather conditions and get the players to run with the wind behind them. Players should run in small groups to ensure a competitive element and maximal training stimulus. There should be a smooth build-up over 25–30 m to produce top speed for a further 30 m. Six to ten repetitions per session can be adequate.

Downhill running

Uphill runs are utilised for muscle strength training. Downhill running on steep declines induces severe 'delayed onset muscle soreness' as a result of the eccentric contractions in the lower limbs to decelerate the body and maintain balance. A small decline of about 2–3 degrees will allow players to go faster than normal without the braking effect of eccentric muscle contractions. There is therefore a requirement to seek out natural terrain for conducting this kind of session. Performance of about eight repetitions would constitute a good training stimulus.

'Wind-sprints'

These runs are so called because they allow the player to 'wind-up' to top speed. They are also referred to as 'flying starts', being preceded by a maximum acceleration. Players should move smoothly at progressive speed over 15–25 m up to top speed and maintain running all-out for 15–35 m. They can recover fully by decelerating, turning round and repeating. Typically, 8–10 repetitions are performed.

'Fast-feet' drills

Such drills might include running on the spot at a cadence much faster than normal running. Emphasis can be placed on the maximum number of ground contacts (foot-tapping) or on lifting the thigh more quickly than normal (high knee pick-up). Lateral and diagonal movements to negotiate flat discs or cones can be incorporated into these drills. Sessions are best conducted in sets, for example 10 sets of 6-s efforts.

Contrast drills

'Resistance' drills are performed with a partner providing tension by means of an elastic cord attached to the player and acting as a running harness. After two or three repetitions the drill is performed without resistance, the contrast between the two designed to improve speed of movement. The drill is more appropriate for work on acceleration than for top speed and is relevant to the kind of speed 'off-the-mark' needed in soccer.

Quasi-plyometric routines

Controlled runs over 30 m can be repeated but with knee pick-ups faster than normal and pushing off the toes.

Planning measures

Speed training drills should be incorporated into the early part of training sessions when players are fresh. They must be preceded by an appropriate warm-up that would include stretching exercises for the major muscle groups. Players should have a good base of conditioning work before focusing on speed training and other aspects (such as improving acceleration and explosive power) must not be ignored. The period devoted to speed training need not be long since the quality of movement rather than the volume of training is emphasised. The focus on speed becomes increasingly relevant as the competitive season progresses, when speed elements can be incorporated into training programmes at least twice a week.

Effects of training on speed can be realised relatively quickly, within 4–6 weeks, provided the background of conditioning work and general fitness is in place. Speed training should then be maintained within the training schedule if the benefits are to last.

Plyometric training

There are many occasions in a game where getting to the ball before an opponent becomes important. The rate of force development and the ability to generate power are relevant to success in these instances. These characteristics may be trained by employing stretch-shortening cycles of muscle actions, as in so-called plyometric exercises.

A stretch-shorten cycle of muscle action occurs when the muscle is first stretched and is then immediately required to shorten. The support muscles of the leg contract eccentrically on contacting the ground, being forced to stretch to take up the force of impact. Energy is briefly stored in the muscle's elastic elements and released in the subsequent shortening or concentric contraction as the body is driven upwards against gravity in the next action. The concentric action is more powerful when preceded by an eccentric phase than if performed without the counter-movement.

As stretch-shortening cycles occur in natural movements such as running and jumping, these activities can be modified to provide an overload for training purposes. Bounding, hopping and jumping activities can be organised into a plyometric training regimen (see Table 6.1). Excessive knee flexion should be avoided since it slows down the movement and may cause generation of high forces across the patella tendon. The surface used for landing or jumping should not be too hard; concrete is unsuitable whereas a firm pitch or an artificial polymer surface or a sprung floor is acceptable.

The muscles engaged in plyometric exercises should have some preliminary strength training, using weights or other form of resistance. It is prudent to start with low-impact exercises before attempting more arduous exercises such as drop-jumping that entail high impact. Plyometric exercises can be used during the late pre-season period or within the season in order to maintain or develop further muscular power.

Table 6.1 A sample of exercises that can form a plyometric training programme

Bounding	The player springs off the ground into the air. Vigorous arm action and use of the free leg can enhance the leap. Five bounds on each leg form one set
Hopping	The player hops for distance on one leg for five hops, turns and repeats the sequence with the other leg. These 10 hops form one set
Bunny hops	The player hops on both feet for distance five times. The total distance may be used as a performance measure
Hurdle jumps	The player jumps from both feet over obstacles such as low hurdles. Ten jumps form one set
Side hops	The jump is performed sideways over a bench and immediately back to the initial position. One set is comprised of five jumps in each direction
Run and jump	The player takes a short run before jumping vertically for maximum height, as if to head a ball. Five jumps off each leg form one set
Drop jumps	The player drops 20–40 cm off a bench or box onto the ground and rebounds to reach a maximum height. Ten jumps form one set
Lift jumps	A short run onto a box-top or bench (20–40 cm high) is followed by a vigorous jump off one leg into the air as if to head a ball. On landing on both feet, a second jump into the air is performed for maximum height. Ten jumps represent one set
Rebound jumps	The player starts on top of one box (20–40 cm high) and drops onto the ground, to jump immediately on to a second box nearby. Sets are comprised of 10 jumps
Ricochets	The player stands on the perimeter of a marked circle 1 m in diameter with set points marked along the circumference. The player jumps with both feet onto another point at random and continues to do so until 10 jumps are completed

Eccentric contractions cause microtrauma to the muscles engaged in the actions. The damage is reflected in disruption of the Z-discs within the sarcomeres and leakage of creatine kinase through the sarcolemma. Creatine kinase concentrations in blood rise to reach a peak about 48 h after exercise. An inflammatory response contributes to the phenomenon of delayed onset muscle soreness which is worst about 48–72 h post-exercise. The soreness is less pronounced at subsequent training sessions, and the activities become easier to perform. Nevertheless, it is prudent to avoid formal plyometric training sessions for the two days prior to a competitive match as a reduction in the force generating capacity of the muscle accompanies the ultrastructure damage (Clarkson et al., 1992).

Agility

Agility refers to the ability to change direction quickly without losing balance. It is an important attribute of good soccer players, both when dribbling a ball past an opponent and countering the movements of an opponent in possession of the ball. On comparing elite 15–16-year old players with age-matched sub-elite soccer players, Reilly et al. (2000) found that performance in an agility run test was the best distinguishing feature of the elite individuals. Agility is a function of the nervous system, incorporating proprioception and co-ordination of muscle activity in both lower limbs and in upper body for control of balance. There has not been comprehensive research investigations of agility training due to the difficulty of identifying the mechanisms of adaptation. Nevertheless it is clear that top soccer players perform well on tests of agility and that this function is amenable to training.

Various drills can be designed for the improvement of agility. Typically they entail zig-zag runs, fast tracks through a maze of obstacles or negotiating low hurdles in alternating directions. Partners may be included with the object of mimicking the shuffling actions of the opposing player. Activities may be specific to soccer, as in getting up quickly from sitting on the ground, or performing zig-zag runs with the ball.

Agility may be combined with fast-feet drills in movements specific to soccer. A series of cones may be placed over 10–12 m with players first manoeuvring their way through with strides shorter but faster than normal. The movements are then performed backwards, sideways to the right and sideways to the left. Players can do the sequences in pairs to provide an element of competition between them. A whole variety of such drills can be designed by the trainer.

Pearson (2001) described a range of drills that might be used for agility training using various items of portable equipment. These items included roped ladders for 'fast-feet' work, cones and poles for marking turning points in a run and belts or harnesses for assistance or resistance work. Plyometrics and speed work are included as components of the exercises recommended. Many of the coaching drills used in small-group work incorporate agility exercises whereby players are required to change direction abruptly. Exercises for agility are best incorporated early in the training session when players are still relatively fresh.

Speed endurance

Improvement of anaerobic capacity would be reflected in an increased average power output in a single exhaustive effort. In order to enhance the 'production' of anaerobic power, the exercise intensity should be near maximal. Even so, blood lactate may not reach very elevated levels although the muscle lactate concentrations can be very high (Reilly and Bangsbo, 1998). The exercise duration can be up to 40 s but the rest period between bouts should be about 4–5 times the exercise duration to allow recovery to take place. Six to eight repetitions are recommended.

'Retention' training is designed to aid the maintenance of speed during a sequence of efforts. The player becomes more able to retain performance when a short sprint is repeated. In this instance the exercise duration can be longer (30–90 s) but the rest interval should only be about the same as the exercise duration. The session may be divided into two sets, for example 5 × 40 s with 4 min between the two sets. The blood lactate concentrations should increase progressively with successive repetitions.

These speed–endurance sessions should enhance activities of glycolytic enzymes. They are also effective in increasing the buffering capacity of muscle. The training effects are localised to the muscles engaged in the exercise. Speed–endurance training for 'retention' purposes is likely to have some effect on the aerobic system since the regimen has some similarities to intensive aerobic interval training.

Multiple benefits of repeated sprints were demonstrated by Dawson et al. (1998). Subjects did six weeks of repetitive sprint training, completing 16–18 sessions in that time at 90–100% maximal running velocity. The distance varied from 30–80 m, the number of sets and total repetitions increasing from 4 and 24 in week 1 to 6 and 42 in week 6, respectively. The work–rest ratio was 1:6 in week 1 and 1:4 by week 6. The programme of training improved running speed over 10 m and 40 m, and running duration in a supra-maximal run representative of anaerobic capacity from 49.9 (±3.5) to 55.5 (±4.0) s. These changes were accompanied by improvements in a repeated-sprints test (6 × 40 m every 30 s) and increases in phosphorylase activity of the vastus lateralis muscle. With this type of programme designed to improve speed and speed–endurance, an improvement was also evident in $VO_{2 \, max}$, from 57.0 (±2.4) to 60.5 (±1.9) ml·kg·min.

Williams et al. (1997) outlined a series of drills for speed–endurance training that utilised the markings of the soccer pitch as cues. For example, the length of the pitch was recommended for 'hollow sprints' of 6–8 repetitions with a short walk between sprints. In another drill, the penalty spot was the local base for a sequence of sprints to each corner of the penalty box, repeated 4–6 times in 3–4 sets per session.

Soccer-specific soccer drills

Various drills are available within soccer (football) coaching manuals which can be modified to provide the desired training stimulus (Reilly, 2005a). The exercise to rest ratio can be manipulated to form a high-intensity speed–endurance session. An example of such a high-intensity was provided by Bangsbo (1994). Players alternate in a 2 vs 2 set-up and an exercise to rest ratio of 1:1. The data in Figure 6.2 demonstrate a progressive rise in heart rate and in blood lactate, sampled in the 1 min recovery after each 1 min of exercise.

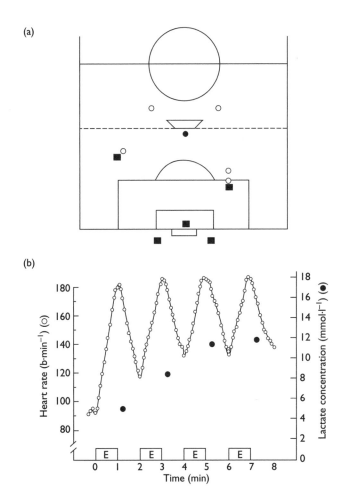

Figure 6.2 Heart rate (o) and blood lactate (•) responses to an intermittent drill (illustrated on top).

Source: Reproduced with permission, from T. Reilly and J. Bangsho (1998) 'Anaerobic and aerobic training' in *Training in Sport: Applying Sport Science*, edited by B. Elliott. © John Wiley & Sons Limited.

Bangsbo (1994) described another training drill for speed–endurance retention. Teams consisted of two players, with both teams attacking the same goal (defended by a goalkeeper). A server passes the ball into the playing area, a marked zone which starts outside the playing area. If a team loses possession, the opposing pair takes over. A team scoring a goal may retain possession. The exercise can be maintained for 1 min and again an equivalent rest period allows another group onto the playing area. The drill may be modified for use of person-to-person marking. Choice of appropriate matched pairs is important if this exercise is to be effective.

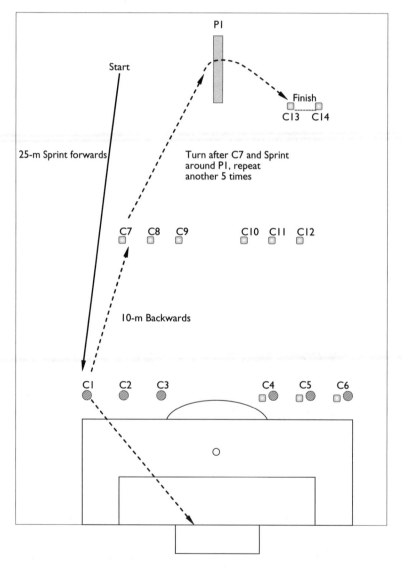

Figure 6.3 A speed-endurance drill, modified from Wilson (2001).

A specific speed–endurance (production) drill was described by Wilson (2001). The overall distance covered is about 300 m but is performed in six discrete sections (see Figure 6.3). The player runs from a starting point, sprints 25 m to kick a ball at goal from an acute angle on the right side of goal, returning backwards for 10 m then turning to sprint round the start point and repeat the process another five times. Three balls are hit with the right foot, the three placed to the left side of the goal with the left foot. The drill may be modified for midfield players to sidefoot the ball or defenders to jump to head it. The drill should be performed under time pressure and its intensity checked by monitoring heart rate.

Repeated speed drills can be organised for the improvement of running speed over short distances (Reilly, 2005b). Players may be organised in pairs about 35 m from the goal line. A server passes the ball about 15 m ahead of the front pair who immediately run to contest possession and drive forwards on goal (Figure 6.4). Once an outcome is achieved the same process is applied to the next pair and the activity is repeated. The exercise to rest ratio may be varied

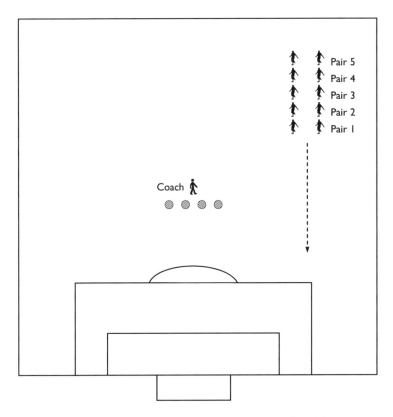

Figure 6.4 A drill for speed training where players operate with a 1:5 exercise to rest ratio.

Source: Reproduced with permission, from Reilly, 2005b.

from 1:3 to 1:5 depending on the number of players engaged in the drill. The entire drill may be performed 10–12 times.

Overview

Fast movements are critical in many situations that arise in playing soccer. These actions rely on a rapid development of force and anaerobic energy production. Whilst speed of movement depends to a great extent on utilisation of FT motor units, speed of motion can be improved by appropriate training methods.

Quick reactions may best be developed in a game context whereas anaerobic power output can be enhanced by strength training and influencing the force–velocity characteristic of muscle. Some movements may be executed ballistically, force being applied concentrically to initiate the action and eccentrically to decelerate and stop the ensuing limb motion. Plyometric training is relevant as soccer entails stretch-shortening cycles of muscle action in a dynamic fashion. Darting runs and changes in direction can be practised and their speed of execution can be increased. Assistance methods can be used to increase all-out running velocity, full recovery being advocated between repeated efforts. Speed–endurance efforts may be all-out to exhaustion or structured in sets to enhance tolerance to metabolic consequences of anaerobic work.

Speed activities such as agility can be accommodated in soccer-specific drills whereas peak running velocity requires a focus on linear running. Speed work can be done early in the training session, following the warm-up while the players are still fresh. Speed–endurance (retention) training is more exhaustive and can be done later in the session, or in a separate session when players train twice in the one day.

References

Bangsbo, J., 1994, *Fitness Training for Soccer*. Copenhagen: Storm.

Cavanagh, P.R. and Williams, K.R., 1982, The effect of stride length variation on oxygen intake during distance running. *Medicine and Science in Sports and Exercise*, **14**, 30–35.

Clarkson, P., Nosaka, D. and Braun, D., 1992, Muscle function after exercise-induced muscle damage and rapid adaptation. *Medicine and Science in Sports and Exercise*, **24**, 512–520.

Dawson, B., Fitzsimons, M., Green, S., Goodman, C., Carey, M. and Cole, K., 1998, Changes in performance, muscle metabolites, enzyme and fibre types after short sprint training. *European Journal of Applied Physiology*, **78**, 163–169.

Pearson, A., 2001, *Speed, Agility and Quickness for Soccer*. London: A. and C. Black.

Reilly, T., 2005a, On-field training for football. In: *International Football and Sports Medicine* (edited by J. Dvorak and D.T. Kirkendall), Rosemont, IL: The American Orthopaedic Society for Sports Medicine, pp. 43–51.

Reilly, T., 2005b, Training specificity for soccer. *International Journal of Applied Sports Sciences*, **17**(2), 17–25.

Reilly, T. and Bangsbo, J., 1998, Anaerobic and aerobic training. In: *Training in Sport: Applying Sport Science* (edited by B. Elliott), Chichester: John Wiley and Sons, pp. 351–409.

Reilly, T., Williams, A.M., Nevill, A. and Franks, A., 2000, A multidisciplinary approach to talent identification in soccer. *Journal of Sports Sciences*, **18**, 695–702.

Stein, N., 1998, Speed training in sport. In: *Training in Sport: Applying Sport Science* (edited by B. Elliott), Chichester: John Wiley, pp. 287–349.

Strudwick, A., Reilly, T. and Doran, D., 2002, Anthropometric and fitness characteristics of elite players in two football codes. *Journal of Sports Medicine and Physical Fitness*, **42**, 239–242.

Williams, A.M., Borrie, A., Cable, T., Gilbourne, D., Lees, A., MacLaren, D. and Reilly, T., 1997, *Umbro Conditioning for Football*. London: Ebury Press.

Wilson, D., 2001, The physiological basis of speed endurance. *Insight: The Football Association's Coaching Association Journal*, **4**(3), 36–37.

Chapter 7

Alternative training methods

Introduction

It is reasonable to consider whether alternatives to soccer-specific training and to formal conventional training methods have a role to play in the preparation of players. Such activities could contribute to play in generic fitness training as a supplement to a formal training programme. The existence of overlap between different training methods offers the possibility of cross-training, for example deriving a similar stimulus to the circulatory system from either of the training modes. Sports such as volleyball entail regular jumping and anticipation of ball flight and these faculties can also have relevance for soccer players.

Variation of activity within the training programme can offer respite to players from regimented conditioning work. There are also possibilities that a change in activity can reduce the risk of 'overtraining injuries', for example when low-impact aerobics exercises replace running sessions. The benefits of the various alternative training modes are outlined along with the circumstances when they may be most effective. The physiological effects of cross-training are first explained and each activity is placed in an overall context.

Cross-training

Cross-training has a long history dating back to ancient Greece when a combination of activities was promoted for purposes of acquiring physical fitness. Endurance running, weight-training and wrestling with animals were encouraged as a means of achieving all-round fitness. The concept of multi-mode activities gave rise to the sports of decathlon and heptathlon and to the current triathlon competitions.

Use of cross-training for health-related benefits differs in principle from its use by the elite performer. In the former, the individual is interested in engaging as many of the body's musculoskeletal components as possible. In contrast the high performer is oriented towards sports specificity and so the soccer player might combine an alternative training mode with soccer-specific training.

For general fitness and cardiovascular health, the recommendations have been that 30–40 min, 3–5 times per week at 60% $\dot{V}O_{2\,max}$ (or 70% HR_{max}) of exercise is prescribed. These guidelines have been revised for the general population to incorporate segmented activities at low intensity during the day which altogether amount to a cumulative health benefit. The recreational player would need a sustained work-out as preparation, and extend training sessions with games. A gymnasium-based fitness session could include weight-training interspersed with ergometric exercise (see Table 7.1). Outdoor sessions designed for community purposes incorporate exercise stations or points of a running trail where exercises for muscle strength or endurance, or flexibility are prescribed in illustrated displays. A 4-km running trail might include 12 stops for such activities. The major benefit of the multi-mode activity is the reduced likelihood of over-use injury due to repetitive actions. The variation in activity is thought to reduce boredom and improve adherence to the exercise regimen.

The elite player will have soccer-specific training as the greatest part of the training load. Activities with a broadly similar mode form an adjunct to this core training. The overall objective is to help maintain fitness rather than improve it by focusing solely on specific training sessions that might induce overuse. Activities with dissimilar modes of activity are used predominantly during rehabilitation and during the off-season. They can also have a place as recovery training.

Cycling and swimming are useful activities for soccer players at certain stages of rehabilitation. Their main benefits are in preventing muscle atrophy through disuse and in activating the oxygen transport system. Their benefits for elite players at peak fitness are limited since both histochemical changes in muscles and effects on $\dot{V}O_{2\,max}$ tend to be specific to the activity in already well-trained individuals.

Soccer players need to develop aerobic capacity and muscle strength at the same time. Gains in strength and power output can be acquired at the same time

Table 7.1 A typical total-body cross-training session for use in a gymnasium setting

Warm up for 10 min using a cycle ergometer		
Bench press	3 × 10 repetitions	60% 1-RM
Back squats	3 × 10 repetitions	60% 1-RM
Use treadmill for 10 min at 70% $\dot{V}O_{2\,max}$		
Upright row with barbell	3 × 10 repetitions	65% 1-RM
Shoulder press	3 × 10 repetitions	65% 1-RM
Use rowing ergometer for 10 min at 75% $\dot{V}O_{2\,max}$		
Sit ups	3 × 16 repetitions	
Deadlifts	3 × 10 repetitions	70% 1-RM
Use cycle ergometer for 10 min at 80% $\dot{V}O_{2\,max}$		
Overhead press	3 × 10 repetitions	65% 1-RM
Power cleans	3 × 10 repetitions	65% 1-RM
Warm-down jog on treadmill at 55–60% $\dot{V}O_{2\,max}$		
Light stretching		

as endurance is improved, provided neither is neglected. Increases in muscle strength tend to be greater when strength training is conducted on its own than when it is combined with endurance training (Dudley and Fleck, 1987). In contrast endurance training does not seem to be affected by conducting a resistance training programme in combination with it (Hickson *et al.*, 1988).

Aerobics

Aerobics training refers to exercise that provides a challenge to the oxygen transport system. The minute ventilation is increased over resting values, cardiac output is raised – including increases in both stroke volume and heart rate – and the oxygen supplied to the active muscles is thereby increased. Exercise that is sufficient in intensity and duration and performed at least three times a week will induce changes in cardiac function and in the ability of the skeletal muscle to take up the oxygen that is supplied. The local adaptations include increased capillarisation and increased activity of oxidative enzymes in the mitochondria. Benefits of aerobic training in its own right, as opposed to its place in a cross-training strategy, were covered in Chapter 4.

Aerobics training is most effective in those starting from a low base of fitness. Generally other fitness indices tend to be poor in company with the low aerobic capacity, and include inflexibility and muscle weakness. For this reason jogging as the original means of promoting exercise was replaced by aerobics work-outs. These comprised a series of exercises conducted as a sequence without any breaks. The exercises entailed gross body movements, extending joints through the range of motion and periodically holding positions of balance for postural control.

The communal aerobics classes conducted under formal instruction are mainly of benefit to individuals who are otherwise sedentary. The energy expended is relatively moderate so that the programme must be linked with nutritional intake if used for purposes of weight control. Musical accompaniment can be used by the instructor to enliven the exercise and maintain compliance. Exercise to music has positive physiological benefits compared to the same exercise protocol performed without the music. Atkinson *et al.* (2004) showed that subjects on a cycle ergometer chose to exercise at a higher work-rate when there was musical accompaniment compared to without music. The music used was known as 'trance', with a tempo of 142 beats·min^{-1} and a volume at the ear of 87 decibels. The participants rated the 'tempo' and 'rhythm' of the music as more motivating than the 'harmony' and 'melody'.

Activities that entail high impacts stimulate the skeleton and can increase bone mineral density. There is also a risk that high-impact activities such as jumping on a hard floor can cause overuse injuries or tendonopathies. Vigorous activities like jumping were eliminated in programmes that were then designated as low-impact aerobics. Aerobics programmes have also been adapted for performance in swimming pools and are promoted as water-aerobics. The programmes are suitable for those at the lower part of the fitness continuum but are relevant for players recovering from injury.

Circuit weight training

Circuit-training is so called because a series of separate exercises is organised for performance in a circle. Individuals rotate around the circle as they progress through the training session. The idea is that moving straight from one exercise to the next maintains a high stimulus for the circulatory system (Reilly, 1981). The notion of an integrated training stimulus differs from the use of multi-stations (see Chapter 4) as a means of focusing on individual exercises for strength-training purposes. The circuit should allow variation of muscle-groups involved between work stations to avoid cessation of activity due to local muscular fatigue. In theory this method is ideal for team training provided the number in the group does not exceed the number of work stations laid out. In practice group organisation invariably presents some problems as do inter-individual differences. Where weight training is included in the circuit, a fixed load may not be suitable for all or many of the group while altering the loads slows up performance and allows untimely recovery. Ideally a homogenous group, a thoroughly well-organised routine and repetition of the circuit or supplementary training are necessary to achieve objectives.

Garbutt et al. (1994) examined physiological responses to a circuit weight-training regimen consisting of nine exercises (Figure 7.1), the whole set being performed three times. The sequence of exercises was designed to maintain a high exercise intensity while avoiding local muscular fatigue. The loading for the circuits was set at 40% 1-RM for each exercise, leg exercises being performed 15 times and arm and trunk exercises 10 times. The circuit took 18 min to complete during which mean heart rate and $\dot{V}O_{2\,max}$ were 70% and 50% of respective maximal values. Blood lactate concentrations reached 6.9 ($\pm$3.6) $mmol \cdot l^{-1}$ on average. Whilst $\dot{V}O_{2\,max}$ was constant between the three sets, both heart rate and blood lactate were higher at the end of the final set than after the first set. There was a progressive increase in the time to complete each set, demonstrating the subjects' inability to maintain the initial pace and the need for short recovery periods between exercises.

Many of the circuits used by amateur soccer players include too much arm exercise to provide a high enough stimulus to improve maximal oxygen uptake. A higher number of repetitions for leg exercises compared to arm exercises helps to stimulate the oxygen transport system. In contrast arm exercise causes a higher lactate production than does large muscle group exercise at the same oxygen uptake. It is important to keep the recovery period between exercises short and also minimise the interval between sets. A recovery exceeding 30 s reduces the physiological stress and also diminishes the training effect.

Circuit-training is frequently applied in squad training for soccer, especially pre-season. Many players maintain this type of session throughout the season.

1 Squat

2 Bench press

3 Lateral pull down

4 Sit-up

5 Seated row

6 Leg press

7 Dead lift

8 Shoilder press

9 Back extension

Figure 7.1 The exercises incorporated in the circuit weight-training regimen in the order performed (Garbutt *et al.*, 1994).

Source: Reproduced with permission, from Garbutt *et al.*, 1994 (http://www.tandf.co.uk/Journals/titles/00140139.asp).

As fitness improves the load can be increased progressively and the pace of exercise raised. Progress is readily apparent and so the player is easily motivated by this form of training.

Exercise in water

Hydrotherapy forms an important element in restoring normal function in injured skeletal muscle. The water provides resistance to the motion of the limb involved without imposing a weight-bearing load upon it. The body is buoyed up in water and so exercise in this medium has little risk of incurring injury.

Trainers have exploited the buoyant properties of water for athletic conditioning purposes. Running in the shallow end of the swimming pool can be of value for increasing muscle strength. The individual may also be connected to a harness linked to the coach at poolside. In this tethered position he/she attempts to run away from the coach and goes through a brief period of running on the spot. The exercise is geared towards improving the ability to accelerate over a short distance.

Swimming is best considered purely as a recreational activity for soccer players. Nevertheless exercise in water can have value particularly on recovery days. The whole team can be engaged and a modification of water polo games introduced for enjoyment. One limitation is that non-swimmers cannot be fully involved although they can participate in water-based exercise by wearing buoyancy aids.

Deep-water running

Deep-water running can introduce novelty into the training programme of players. It is performed in a deep hydrotherapy pool or in the deep end of a swimming pool. The individual tries to simulate the normal running action used in land whilst wearing a buoyancy vest to assist flotation. Due to biomechanical differences between running in water and on land, a definite attempt must be made to keep the hips pushed forward in order to maintain good posture. This training modality is used as a means of preventing injury, in promoting recovery from strenuous exercise and as a form of supplementary training for cardiovascular fitness (see Table 7.2).

As the feet do not touch the floor of the pool, impact is avoided and the risk of injury to the lower limbs eliminated. The added buoyancy while performing deep-water running has the potential to decrease the compressive forces on the spine that are evident during running on land. Dowzer et al. (1998) reported that, while participants exercised at 80% of mode-specific $\dot{V}O_{2\,peak}$, spinal shrinkage was less during deep-water running than treadmill running as a result of reduced axial loading on the vertebral column (Figure 7.2). Running in deep water will enable individuals to reduce impact loading while maintaining training intensity.

Table 7.2 The uses and benefits of deep-water running

Population	Purpose	Benefit
Injured	Rehabilitation	Prevents detraining Accelerates rehabilitation
Games players	Recovery from delayed-onset muscle soreness	Accelerates recovery from matches Promotes pain-free exercise Maintains flexibility
Athletes	Complementary training	Avoids overtraining effects Maintains 'central' training stimulus
Untrained	Aerobic training Strength training	Avoids injury resulting from the initiation of land-based training Increases shoulder strength
Physically debilitated	Allows movement	Freedom from risk of falling Subjective sense of comfort and security
Overweight	Aerobic training	Aids weight reduction by increasing energy expenditure Reduces load bearing on the joints Allows exercise to be performed without embarrassment

Source: From Cable 2000.

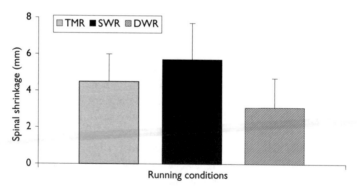

Figure 7.2 Spinal shrinkage during a training session is reduced when deep-water running (DWR) is compared to running in shallow water (SWR) or on a treadmill (TMR).

Deep-water running can also accelerate the recovery process after matches or after strenuous training. In particular the recovery of muscle strength after stretch-shortening exercise designed to induce muscle soreness was accelerated compared to treadmill running (Reilly *et al.*, 2003a). It was concluded that deep-water running is effective in temporarily relieving soreness while enhancing the process of recovery. The temporary relief of muscle soreness allows training to be continued at a time that training on land would be uncomfortable.

The physiological responses to exercise in water and in air differ largely due to the hydrostatic effect of water on the body in deep-water running. There are changes in blood compartments, cardiovascular responses, pulmonary and renal function that have been reviewed by Reilly *et al.* (2003b). Briefly, the heart rate is reduced by reflex action immediately on immersion. Both stroke volume and cardiac output increase during water immersion: an increase in blood volume largely offsets the cardiac decelerating reflex at rest. At sub-maximal exercise intensities, blood lactate responses to exercise during deep-water running are elevated in comparison to treadmill running at a given oxygen uptake (VO_2). While VO_2, minute ventilation and heart rate are decreased under maximal exercise conditions in the water, deep-water running can nevertheless be justified as providing an adequate stimulus for cardiovascular training. Responses to training programmes have confirmed the efficacy of deep-water running, although positive responses are most evident when measured in a water-based test. Aerobic performance is maintained with deep-water running for up to 6 weeks in trained endurance athletes; sedentary individuals benefit more than athletes in improving maximal oxygen uptake. There is some limited evidence of improvement in anaerobic measures and in upper-body strength in individuals engaging in deep-water running.

As deep-water running is safe, it is suitable for a range of soccer-playing populations. It may be used by recreational and veteran players and has a role also in the regimen of professional players. Its uses are listed in Table 7.2, emphasising that it can serve different purposes for different groups.

Ergometers

Ergometers refers to devices which enable the power output to be calculated. The resistance against which the individual exercises is set, from which the mechanical work done to overcome this resistance is measured. The amount of mechanical work done per unit time indicates the power output and this function is calculated in watts. The greater the power output, the higher is the exercise intensity.

The ergometer is a fundamental item of apparatus in a sports physiology laboratory since it indicates the exercise intensity very precisely. Ergometers used for experimental studies include cycles and motor-driven treadmills. The exercise intensity can be controlled on the treadmill by varying the belt speed and increasing the gradient but calculating the power output is quite complex. For exercise purposes the value of power is not necessary.

Whilst ergometry was first employed for scientific purposes, the devices have found favour for health-related exercise. In such cases the designs have been modified for gymnasium use, have facilities for grading the exercise intensity but not usually for measurement of power output. The ergometers used in fitness centres may range from relatively inexpensive resistance systems to relatively sophisticated computer-controlled devices which allow the user to pre-set the dimensions of the exercise session.

The cycle ergometer is the most basic of the fitness devices. It has the advantage that body weight is supported and so the lower limbs are not subject to the repetitive impact loading that occurs in running. Exercise can be performed at a high intensity if needed, or sustained for a long duration at a lower intensity. Sessions can be set up as continuous exercise for a fixed duration. As fitness improves the intensity and duration may be increased in a progressive manner. Alternatively, the intensity may be varied systematically to correspond with interval training, for example 60 s at a high intensity followed by 120 s at a low intensity performed for 12 repetitions.

Cycle ergometry is an ideal form of exercise for maintaining aerobic fitness during rehabilitation from lower-limb injury. In such circumstances it is also useful for restoring muscle strength. It can have value as part of a warm-up regimen for elevating the metabolic rate and core body temperature. Cycle ergometry can also be employed as recovery training, for example in between matches scheduled close together.

Rowing ergometers have also found favour as training aids. The power output may be displayed in watts or for performance purposes may be indicated on a digital display as equivalent distance covered in metres. This feedback is valuable to the performer in gauging the session and monitoring improvement with repeated use.

An advantage of rowing exercise is that major muscle groups are engaged. The power is generated by the extension of the quadriceps complemented by activity in the trunk muscles and in the upper body. The starting posture for the next effort is resumed in a controlled manner. The exercise should be conducted in a co-ordinated and smooth manner so that injury to the lower back is not incurred.

A well equipped fitness centre generally has a number of treadmills available to users. Programmable treadmills allow the individual to set the target load and exercise duration. In some set-ups the treadmill speed may be controlled by the heart-rate response of the individual. An alternative treadmill design is where the belt is propelled by the person who runs on it and who dictates the exercise intensity by his/her own effort. It is therefore completely safe to use since the belt stops immediately the individual halts.

Professional soccer clubs tend to have a treadmill available so that injured players may gradually return to running. Treadmills may also be used for additional training by players for whom more endurance exercise is prescribed. In such cases running outdoors, in parkland or forest paths, may be preferable although there may be professional reasons for completing the activity on the club's premises.

Laddermills and stair-steps have also been designed as modes of exercise for health promotion purposes. Care is needed when the step height approaches 45 cm in case the lead leg slips or the strain through the patellar tendon becomes excessive. The legs should be used alternately in stepping down, otherwise delayed-onset muscle soreness is experienced unilaterally.

The work done in stepping up onto a bench or set of stairs may be calculated once the body mass and the vertical distance it is moved against gravity are known. Completing repetitive step ups in a given period of time enables the power output to be calculated in kgm·min^{-1} and converted to watts. As the rate of stepping can be controlled, this activity was employed in fitness assessments such as the Harvard Step Test. This test involved stepping onto a bench 20 in (50.8 cm) high at a rate of 30 steps per min for 5 min. The pulse rate was recorded for 30 s at 1 min, 2 min and 3 min post-exercise and a fitness score calculated. The test is hardly now used as a measure of fitness in soccer players. As a mode of exercise for fitness, step ups may be of most use for recreational players or incorporated as a simple station in circuit training. Benches still have a use by professional players who may bound over them or drop from them onto the ground when doing plyometric exercises.

Complementary sports

There are many components of fitness for soccer and there are many skills that are relevant to the game. It is not surprising therefore that many soccer players have a good all-round athletic ability and can participate with reasonable competence in a range of sports. Invariably they have to abandon these other interests to concentrate on soccer if they are to realise their aspirations in the game.

The value of a specific sport as a training stimulus is reflected in its average energy expenditure. Even so, sports that are physiologically demanding may be unsuitable if there is a risk of injury. For this reason cross-country and downhill skiing as well as contact sports should be avoided.

Sports such as volleyball include jumping and co-ordination activities without a necessity for physical contact. These games may be employed for low-intensity activity the day following a hard training session. Alternatively, the principles of play may be modified with the ball being played with the feet or the head. In this way games skills are practiced in an unobtrusive manner and in a relaxed circumstance.

Of the sports listed in Table 7.3, golf is one that is suitable for players on days off. The energy expenditure is light so the training effect is negligible. Nevertheless, the activity may take 3 h or more for 18 holes of play to be

Table 7.3 Energy expenditure in different sports

Light (kJ min^{-1})		Moderate (kJ min^{-1})		Heavy (kJ min^{-1})		Very heavy (kJ min^{-1})	
Archery	13–24	Baseball	20–27	Boxing	46–60	Cross-country running	63–67
Billiards	11	Cricket	21–33	Handball	46–50		
Bowls	17	Fencing	21–42	Hockey	36–50	Cross-country skiing (uphill)	78
Croquet	13–17	Gymnastics	10–50	Judo	41–55		
Fishing	13–18	Horse riding	13–42	Wrestling	50–59	Orienteering	60
Golf	20	Mountain-climbing	42				
Softball	17						
Table tennis	15–22	Tobogganing	30				

completed so that a round of golf can constitute activity suitable for recovery on the day following a match.

Overview

There are occasions when soccer players may not be able to take part in normal practices and have to find temporary alternatives. These circumstances include times after injury, times when travelling or staying in accommodation which has gymnasia facilities and times when weather conditions preclude training outdoors. In such cases good use can be made of various exercise ergometers. Alternative modes of exercise may also be incorporated into the training programme either to promote recovery, reduce the intensity of training or avoid monotony. In all cases there should be a clear purpose to changing a routine so that the activity conducted is beneficial rather than detrimental to the soccer player.

References

Atkinson, G., Wilson, D. and Eubank, M., 2004, Effect of music on work-rate distribution during a cycling time trial. *International Journal of Sports Medicine*, **25**, 611–615.

Cable, T., 2000, Deep-water running. *Insight: The Football Association's Coaching Association Journal*, **3**(2), 45.

Dowzer, C.N., Reilly, T. and Cable, N.T., 1998, Effects of deep and shallow water running on spinal shrinkage. *British Journal of Sports Medicine*, **32**, 44–48.

Dudley, G.A. and Fleck, S.J., 1987, Strength and endurance training: are they mutually exclusive? *Sports Medicine*, **4**, 79–85.

Garbutt, G., Boocock, M.G., Reilly, T. and Troup, J.D.G., 1994, Physiological and spinal responses to circuit weight-training, *Ergonomics*, **37**, 117–125.

Hickson, R.C., Dvorak, B.A., Gorostiaga, E.M., Kurowski, T.T. and Foster, C., 1988, Potential for strength and endurance training to amplify endurance performance. *Journal of Applied Physiology*, **65**, 2285–2290.

Reilly, T., 1981, *Sports Fitness and Sports Injuries*. London: Faber and Faber.

Reilly, T., Cable, N.L. and Dowzer, C.N., 2003a, The effect of a 6-week land- and water-running training programme on aerobic, anaerobic and muscle strength measures. *Journal of Sports Sciences*, **21**, 333–334.

Reilly, T., Dowzer, C.N. and Cable, N.T., 2003b, The physiology of deep-water running. *Journal of Sports Sciences*, **21**, 959–972.

Chapter 8

Recovery from exercise

Introduction

The typical week of a soccer player during the competitive season includes a period for training, a taper, the competitive match and recovery from it. This weekly cycle is often disrupted by an irregular schedule of games, match day being not necessarily the same from one week to another. Players in the top professional clubs may have extra commitments such as cup and other knock-out matches, competing in continental leagues or representing their country in international matches. University players may have fixtures for their institution in mid-week and for their club at weekends. The unrelenting fixture schedule, the hassle and stress of travel increase the risk of experiencing 'burn-out' whereby players lose 'form' and enter an underperformance spiral. When matches are too frequent, there is insufficient time between them for real training to take place.

A relentless grind of matches can place enormous strain on players and so they are unlikely to be at their best in all matches. During the Christmas–New Year period of 2005–2006, teams in the English Premier League played four games in eight days so that the season would be completed one week earlier than usual and allow the national team a longer period of preparation for the World Cup (see Table 8.1). Some national leagues in Europe contain a mid-season intermission; this period offers a respite to those who are in the first team squad. The argument for the break is that it enables players to recover from the first half of the season and its scheduling coincides with the time when climatic conditions in Europe are usually at their worst. The richest clubs in the European leagues tend to have the largest squads, allowing some scope for 'squad rotation' and allowing certain players to have an occasional break. In 2004 the lowly fancied Greek team without any individual stars won the European nations championship, defeating teams composed of players from among the top clubs that have arduous competitive schedules towards the end of the domestic League season. The World Cup finals in Korea and Japan took place shortly after the completion of the 2002 domestic league season on the European continent. In a study of factors causing an apparent 'underperformance' of teams in this tournament, it was concluded

Table 8.1 An example of fixture list over the Christmas and New Year period for two English Premier League teams during the 2005–2006 season. Start times are indicated

	Everton		Chelsea	
26 December	Aston Villa (away)	17:15	Fulham (home)	15:00
28 December	Liverpool (home)	20:00	Manchester City (away)	20:00
31 December	Sunderland (away)	15:00	Birmingham City (home)	13:00
2 January	Charlton (home)	15:00	West Ham (away)	12:45

that it was the congestion of fixtures towards the end of the professional League season followed by a short period before mid-season international tournaments that caused some players to underperform in those latter competitions (Ekstrand *et al.*, 2004).

Certain players can now be used sparingly in a game by the coach, with substitutions based on tactical grounds so that key individuals are not exhausted at the end of the match. The rules of play allow three players to be replaced during the game, but the majority are obliged to compete for the full 90-min duration. Rule changes in the 1990s, an increased emphasis on fitness training and on a high workrate have contributed to a high tempo of match-play (Williams *et al.*, 1999). The outcome is that competitive engagements take participants to the verge of exhaustion, from which they must recover quickly to be prepared for the next game. When competitive fixtures are congested, the recovery process should be optimised and some of the strategies for doing so are considered in this review.

Ensuring recovery between matches

Playing a competitive soccer game places all of the body's major organs and systems under some measure of stress. The renal system is spared, blood flow to the kidneys being reduced during exercise and being shunted to serve the more urgent needs of active skeletal muscles and requirements for thermoregulation. The main physiological systems engaged include energy systems (liver and muscle glycogen, free fatty acids and muscle tryglycerides), the musculoskeletal system, the cardiovascular, endocrine and nervous systems. Players are often near to exhaustion at the end of a game, being low in glycogen depots in their liver and skeletal muscles (Saltin, 1973). They may also feel mentally drained of their 'nervous energy', even though subjective states are often mediated by the outcome of the match. Various factors influence the rate of recovery between games, particularly when matches are scheduled twice in one week.

Methods for hastening the recovery process include warm-down, replacement of fluid lost and restoration of energy levels. Active and passive means of intervention to accelerate the recovery process are also relevant. The immune system can be compromised by competitive stress (Gleeson *et al.*, 1997): whether it is possible to boost the body's resistance to infection or damage is also briefly addressed.

Warm-down

Lactate is removed more quickly from the blood when recovery is active rather than passive. Clearance of lactate from the circulation is related directly to the exercise intensity (Monedero and Donne, 2000) up to about 50% of the maximal oxygen uptake ($\dot{V}O_{2\,max}$). An active warm-down also facilitates a smoother decline in body temperature and blood flow than happens if activity is terminated abruptly, as core temperature continues to rise for a few minutes once the participant stops exercise (Reilly and Brooks, 1986). It also helps to damp activity in the nervous system and this effect promotes sleep afterwards: sleep could be adversely affected after a match due to a maintained elevation in the level of arousal of the central nervous system (Smith and Reilly, 2005). It is thought that a warm-down can benefit the immune system as the individual might otherwise be more vulnerable to minor infections for some hours after finishing hard exercise if the drop in body temperature is too abrupt (Reilly and Ekblom, 2005).

The effects of an active warm-down were examined in two groups of university soccer players by Reilly and Rigby (2002). One group did an active warm-down after a first match and a controlled recovery regimen the week afterwards before competing in a second game after which no formal warm-down was conducted. The procedure was reversed in a second group to balance the order of administering the experimental warm-down. There were three phases in the active warm-down which consisted of:- jogging for 5 min, stretching for 5 min, followed by a further 2 min lying prone with legs raised and 'shaken down' by another player. This procedure was contrasted with a control recovery, in which the participants returned to the changing rooms and rested (seated) for 12 min. Various physical performance tests were administered following the game and for the three days afterwards and results were compared to a reference pre-game condition. Impairments in vertical and broad jumps were observed in both groups, but less so in the group that had warmed down. This group recovered to pre-match values more quickly than the inactive subjects whose performances were still below reference levels 48 h post-game. Speed over a 30-m sprint followed a similar trend, the deterioration being almost 50% greater in the control subjects compared to the experimental group. Performance in a sprint-fatigue test consisting of seven 30-m sprints (with 20 s for active recovery in between sprints) was unaltered in the experimental group 48 h after the game, whereas a marked difference from baseline values was observed in the control subjects. By 48 h after playing, muscle soreness had almost disappeared in the individuals who had warmed down in contrast to the increased ratings with successive days in the control group. The data suggested that players warming down after a mid-week match would be adequately recovered for a week-end game 72 h later, in contrast to the inactive group who would not have fully recovered to baseline values by this time.

An effective warm-down after a match need only be brief in duration, for example 7–10 min. It should also be light in intensity. Jogging is probably the best form of exercise, unless a player has muscle problems. Stretching is not necessary, especially if it is in the early part of the season as the muscle may be already damaged from 'stretch–shortening' cycle exercise. This term refers to stretching a muscle following its shortening (eccentric and concentric actions) as happens when a player crouches prior to leaping to win the ball in the air. The consequence is 'delayed onset muscle soreness' which usually peaks 48 h after a game before recovery of its own accord.

Deep-water running

Stretch–shortening cycles of muscle actions in which the muscle is stretched prior to its shortening in a concentric contraction, occur frequently during match-play and training. These actions induce 'delayed-onset muscle soreness' which may be compounded by bruises and contusions following physical contact with other players during the game. In novice and recreational players, severe soreness is induced by actions such as kicking the ball, accelerating and decelerating, jumping, turning and tackling. The microtrauma suffered by the muscles engaged is later reflected in a leakage of substances, notably creatine kinase and myoglobin, from the muscle cells into the blood.

Physical training programmes often include deep-water running, particularly during rehabilitation from injury and as light recovery sessions immediately after or the day following competitive games. The exercise is conducted in the deep end of a swimming pool with the body kept afloat by means of a buoyancy belt. This mode of exercise is employed as a means of preventing soft-tissue injury in the lower limbs, since impact with the ground is avoided, thereby reducing the load on skeletal structures (Dowzer et al., 1998). Its use as an exercise modality for recovery is attractive to players due to its non-weightbearing nature.

Deep-water running has proved to be superior to other putative methods of alleviating muscle soreness and restoring muscle strength following 'plyometric exercise' in one study of 30 previously untrained subjects (Reilly et al., 2002). The regimen used to induce soreness consisted of drop jumps from a platform 50 cm in height once every 7 s until voluntary exhaustion. During the three subsequent days training consisted of runs for 30 min at 70–80% of heart rate reserve (the difference between maximal and resting heart rate). The methods of recovery studied were (i) rest on all days; (ii) rest on day one, deep-water running on remaining days; (iii) rest on day one, treadmill running on later days; (iv) treadmill run on all days; (v) deep-water running on all days. The most effective recovery protocol was when deep-water running was incorporated in the training programme for all three days following the plyometric regimen. Deep-water running did not prevent delayed-onset muscle soreness but appeared to speed up the process of recovery for muscle strength (determined using isokinetic dynamometry) and perceived soreness. Creatine kinase levels peaked 24 h earlier and at a lower value in the group employing deep-water running compared to the other groups. Soreness was eliminated whilst subjects were running in deep water but re-appeared post-exercise, having allowed exercise to proceed pain-free meantime. Use of deep-water running also enabled subjects to maintain range of motion at the hip joint even though they were experiencing soreness. These factors were linked with the smaller impairment in leg muscle strength when deep-water running was employed. Professional soccer players are more used to stretch–shortening cycle exercise than are typical experimental subjects, nevertheless results highlight likely benefits of deep-water running in reducing impact stresses during recovery. Besides, a training stimulus for the oxygen transport system can be provided by this type of exercise in water using suitably designed exercise programmes (Dowzer et al., 1999). Other uses of deep-water running as an alternative training modality were covered in Chapter 7.

Restoration of energy

Players who complete the entire game or participate in a prolonged training session are likely to have nearly depleted their glycogen stores in active muscles and liver by the end. Blood glucose may also be lowered in some players. Ekblom (1986) reported blood glucose concentrations of 3.8 mmol·l^{-1} in players of the Swedish First Division at the end of a game, three individuals displaying values in the range 3.0–3.2 mmol·l^{-1}. It is thought that such sub-normal glucose concentrations could contribute to impairments in cognitive function towards the end of a game (MacLaren, 2003).

Those players who train hard the day before a match are likely to experience fatigue earlier than the ones who rest. The lowered muscle glycogen levels caused by training have been associated with an impaired work-rate, notably less sprinting 'off-the-ball' (Saltin, 1973). When normal glycogen levels are reduced, players are ill-prepared for continuing their training programmes in an optimal manner and glycogen stores should be fully restored before the next match.

The optimal time for beginning the replacement of energy is in the first 2 h after exercise ceases because the enzymes associated with glycogen synthesis are most active during this period. Glucose sensitivity and muscle GLUT4 expression are increased in the early post-exercise period (Dohm, 2002). Nutritional guidelines suggest a carbohydrate intake of 1.5 g·kg^{-1} body mass over the first 30 min of recovery: this figure would amount to 120 g carbohydrate for a player weighing 80 kg. The glycogen resynthesis rate is itself limited (Coyle, 1991), suggesting that an intake exceeding 50 g carbohydrate every 2 h post-exercise provides no extra benefit. A concentrated carbohydrate beverage can be influential in initiating the recovery of energy and can compensate for the suppression of appetite due to strenuous exercise. Individuals experiencing mental fatigue can be given solid foods with a high glycaemic index which can be provided in the

Table 8.2 Classification of some foods based on their glycaemic index

High index	Moderate index	Low index
Bread	Pasta	Apples
Potato	Noodles	Beans
Rice	Crisps	Lentils
Sweetcorn	Grapes	Milk
Raisins	Oranges	Ice cream
Banana	Porridge	Yoghurt
Cereals	Sponge Cake	Soup
Glucose		Fructose

dressing room for eating after showering. Foods with a high glycaemic index are listed in Table 8.2. The inclusion of essential amino acids along with carbohydrate provides a significant means of enhancing protein synthesis, especially if ingested 1–3 h post-exercise (Rasmussen et al., 2000). Protein degradation may also be increased after exercise and so a net protein gain is important (Tipton and Wolfe, 2001).

Wong et al. (1998) studied the effects of a carbohydrate–electrolyte solution during 4 h recovery from running at 70% of maximal oxygen uptake. After the 4-h recovery, the subjects continued running at the same speed to voluntary exhaustion. Drinking a prescribed volume of the experimental solution (6.9% carbohydrate, 300 mOsm osmolality) after 90 min exercise, calculated to replace body fluid losses, restored endurance capacity to a greater extent compared to rehydration ad libitum, even though the total volumes ingested were the same.

The restoration of energy must be continued next day in order to become effective. The protocol may entail ingesting 8–10 g·kg^{-1} or more of carbohydrate over the day, representing a proportionate carbohydrate intake of 60% of the daily energy intake.

Restoration of body water

Core body temperature may rise to over 39°C during a game (Ekblom, 1986). The intensity of exercise as well as environmental temperature affects the increase in core temperature, both ambient dry bulb temperature and relative humidity being relevant. "Globe temperature" indicates the radiant heat load and its value should also be taken into consideration as games are outdoors and solar radiation is a relevant factor. In environmental temperatures in the range 20–25°C, Ekblom (1986) observed mean rectal temperatures of 39.5°C for Swedish top League players, whereas values were in the range 39.2–39.4°C for players from lower divisions.

In order to offset heat gain, the body's heat loss mechanisms come into play. Evaporation of sweat from the skin surface becomes the main route of heat loss during exercise, this avenue of heat exchange with the environment being impeded when relative humidity is high. The type of clothing (loose or tight fit, long or half-sleeve, shirt material and so on) could restrict the effective evaporation of sweat from the skin surface. At an average exercise intensity of 75% $\dot{V}O_{2\ max}$, corresponding to the intensity estimated for match-play in a game, soccer players may lose sweat at a rate approaching $2\ l\cdot h^{-1}$ (Reilly and Cable, 2001). Ingestion of fluid during competition cannot keep pace with this amount of fluid lost and so a deficit in body water is incurred.

Physical performance capability may be impaired when water losses exceed 2% of body mass (Barr, 1999), so it is important that players start the game already hydrated and that the fluid deficit is minimised. To do so requires periodic drinking during the natural breaks occurring during the game and more substantial fluid intake at the half-time intermission. The opportunity to take drinks at the sideline is not helpful to those players in central areas of the pitch who are reluctant to leave their positions for tactical reasons. When trying to restore fluid balance by drinking in the half-time interval, gastric discomfort constitutes a practical limitation. A rough guideline is contained in the schedule employed by Clarke et al. (2003). A total volume of 1065 ± 76 ml (administered at 0, 15, 30, half-time, 60 and 75 min) given in six equal small volumes eliminated feelings of gut fullness that were evident when the same total amount of fluid was given in two drinks, before the game and at half-time.

The fluid deficit incurred during the game should be reversed as soon as possible afterwards. Drinking pure water in the period after finishing the game lowers plasma osmolality and plasma sodium levels; the effects are a reduction in thirst and an increase in urine production, both of which tend to delay effective rehydration (Maughan, 1991). Drinks that include electrolytes, notably sodium, facilitate absorption of water through the intestinal wall. The electrolyte content of sweat varies between individuals, some players may be in particular need of electrolyte replacement, notwithstanding that sweat tends to be hypotonic. If sodium and chloride are not included in the drink, part of the fluid ingested is lost again in the urine. As body water content begins to fall, the secretion of vasopressin (a posterior pituitary hormone) stimulates renal retention of fluid whilst the adrenal glands secrete aldosterone in an attempt to preserve sodium. Nevertheless, the body's total electrolyte reserve can handle some short-term losses without any evident effect on physical performance. Most meals that cover the daily energy expenditure also include enough electrolytes to compensate fully for losses that occur during training. As there is a marked variation between individuals in the sodium content of sweat and in the amount of sweat lost, some additional salt (added to food or in drinks ingested) may be needed for those players incurring high salt losses.

The loss of body water during exercise (dehydration) can impair performance in training and match-play. As thirst is satisfied before body water is fully restored, players should be encouraged to drink more than they feel is needed. The deficit may carry over into the following day and affect performance in training. The imbalance may become acute when matches or training are held

Table 8.3 Potential markers in urinary and blood indices of hydration status considered by Shirreffs (2000)

Haematological and circulatory indices	Urinary indices of hydration status
Haemoglobin	Urine volume
Haematocrit	Osmolarity
Alteration in pulse rate	Specific gravity
Alteration in blood pressure	Colour
Plasma osmolarity and Na concentration	
Plasma hormones (testosterone, noradrenaline, atrial natriuretic peptide)	

in hot conditions, or in the days following air flight. The dry air on board the aircraft causes increased respiratory evaporative water loss and has been reflected in reduced urine volume in athletes travelling across five time-zones to a warm-weather training camp (Reilly *et al.*, 2003). In such instances monitoring urine osmolality, or its specific gravity or conductance can provide a good indication of hydration status (Pollock *et al.*, 1997). There is no current 'gold standard' measure of hydration status, although a urine osmolality greater than about 900 mosmol·kg^{-1} could reasonably be taken to indicate a hypohydrated state (Shirreffs, 2000). The urinary measures were deemed more appropriate than blood markers and urine osmolality was the preferred measure (see Table 8.3). Simple measurements could include monitoring of body mass (in the morning) or assessment of urine colour (Armstrong *et al.*, 1998).

In summary, whilst the major need is for water to restore the body's hydration status post-exercise, absorption is improved when drinks contain some electrolytes. There is evidence that energy in the drink also helps. Thirst is not a perfect gauge of body water needs and players should be encouraged to drink more than they feel they want after exercise has been performed in the heat. Alcohol is a diuretic, promoting body water loss, and so is not an appropriate means of replacing fluids lost in a game or during strenuous training.

Immune status

The time between matches is often inadequate for complete recovery to homeostasis. Such overload can arise when fixtures are congested for adult players, in tournament play at the end of a season or during intensive training camps for young players. Competitive matches stimulate the secretion of stress hormones and elevate concentrations of substances known to influence the function of leucocytes whose number and functional capacities are reduced post-exercise (Gleeson *et al.*, 1997). For several hours after heavy exercise, both the innate (natural killer cell activity and neutrophil oxidative burst activity) and adaptive (T and B cell function) immune systems are suppressed (Nieman and

Bishop, 2006). Natural killer cells fall in number and activity below pre-exercise levels. Other changes in immune function contribute to a weakening of the response to pathogens and increase the vulnerability to infections for some hours after exercise ceases. This period of increased susceptibility is often described as the 'open window' theory (Figure 8.1).

Adequate time should also be allowed between strenuous training sessions for normal homeostasis to be restored. In such circumstances catabolic processes may dominate over anabolic systems and cause 'underperformance'. Compromising the immune system may lead to upper respiratory tract infections and other ailments. Nakamura *et al.* (2004) recommended monitoring secretory immunoglobulin A levels in saliva samples as a useful method for managing risk of upper respiratory tract infection, after studying Japanese soccer players during a period of training for 2 h each day.

Adverse physiological effects are experienced by young players when full competitive matches were played on consecutive days and within 20 h of each other (Ekblom, 2005). Measurements were made leading up to the first game and up to 72 h after the second game. These measurements included energy balance, endocrine responses, markers of immune function determined by means of flow cytometry, and lymphocyte receptors. The players incurred an energy deficit as a

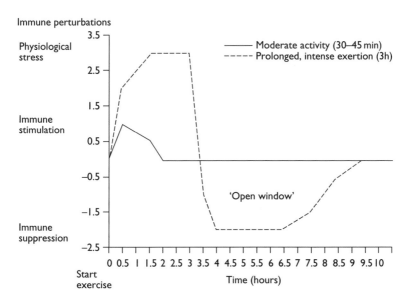

Figure 8.1 The 'open-window' theory of immune perturbations following strenuous exercise.

Source: Reprinted with permission, from Nieman and Bishop, 2006 (http://www.tandf.co.uk/journals/titles/02640414.asp).

result of the congestion of matches. The findings underline once again the value of drinking beverages containing carbohydrates where possible during and after intensified training. Both testosterone and cortisol were downregulated for 72 h after the second game. The populations of natural killer cells and T-helper cells were also decreased, representing a negative effect on the body's immune system. Relative to resting values the number of cells in all natural killer subpopulations showed a consistent fall of 20–60% for a period immediately after the second match: the number of CD57$^+$ and CD56$^+$ CD16$^+$ CD57$^+$ CD3$^-$ cells were still decreased at 72 hours (see Figure 8.2, Reilly and Ekblom, 2005). The changes in these markers of immune function lend support to the 'open window' theory.

Malm *et al.* (2004) later identified a delayed phase 48 h after the second game, in which the expression of both adhesion and signaling molecules increased on lymphocytes and monocytes. These changes in adhesion and signaling molecules at 48 h were negatively correlated with the subjects' $\dot{V}O_{2\,max}$. This finding suggested a larger immunological response to similar exercise in players with lower aerobic power and implied a benefit associated with aerobic fitness.

The extent to which young players experience adverse reactions during a 7-day training camp was reported by Ekblom (2005). The players displayed a negative calorie balance of 2–2.8 MJ·day^{-1} even though their diet was supervised. Signs of 'over-reaching' included a decreased appetite, alterations in mood and reduced stamina. The inability of the players to recover from their daily training regimens demonstrates the need to build in recuperative elements to the activities of young players attending camps for specialist training.

The training programme during week-long camps is likely also to expose participants to oxidative stress and the potentially damaging effects of oxygen free radicals. Sources of oxidative stress include mitochondrial superoxide production, ischaemia-reperfusion mechanisms and auto-oxidation of

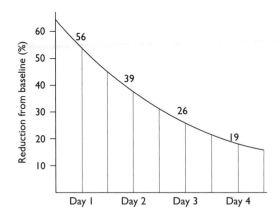

Figure 8.2 Change in NK cell numbers from before to after two soccer games in two days. The second game was played on Day 1

catecholamines. Antioxidant defences are located in body water pools and in the body's lipid stores. The major antioxidant vitamin in aqueous environments is vitamin C, whereas vitamin E is the main antioxidant vitamin in lipid environments which works by breaking the chain of lipid peroxidation. However, supplementation of lipid soluble anti-oxidants can have a negative effect. Malm *et al.* (1997) examined the effects of supplementation with ubiquinol (co-enzyme Q10), a substance with lipid anti-oxidant properties. Those players using the supplement fared worse than a placebo group when the training load was increased, a result that was unexpected. The players using supplementation were inferior to the control group in selected exercise performance tests, showed greater muscle damage and slower rates of recovery after the period in which the training load was elevated.

It is thought that other anti-oxidants may benefit recovery processes after a competitive match. Thompson *et al.* (2003) investigated whether post-exercise supplementation with 200 mg of vitamin C influenced recovery from 90 min of shuttle running designed to correspond to the average exercise intensity of playing a match. No differences were found between the group receiving supplementation and a placebo group in the rate of recovery for the three days following exercise. Serum creatine kinase activities, myoglobin concentrations, muscle soreness, and recovery of muscle function in leg extensors and leg flexors were similar between the two groups. Plasma concentrations of malondialdehyde (reflecting oxidative stress) and interleukin-6 increased post-exercise equally in the placebo and supplemented groups. It seems that either free radicals are not involved in delaying recovery from such exercise protocols, or that the consumption of vitamin C wholly after exercise is unable to deliver an antioxidant effect at the appropriate sites with sufficient expediency to improve recovery. It seems that the benefits of antioxidant supplementation may be for the long term rather than the short term.

Carbohydrate supplementation during periods of heavy exercise is a potential effective counter-measure to becoming susceptible to illnesses attributed to the 'open-window' period. It has been shown to attenuate increases in blood neutrophil counts, stress hormones and inflammatory cytokines. Nevertheless carbohydrate does not convey immunity since it is largely ineffective against other immune components, including natural killer and T-cell function (Nieman and Bishop, 2006).

Restoration of muscle comfort

Movement during match-play entails frequent stops and starts, angled runs and deceptive sidesteps. Musculoskeletal control of these movements incorporates stretch–shortening cycles of muscle actions, the eccentric components of which lead to the phenomenon of delayed-onset muscle soreness referred to earlier in the chapter and in Chapter 4. Such actions are also implicated in kicking a ball, which stretches the hamstrings and jumping which stretches the calf muscles and the quadriceps. The microtrauma in the muscles is later reflected in the leakage

Table 8.4 Methods of alleviating delayed-onset muscle soreness
(DOMS) reviewed by Cleak and Eston (1992)[a]

- Stretching
- Cold application
- Ultrasound
- Transcutaneous electrical nerve stimulation (TENS)
- Application of anti-inflammitant creams
- Pharmacological agents
- Exercise
- Massage
- Training

Note
a Although some success was found by a few authors using stretch,
  TENS and topical anti-inflammitant creams to alleviate DOMS, the
  majority view was that there seemed to be no single effective way of
  reducing the soreness once it has occurred. Prevention was best
  secured by training according to the 'repeated bouts effect'.

of creatine kinase, myoglobin and other substances through the sarcolemma into the blood. Concentrations of creatine kinase in the blood usually reach a peak about 24–48 h post-exercise, and precedes the highest subjective soreness. These physiological sequelae may delay the restoration of muscle glycogen stores.

Regular performance of plyometric training offers some protection against delayed onset muscle soreness, the phenomenon being referred to as the 'repeated bouts effect' (Cleak and Eston, 1992). The protective effect of a single session of plyometric training can last at least three weeks. Professional players are likely to experience less muscle soreness of this type than do novice or recreational players inexperienced in training programmes that utilise stretch–shortening cycle exercises (Foley et al., 1999). Experienced players would still be advised not to do any plyometric training in the days following matches until soreness has passed its peak and plyometrics should be omitted also when players have games in mid-week and at the weekend in the same week.

Strength and conditioning work provide the best means to reduce the impact of delayed-onset muscle soreness (see Table 8.4). This type of soreness may even be compounded by suffering contusions and bruises due to physical contact whilst competing. Pharmacological means (such as non-steroidal anti-inflammitants) of treating muscle soreness due to eccentric exercise have proved largely ineffective (Gleeson et al., 1997). Ultrasound may be effective therapy for other muscle complaints but has not proved beneficial for this form of soreness.

Iced baths

The low water temperatures used in iced baths are in contrast to the higher temperatures associated with deep-water running which are more compatible with thermal comfort. As explained above, deep-water running has been shown to provide some relief in the days following a hard plyometric exercise session, without affecting the creatine kinase response (Reilly *et al.*, 2002). Such an exercise mode would therefore reduce discomfort during training on recovery days and help avoid any detraining effects.

Only limited benefits have been reported for cold-water immersion and no effect on the perception of tenderness or strength loss following damage-inducing eccentric exercise of the elbow flexors (Eston and Peters, 1999). Their cryotherapy technique entailed submersing the exercised arm in a plastic tub of ice water for 15 min. Similarly, Howatson and van Someren (2003) found that although ice massage reduced the appearance of creative kinase (CK), it had no other effect on signs and symptoms associated with exercise-induced muscle damage.

Immersion in cold water induces a host of physiological responses that include hyperventilation, bradycardia and alterations in blood pressure and blood flow (Reilly and Waterhouse, 2005). Heat is lost much more quickly in water than it is in air so that voluntary immersion in cold water must be short term, for a matter of minutes. Cold and heat treatments have a long history in physical therapy. The use of iced baths to promote recovery from strenuous muscular exercise gained credence in other sports before being adopted by some soccer teams. Others have preferred contrast bathing, again a conventional practice within physiotherapy, whereby periods of immersion in cold water are interspersed with exposure to water at a temperature close to mean skin temperature.

Contrast bathing, alternating immersion up to the trunk in barrels of cold water with warmer water or air, is currently being practised by Australian Rules players, but without convincing evidence of its benefits. The protocol used by Dawson (2002) consisted of alternating between standing in a hot shower (~45°C) for 2 min with standing waist deep in icy water (~12°C) for 1 min, repeated until five hot and four cold exposures had been completed. The England Rugby Union team used the strategy of immersion in iced water following its matches in the 2003 International Rugby Union World Cup tournament. Typically, water temperature of 11°C is employed in iced water baths for games players, but the duration and frequency of immersions seems to be more determined by local preferences than scientific influence. Where contrast baths are used in preference to iced baths, a protocol of 1–2 min in each medium for 4 successive immersions is common.

Massage

Masseurs are used in many sports in the belief that they can assist in ensuring muscles are prepared for forthcoming exercise and in accelerating their recovery following exercise. Surface massage has a two-fold effect, first it stimulates blood flow in the underlying muscle and secondly, it can promote re-absorption of any haematoma that is present. Its soothing effects can relieve muscles of ache due to minor trauma or tears. It can increase muscle temperature more effectively than ultrasound, although both methods have only limited effects on deep muscle temperature (Drust *et al.*, 2003).

Hilbert *et al.* (2003) reported that massage offered subjective relief of symptoms associated with delayed-onset muscle soreness but had no effect on reducing muscle damage and the inflammatory response. Whilst it may have a role in physiotherapy, there is no evidence that it facilitates the recovery of physiological processes following soccer match-play.

Recovery from spinal shrinkage

Weight-bearing exercise imposes axial loading on the spine and the intervertebral discs lose height as they are compressed. The loss of height is referred to as spinal shrinkage and can be recorded using precision stadiometry. Shrinkage occurs during the day due to domestic, habitual and occupational activity and can approach 1% of stature in magnitude. Recovery occurs during rest pauses when the spine is unloaded and is completed during nocturnal sleep.

Many activities incorporated in match-play have been found to induce spinal shrinkage. The amount of shrinkage is influenced by the velocity of running but the rate of loss in height decreases with the duration of exercise as the discs become stiffer than normal. Training activities such as weight-training and drop-jumping also induce appreciable spinal loading (see Reilly, 2002). The individual may be at increased risk of injury on exertion unless the spinal structures involved are allowed to recover.

The standard posture for regaining height in the intervertebral joint complex is known as Fowler's position. In this posture, the individual lies supine, legs raised to an angle of 45° at the hip whilst resting on a bench or chair. Gravity inversion systems (such as hanging upside down suspended by the ankle) also unload the spine (see Figure 8.3). A suspension angle of 45° is more effective

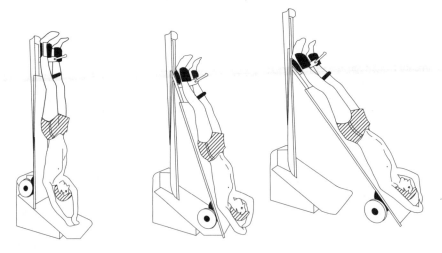

Figure 8.3 Gravity-inversion system used in some commercial gymnasia for unloading the spine. The angle of 45° has been found to promote best effects.

than more acute angles while an angle of 90° is felt by many to be too uncomfortable. Sitting in a comfortable chair can promote recovery of stature but many domestic and office chairs are not conducive to spinal unloading. Use of short naps or lying in bed resting constitute the more practical methods of relieving the spine from the consequences of physical loading.

Modifying training

It is important that training between matches facilitates recovery and does not increase the risk of injury. Light training is advised and a day of rest at this stage is not essential. Training can commence with a systematic warm-up which incorporates flexibility exercises and soccer-specific movements (see Table 8.5).

High-intensity training should be avoided the day after a game but can be gradually stepped up in subsequent days. The intensity can be at a level which raises the heart rate to about 150 beats·min^{-1}. Strenuous training on successive days may place high demands on energy stores and prevent the restoration of normal energy depots.

Conditioned drills and restriction of games that eliminate physical contact are advised in the recovery period. Teams that have access to swimming pools may utilise deep-water running. This modification allows players to exercise hard whilst avoiding the stresses associated with ground impact. Both deep-water training and other forms of hydrotherapy have been used successfully by some international rugby and association football (soccer) teams in the days between tournament matches to help maintain fitness whilst recovering from the previous match.

Lifestyle factors

Lifestyle and habitual activities can influence the speed of recovery from strenuous exercise. These important aspects include adherence to proper nutritional strategies, embracing fluid and energy, and moderation when drinking alcoholic beverages. Reilly (1994) reported a value of alcohol intake for an international

Table 8.5 Training principles to facilitate recovery

- Identify players prone to re-injury
- Introduce flexibility exercises (slow)
- Warm-up should include soccer-specific exercises
- Avoid intense plyometric programmes
- Avoid high-intensity training
- Consider 'conditioned' drills and games such as restricted contact
- Consider deep-water running and hydrotherapy

Table 8.6 Mean percentage decrease in weight lifted over four days of partial sleep loss

Exercise	Order in session	Days 1–2	Days 1–3	Days 1–4
Biceps curl	1	2	5	10
Bench press	2	4	10	12
Leg press	3	3	10	14
Dead lift	4	1	13	17

Source: Data from Reilly and Piercy, 1994.

player constituting almost 10% of daily energy intake in the evening following a league game, even though carbohydrates represented 60% of the average daily macronutrient intake. Its diuretic and depressant effects render alcohol an inappropriate beverage for professional players, either leading up to competition or recovering from matches.

Consideration should be also be given to appropriate sleeping patterns. Most individuals have a good tolerance to sleep disruption, but sleep loss following match-play can interfere with performance in training on the following day (Reilly and Piercy, 1994). The fall-off in performance was progressive within a weight training session as subjects lost motivation to continue their more strenuous efforts (see Table 8.6). Whilst players may have a prolonged sleep latency after a game, any loss of sleep is likely to be compensated for the next night. An alternative is to have a late afternoon nap on the recovery day to exploit the recuperative properties of sleep. Disrupted or reduced sleep can suppress immune functions (Smith and Reilly, 2005) and accentuate the immunodepression associated with the 'open-window' period post-exercise.

The timing of kick-off, return travel schedules and other external factors may cause disturbance in the players' normal sleep–wake cycle. Severe exercise during the daytime is sometimes associated with changes in slow-wave sleep and growth hormone secretion during the following night (Waterhouse *et al.*, 2002). These observations imply restorative characteristics of sleep. Slow-wave sleep predominates in the first half of the night, underlying the benefit of getting to bed in reasonable time after competing in a match for restoration of homeostasis.

Overview

Strenuous training and match-play place enormous demands on the mental, physical and physiological reserves of players. Players vary in their abilities to cope and in their tolerance of competitive stresses. Whilst adapting to these physiological demands, additional stresses due to hard training or other games in quick succession may overtax individual capabilities and impair performance or even increase injury risk. The emphasis therefore in training must be on establishing the correct balance between recovery and training stimulus in the days intervening between matches.

Where there are multiple matches within a congested schedule of engagements it is essential that the complete recovery of physiological and psychological capacities occurs. Special consideration may be needed to restore the self-confidence of players before the next match and specific coaching may be necessary to correct tactical deficiencies in the event of defeat or poor performance.

Regeneration of normal metabolic reserves is a priority and practices to promote recovery should commence once the game (or formal training) is finished. The replacement of fluid lost during exercise is also important so that net losses are reduced. The benefits of physical therapy are unclear, except where minor soft-tissue trauma has been incurred. It is prudent to modify the training programme to take into account the transient reduction in physical capacities and incorporate recovery sessions into the weekly regimen. Unless complete recovery is achieved, the team will enter the next contest with some of its players at a disadvantage. In order to avoid this possibility, recovery strategies should incorporate specific hydration, nutritional, psychological, training and lifestyle factors (see Table 8.5). There are numerous interactions among the factors influencing recovery, and so a knowledge and appreciation of the principles involved are important.

References

Armstrong, L.E., Herrera-Soto, J.A., Hacker, F.T., Casa, D.J., Kavouras, S.A. and Maresh, C.M., 1998, Urinary indices during dehydration, exercise and rehydration. *International Journal of Sport Nutrition*, **8**, 345–355.

Barr, S.I., 1999, Effects of dehydration on exercise performance. *Canadian Journal of Applied Physiology*, **24**, 164–172.

Clarke, N.D., Drust, B., MacLaren, D.P.M. and Reilly, T., 2003, Hydration and energy provision during soccer-specific exercise. *Proceedings of the Physiological Society* P555, 28P.

Cleak, M.J. and Eston, R.G., 1992, Delayed onset muscle soreness: mechanisms and management. *Journal of Sports Sciences*, **10**, 325–341.

Coyle, E.F., 1991, Timing and method of increased carbohydrate intake to cope with heavy training, competition and recovery. *Journal of Sports Sciences*, **9**, 29–52.

Dawson, B., 2002, Effects of immediate post-game recovery procedures on muscle soreness, power and flexibility levels over the next 48 hours. *Communication to the Annual Meeting of the Australian Society for Sports Medicine*.

Dohm, G.L., 2002, Exercise effects on muscle insulin signaling and action – regulation of skeletal muscle GLUT-4 expression by exercise. *Journal of Applied Physiology*, **93**, 782–787.

Dowzer, C.N., Reilly, T. and Cable, N.T., 1998, Effects of deep and shallow water running on spinal shrinkage. *British Journal of Sports Medicine*, **32**, 44–48.

Dowzer, C.N., Reilly, T., Cable, N.T. and Nevill, A., 1999, Maximal physiological responses to deep and shallow water running. *Ergonomics*, **42**, 275–281.

Drust, B., Atkinson, G., Gregson, W., French, D. and Binningsley, D., 2003, The effects of massage on intra-muscular temperature in the vastus lateralis in humans. *International Journal of Sports Medicine*, **24**, 395–399.

Ekblom, B., 1986, Applied physiology of soccer. *Sports Medicine*, **3**, 50–60.

Ekblom, B., 2005, Assessment of fitness and players' profiles. In: *International Football and Sports Medicine: Caring for the Soccer Athlete Worldwide* (edited by J. Dvorak and D.T. Kirkendall), Rosemont, Il, American Orthopaedic Society for Sports Medicine, pp. 37–42.

Ekstrand, J., Walden, M. and Hagglund, M., 2004, A congested football calendar and the well-being of players: correlation between match exposure of European football players before the World Cup 2002 and their injuries and performances during that World Cup. *British Journal of Sports Medicine*, **38**, 493–497.

Eston, R. and Peters, D., 1999, Effects of cold water immersion on the symptoms of exercise-induced muscle damage. *Journal of Sports Sciences*, **17**, 231–238.

Foley, J.M., Jayaraman, R.C., Prior, B.M., Pivarnik, J.M. and Meyer, R.A., 1999, MR measurement of muscle damage and adaptation after eccentric exercise. *Journal of Applied Physiology*, **87**, 2311–2318.

Gleeson, M., Blannin, A.K. and Walsh, N.P., 1997, Overtraining, immunosuppression, exercise-induced muscle damage and anti-inflammatory drugs. In: *The Clinical Pharmacology of Sport and Exercise* (edited by T. Reilly and M. Orme), Amsterdam: Excerpta Medica, pp. 47–57.

Hilbert, J.E., Sforzo, G.A. and Swensen, T., 2003, The effects of massage on delayed-onset muscle soreness. *British Journal of Sports Medicine*, **37**, 72–75.

Howatson, G. and van Someren, K.A., 2003, Ice massage: effects on exercise-induced muscle damage. *Journal of Sports Medicine and Physical Fitness*, **43**, 500–505.

MacLaren, D., 2003, Nutrition. In: *Science and Soccer* (edited by T. Reilly and A.M. Williams), London: Routledge, pp. 73–95.

Malm, C., Svensson, M., Ekblom, B. and Sjödin, B., 1997, Effect of ubiquinone-10 supplementation and high intensity training on physical performance in humans. *Acta Physiologica Scandinavica*, **161**, 379–384.

Malm, C., Ekblom, O. and Ekblom, B., 2004, Immune system alteration in response to two consecutive soccer games. *Acta Physiologica Scandinavica*, **180**, 143–155.

Maughan, R.J., 1991, Fluid and electrolyte loss and replacement in exercise. *Journal of Sports Sciences*, **9** (Special Issue), 117–142.

Monedero, J. and Donne, B., 2000, Effect of recovery interventions on lactate removal and subsequent performance. *International Journal of Sports Medicine*, **21**, 593–597.

Nakamura, D., Akimoto, T., Suzuki, S. and Kono, I., 2004, Decreased salivary Sg₉A levels before appearance of upper respiratory tract infection in Collegiate soccer players. In: *Science and Football V* (edited by T. Reilly, J. Cabri and D. Araújo), London: Routledge, pp. 536–543.

Nieman, D. and Bishop, N.C., 2006, Nutritional strategies to counter stress to the immune system in athletes, with special reference to football. *Journal of Sports Sciences*, **24**, 763–772.

Pollock, N.W., Godfrey, R. and Reilly, T., 1997, Evaluation of field measures of urine concentration. *Medicine and Science in Sports and Exercise*, **29** (Suppl. 5), S261.

Rasmussen, B.B., Tipton, K.D., Miller, S.L., Wolfe, S.E. and Wolfe, R.R., 2000, An oral essential amino acid-carbohydrate supplement enhances muscle protein anabolism after resistance exercise. *Journal of Applied Physiology*, **88**, 386–392.

Reilly, T., 1994, Physiological aspects of soccer. *Biology of Sport*, **11**, 3–20.

Reilly, T., 2002, Measurement of spinal loading: shrinkage. In: *Musculoskeletal Disorders in Health-related Occupations* (edited by T. Reilly), Amsterdam: IOS Press, pp. 25–39.

Reilly, T. and Brooks, G.A., 1986, Exercise and the circadian variation in body temperature measures. *International Journal of Sports Medicine*, **7**, 358–362.

Reilly, T. and Cable, N.T., 2001, Thermoregulation. In: *Kinanthropometry and Exercise Physiology Laboratory Manual: Tests, Procedures and Data. Volume 2: Exercise Physiology*, London: Routledge, pp. 193–210.

Reilly, T. and Ekblom, B., 2005, The use of recovery methods post-exercise. *Journal of Sports Sciences*, **23**, 619–627.

Reilly, T. and Piercy, M., 1994, The effects of partial sleep deprivation on weight-lifting performance. *Ergonomics*, **37**, 107–115.

Reilly, T. and Rigby, M., 2002, Effect of an active warm-down following competitive soccer. In: *Science and Football IV* (edited by W. Spinks, T. Reilly and A. Murphy), London: Routledge, pp. 226–229.

Reilly, T. and Waterhouse, J., 2005, *Sport, Exercise and Environmental Physiology*. Edinburgh: Elsevier.

Reilly. T., Cable, N.T. and Dowzer, C.N., 2002, The efficacy of deep-water running. In: *Contemporary Ergonomics 2002* (edited by P.T. McCabe), London: Taylor and Francis, pp. 162–166.

Reilly, T., Edwards, B.J. and Waterhouse, J., 2003, Long haul travel and jet-lag: behavioural and pharmacological approaches. *Medicina Sportiva*, E115–E122.

Saltin, B., 1973, Metabolic fundamentals in exercise. *Medicine and Science in Sports*, **5**, 156–158.

Shirreffs, S.M., 2000, Markers of hydration status. *Journal of Sports Medicine and Physical Fitness*, **40**, 80–84.

Smith, R.S. and Reilly, T., 2005, Sleep deprivation and the athlete. In: *Sleep Deprivation* (edited by C. Kushida), New York: Marcel Dekker Inc, pp. 313–334.

Thompson, D., Williams, C., Garcia-Roves, P., McGregor, S.J., McArdle, F. and Jackson, M.J., 2003, Post-exercise vitamin C supplementation and recovery from demanding exercise. *European Journal of Applied Physiology*, **89**, 393–400.

Tipton, K.D. and Wolfe, R.R., 2001, Exercise, protein metabolism and muscle growth. *International Journal of Sports Nutrition and Exercise Metabolism*, **11**, 109–132.

Waterhouse, J.M., Minors, D.S., Waterhouse, M.E., Reilly, T. and Atkinson, G., 2002, *Keeping in Time with Your Body Clock*. Oxford: Oxford University Press.

Williams, A.M., Lee, D. and Reilly, T., 1999, *A Quantitative Analysis of Matches Played in the 1991–92 and 1997–98 Seasons*. London: the Football Association.

Wong, S.H., Williams, C., Simpson, M. and Ogaki, T., 1998, Influence of fluid intake pattern on short-term recovery from prolonged, submaximal running and subsequent exercise capacity. *Journal of Sports Sciences*, **16**, 143–152.

Chapter 9

Training for different environments

Introduction

Soccer is played throughout the world and in many different kinds of environments. The existence of seasonal variations in climatic conditions mean that sometimes the environment is temporarily unsuitable for playing soccer matches and there is a break in the competitive programme. This intermission in the calendar applies in the winter of northern climates and in tropical countries during the rainy season. When the weather is cold and wet, it becomes impossible to maintain pitches to an adequate standard and the conditions are too harsh for the comfort of players. At the other climatic extreme is the stress imposed by a hot environment and the difficulty of coping with high heat and humidity. The hottest part of the day can be avoided and matches timed for evening kick-offs. This scheduling is not always practical for international tournaments and teams from temperate climates can be required to compete in conditions with which they are unfamiliar. They will not be able to cope well unless they make the necessary preparations.

The elevation above sea level can also make exceptional demands on soccer players. Teams may be obliged to play friendly or international matches at moderate to high altitudes. Temporary training camps for top teams may be based at altitude resorts and this environment constitutes a particular novel challenge to those dwelling at sea-level. South American teams playing in Bolivia, and less so in parts of Mexico, can be hampered by the altitude at which the game is played.

The process of acclimatisation enables the human body to adapt to some extent to environmental challenges. Many physiological functions also adjust during the day in harmony with cyclical changes in the environment. The sleep–wake cycle corresponds with the daily alternation of darkness and light and the majority of the body's activities are suited for action during the day and rest at night. These circadian rhythms are disturbed when the body is forced to exercise at a time it is unused to, for example, after crossing multiple time zones to compete overseas. The rhythms are also disrupted if sleep is disturbed, displaced to a different time of day or lost completely (Reilly and Deykin, 1983).

The major environmental variables that affect soccer play and training are considered in this chapter. These factors include heat, cold, hypoxia, circadian rhythms, air quality and weather conditions. The biological background is provided prior to describing the consequences of environmental conditions for the soccer player.

Thermoregulation

The temperature of the human body is relatively constant, being regulated about a set point of 37°C. Core temperature refers to temperature within the body's central organs and is measured usually as rectal, tympanic, oesophageal or gut temperature. Oral temperature tends to be lower than in these areas and is less reliable since the temperature within the mouth can be affected by drinking cold or hot fluids and by the temperature of the air inspired.

For thermoregulatory purposes the body can be thought of as consisting of a shell around a warmer body core. The mean skin temperature is usually about 33°C, representing a gradient of about 4°C from core to shell. The temperature of the shell is more variable than that of the core and responds to changes in environmental temperatures. The normal temperature gradient from skin to the air facilitates a loss of heat to the environment.

The human body exchanges heat with the environment through different routes to achieve an equilibrium. The heat balance equation is expressed as:

$$M - S = E \pm C \pm R \pm K$$

where M = metabolic rate, S = heat storage, E = evaporation, C = convection, R = radiation and K = conduction.

Heat loss and heat gain mechanisms must be in balance for thermal equilibrium. Metabolic processes produce heat, the basal metabolic rate being about 1 kcal kg^{-1} h^{-1}. One kilocalorie (4.186 kJ) is the energy required to raise 1 kg water through 1°C. Energy expenditure during soccer can increase this value by a factor of 15–16, with about only 20–25% of the energy expended being reflected in external power output. The remaining 75–80% is dissipated as heat within the active tissues, leading to an increased heat storage within the body. The body possesses physiological mechanisms for losing heat so that overheating is avoided. The thermal state of the body can also be maintained in circumstances where heat might be lost very rapidly to the environment, such as occurs when the weather is very cold.

Specialized nerve cells within the hypothalamus are responsible for the control of body temperature. The neurones in the anterior portion constitute the heat loss centre since they trigger initiation of responses that lead to a loss of heat (Figure 9.1). The posterior part of the hypothalamus contains the heat gain centre that operates to preserve body heat when the environment is cold.

When conditions are hot, peripheral vasodilation causes a redistribution of blood to the skin where it can be cooled. A second mechanism is the stimulation of eccrine sweat glands to secrete a solution onto the skin surface where

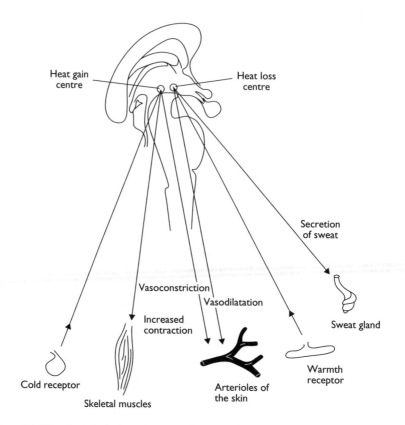

Figure 9.1 The physiological mechanisms that contribute to thermoregulation.

Source: Reprinted with permission, from Reilly and Willams, 2003, figure 12.2.

evaporative cooling can take place. Conversely, in cold conditions vasoconstriction reduces blood flow to the skin, allowing the temperature in the shell to decline but protecting core temperature.

The hypothalamic cells that control thermoregulatory responses are sensitive to the temperature of blood that flows through them. These cells also receive signals from warmth and cold receptors located in the skin. In these ways the heat loss and gain centres receive information about both the body's internal thermal state and environmental conditions.

Exercise in the heat

The temperature within the active muscles and core temperature both rise during exercise. When the exercise is performed in hot conditions the skin temperature is elevated, reflecting the external challenge to the body. An increased portion of the cardiac output is shunted to the skin to facilitate the loss of heat: the body surface can lose heat to the environment (by convection and radiation) due to the warm blood now being diverted through its subcutaneous layers. During intense exercise, the cardiac output may be maximal or near it and the increased cutaneous blood flow may compromise blood supply to the active skeletal muscles. In such instances the soccer player has to reduce the exercise intensity, take longer recovery periods than normal or do less running 'off-the-ball'.

The work-rates of players during matches and in training are affected by high environmental temperatures. The distance covered in high-intensity running during soccer match-play at an ambient temperature of 30°C was 500 m compared to 900 m when the temperature was 20°C (Ekblom, 1986). This lowered work-rate reflects changes in the overall pace of the game. The amount of rise in core temperature is affected by the exercise intensity and the level of play. Rectal temperatures averaging 39.5°C have been reported for Swedish First Division players in ambient temperatures of 20–25°C, whereas the average for players of lower divisions was 39.1°C (Ekblom, 1986).

Dilation of peripheral blood vessels allows blood flow to the skin to be increased. The increased vasodilation reduces peripheral resistance and causes a decrease in blood pressure so that the protection of the blood pressure from too large a fall limits the amount of vasodilation that occurs. The kidney hormone renin stimulates angiotensin which is a powerful vasoconstrictor and this response offsets a drop in blood pressure. The decline in blood pressure is a risk when prolonged training is conducted in the heat and there is a related decrease of body water stores.

When core temperature rises the sweat glands are stimulated, loss of sweat by evaporation being the major route of heat loss to the environment during intense exercise. The sweat glands are stimulated by noradrenaline and secrete a dilute solution containing electrolytes and trace elements. Heat is lost to the environment only when the fluid is vaporised on the surface of the body, no heat being exchanged if sweat drips off or is wiped away. Loss of heat by evaporation is decreased when the relative humidity is high, since the air is already highly saturated with water vapour. Hot humid conditions are especially detrimental to performance and increase the risk of heat-injury.

Up to 3 l or more fluid may be lost during the course of a match played in the heat, although this figure may vary with the climatic conditions and also between individuals. Players who sweat profusely may be dehydrated near the end of the game whereas those who sweat little will be at risk of hypothermia. A fluid loss of 3.1% body mass was reported during a match at 33°C and 40% relative humidity and also when ambient temperature was 26.3°C but humidity was 78% (Mustafa and Mahmoud, 1979). Professional players training in the evening when the temperature was 32°C experienced a net loss of body mass of 1.6 ± 0.6%, despite having free access to a sports drink for the 90 min of training (Shirreffs et al., 2005). It is thought that a loss of 2% body mass is sufficient to affect performance adversely.

Sweating causes an equally proportionate decrease in body water in the cells, in the interstices and in plasma. The reduction in plasma volume compromises the supply of blood available to the active muscles and to the skin for cooling. The endocrine glands and kidneys attempt to conserve body water and electrolytes, but the needs of thermoregulation override these mechanisms and the athlete may become dangerously dehydrated through continued sweating. The main hormones involved in attempting to protect against dehydration are vasopressin (anti-diuretic hormone), produced by the pituitary gland, and aldosterone secreted by the adrenal cortex which stimulates the kidneys to conserve sodium.

Players must be adequately hydrated prior to playing and training in the heat in order to cope best with its conditions. In these circumstances, water is lost through sweat at a faster rate than it can be replaced by means of drinking and subsequent absorption through the small intestine. Besides, thirst is not a very precise indicator of the level of dehydration and players should make a conscious effort to drink regularly, about 200 ml every 15–20 min when training in the heat. The primary need is for water since sweat is hypotonic. Electrolyte and carbohydrate solutions can be more effective than water in enhancing intestinal absorption.

Many components of soccer performance will be adversely affected once core temperature rises above an optimal value. This level is probably around a body temperature of 38.3–38.5°C. Progressive levels of dehydration also cause performance to deteriorate. This drop in performance can be offset to some degree by fluid replacement. Cognitive as well as physical and psychomotor aspects of skill can be affected. Reilly and Lewis (1985) reported that decision-making was best maintained when an energy drink was provided to subjects compared with water only, which itself was superior to a trial when no fluid was provided (see Figure 9.2).

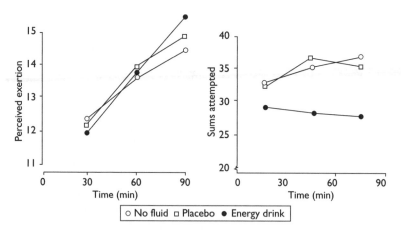

Figure 9.2 Rating of perceived exertion and the speed of adding under three experimental conditions: no fluid, a placebo and an energy drink.

Source: Reprinted with permission, from Reilly and Williams, 2003, figure 12.3.

It is the relative exercise intensity (%$\dot{V}O_{2\ max}$) rather than the absolute work-load that determines the thermal strain on the individual player. The higher the maximal aerobic power ($\dot{V}O_{2\ max}$) and maximal cardiac output, the lower is the thermal strain on the player. A well-trained cardiovascular system helps the individual to cope with the dual roles of supplying oxygen to the active muscles during exercise and serving the needs of thermoregulation. This individual will also acclimatise more quickly than one who is unfit. The training process itself improves exercise tolerance in the heat but does not eliminate the necessity for heat acclimatisation.

One of the metabolic consequences of playing in hot conditions is that muscle glycogen is used up more rapidly than normal. Intermittent exercise at 41°C for 60 min increased muscle glycogen utilisation compared to exercise at 9°C (Febbraio, 2001). There is a corresponding shift in the respiratory exchange ratio and a decrease in the use of intramuscular triglycerides. The outcome is that fatigue occurs earlier than normal, a process accelerated by the effect of heat stress on performance.

In preparing for exercise in hot conditions, an appropriate choice of clothing must be made. Light, loose clothing helps in creating convective air currents to cool the skin. Clothing of natural fibre such as cotton (or at least a cotton–polyester mix) is desirable under warm and radiant environmental conditions. When training takes place in very hot conditions, the use of a 'cooling vest' can be effective in reducing heat stress and maintaining performance. Webster et al. (2005) found that a light-weight cooling vest worn during the rest and warm-up prior to exercise, and the warm-down afterwards provided a significant thermoregulatory advantage to athletes wearing them. The advantage was evident in a decrease in core temperature, skin temperature and sweat rate and in enhanced recovery of the thermoregulatory system post-exercise. Endurance performance was impaired when the cooling vest was discarded after the warm-up. A commercial cooling suit designed for applications in sport may not be available to many teams in hot weather and other strategies may be used to keep the body from getting too hot during exercise. Drust et al. (2000) found that a long period in a cold shower was effective in reducing the rise in temperature during a simulation of the workrate of competitive soccer. The benefit was lost by the start of the second half, the half-time intermission allowing opportunity for thermoregulatory processes to return towards resting values.

Heat acclimatisation

Acclimatisation refers to adaptations of physiological systems to the natural climate. The term *acclimation* is used to refer to physiological changes which occur in response to experimentally induced changes in one particular factor (Nielsen, 1994).

Heat acclimatisation leads to an earlier onset of sweating (sweat produced at a lower rise in body temperature) and a more dilute solution from the sweat

Table 9.1 Physiological changes associated with heat
acclimatisation

- Earlier onset of sweating
- Sweat becomes more dilute
- Increased sweat rate at the same core temperature
- Reduced heart rate at a given exercise intensity
- Improved pacing of effort

glands. The heat-acclimatised individual sweats more at a given exercise intensity than one who is unacclimatised. The distribution of blood to the skin achieves more effective cooling after a period of acclimatisation, although the acclimatised player depends more on evaporative sweat loss than on distribution of blood flow (Table 9.1).

It is possible for acclimatisation to heat to be achieved relatively quickly and a good degree of adaptation takes place within 10–14 days of the initial exposure. Further adaptations will enhance the athlete's capability of performing well under heat stress (Nielsen, 1994). Ideally, therefore, players should be exposed to the climate of the host country for at least 2 weeks before the competitive event. An alternative strategy is to have an acclimatisation period of 2 weeks or so well before the event with subsequent shorter exposures as training is tapered before competition. If these are not feasible, some degree of heat acclimation should be attempted before the players leave for the host country. This goal may be achieved prior to exposure to the competitive environment in various ways (see Reilly, 2003):

1 The player seeks out exposure to hot and humid environments, choosing the hottest or the most humid time of day to train at home.
2 Players may seek access to an environmental chamber for periodic bouts of heat exposure. The players must exercise rather than rest under such conditions for the exposure to be effective. About 3 h per week exercising in an environmental chamber provides a good degree of acclimation (Reilly *et al.*, 1997).
3 Heavy sweat suits or windbreakers may be worn in training to keep the microclimate next to the skin hot. This practice will add to the heat load imposed under cool environmental conditions and induce a degree of adaptation to thermal strain.
4 Exposure to heat is itself a learning experience. The individual gauges how exercise performance is affected and how to pace the effort so that the conditions can be tolerated.
5 The player may make repeated use of a sauna or Turkish bath, but this procedure is only partially effective.

Players should be encouraged to drink copiously to maintain normal hydration status when first exposed to a hot climate. They should drink much more fluid than their thirst dictates and not rely solely on their subjective sensations of thirst. Sunbathing after arrival in the hot country should be discouraged as this itself does not help acclimatisation except by the development of a suntan which will eventually protect the skin from damage via solar radiation. Acquiring a suntan is a long-term process and is not beneficial in the short term, but negative effects of sunburn can cause severe discomfort and a decline in performance. Players should therefore be protected with an adequate sunscreen if they are likely to be exposed to solar radiation.

Training should at first be undertaken in the cooler parts of the day so that an adequate workload can be achieved and adequate fluid must be taken regularly. Arrangements can be made to sleep in an air-conditioned environment if sleeping is disturbed, but to achieve acclimatisation the rest of the day should be partly spent exposed to the ambient temperature other than in air-conditioned rooms. There should be no need to take salt tablets to compensate for the sodium lost in sweat, provided adequate amounts of salt are taken with normal food.

When ingested with water 2 h before exercise, glycerol has been found to increase fluid retention, and reduce cardiovascular strain during exercise (Anderson et al., 2001). The authors concluded that this practice of using glycerol ($1.0–1.5$ g.kg^{-1}) to increase water retention pre-exercise improves exercise performance in the heat by mechanisms other than alterations in muscle metabolism. This ergogenic effect of taking glycerol with a large volume of water has not been shown by others and may not apply to intermittent high-intensity exercise as occurs in soccer. Armstrong (2006) concluded that use of glycerol in a soccer context cannot be recommended, especially if hydration status can be maintained during exercise.

It is good practice to measure body weight each morning and players should try to compensate for weight loss with adequate fluid intake when attempting to acclimatise to heat. Alcohol is inappropriate for rehydration purposes since it acts as a diuretic and increases urine output. Players are reminded to check that the volume of urine is as large as usual and that it is a pale straw colour rather than dark. Sports scientists working with soccer teams may collect urine samples in the morning and use a standard colour chart to assess hydration status. A dark colour indicates dehydration whereas a clear colour or straw colour denotes adequate hydration. Although there is no ideal measure of hydration status, the most suitable methods are osmolarity, specific gravity and conductivity (Pollock et al., 1997).

Heat injury

Hyperthermia (overheating) and loss of body water (hypohydration) lead to abnormalities that are referred to as heat injury. Progressively they may be manifest as muscle cramps, heat exhaustion and heat stroke. Cramps occur more frequently in individual events such as distance running than in soccer but can be observed in matches or training sessions in the heat in young players particularly.

Heat cramps are associated with loss of body fluid, particularly in games players competing in intense heat (Reilly, 2000). The electrolytes lost in sweat cannot adequately account for the occurrence of cramps which seem to coincide with low energy stores as well as reduced body water levels. Generally the muscles employed in the exercise are affected, but those most vulnerable are the leg (upper or lower) and abdominal muscles. Stretching the affected muscle helps to relieve the cramp, and sometimes massage produces a good outcome.

A core temperature of about 40°C is characteristic of heat exhaustion. There is an accompanying feeling of extreme tiredness, dizziness and breathlessness and an increased heart rate. The symptoms may coincide with a reduced sweat loss but they usually arise because the skin blood vessels are so dilated that blood flow to vital organs is reduced.

Core temperatures of 41°C or higher are observed in individuals suffering heat stroke. Hypohydration – due to loss of body water in sweat and associated with a high core temperature – can threaten life. Cessation of sweating, total confusion or loss of consciousness are characteristic of heat stroke which must be considered a true medical emergency. Treatment is urgently needed to reduce body temperature. There may also be circulatory instability and loss of vasomotor tone as the regulation of blood pressure begins to fail.

Competing and training in cold

In countries such as the United Kingdom, soccer is regarded as a winter sport and is often played in near-freezing conditions. Core temperature and muscle temperature may fall and exercise performance will be increasingly affected. Experimental studies indicate that muscle power output is reduced by 5% for every 1°C fall in muscle temperature below normal levels (Bergh and Ekblom, 1979). A fall in core temperature to hypothermic levels is life-threatening: fortunately the body's heat gain mechanisms are designed to arrest the decline and true hypothermia is a rare occurrence in match-play. It is more common for players to experience thermal discomfort due to a fall in body temperature to a level that impairs performance.

The posterior hypothalamus initiates a generalised vasoconstriction of the cutaneous circulation in response to cold, a response mediated by the sympathetic nervous system. Blood is displaced centrally away from the peripheral circulation and this change causes the temperature gradient between core and shell to be increased. The reduction in skin temperature in turn decreases the gradient between the skin and the environment which protects against a large loss of heat from the body. Blood returning from the limbs is diverted from the superficial veins to the vena comitantes that lie adjacent to the main arteries. The arterial blood is cooled by the venous return almost immediately it enters the limb by means of counter–current heat exchange.

A drop in limb temperature adversely affects the performance of motor skills. Muscular strength and power output are impaired as the temperature in the muscle falls and the conduction velocity of nerve impulses to the muscles is retarded. The sensitivity of muscle spindles also declines causing impairment in

Table 9.2 Some effects of cold on human
         performance

- Increased peripheral vasoconstriction
- Periodic shivering
- Muscle spindle sensitivity falls
- Reduced conduction velocity of nerve
  fibres
- Manual dexterity deteriorates
- Muscle strength and power decline
- Errors and injuries increase

manual dexterity. For these reasons, it is important to preserve limb temperature in soccer players during matches. The goalkeeper in particular must maintain manual dexterity for handling the ball. The activity of the goalkeeper is often spontaneous rather than directly imposed by demands of the game. The goalkeeper must stay alert during those periods when not directly involved in play in anticipation of being called quickly into action.

The body's autonomic nervous system stimulates shivering in response to the fall in core temperature (Table 9.2). Skeletal muscles contract involuntarily in order to generate metabolic heat. Shivering tends to be intermittent and may persist during exercise if the intensity is insufficient to maintain core temperature. It may occur during stoppages in training when conditions are cold and especially when compounded by sleet or rain. Coaches should be attentive to the possibility of young players experiencing such behavioural signs of cold, especially if they become increasingly disengaged from activity 'on-the-ball'.

Shivering, fatigue, loss of strength and coordination and an inability to sustain workrate are all early symptoms of hypothermia. Once fatigue sets in, shivering may decrease and the condition worsens to include collapse, stupor and loss of consciousness. This risk applies more to recreational rather than professional players as some individuals might not be able to sustain a workrate to keep themselves warm in extreme cold. In such events, the match official would be expected to abandon play before conditions became critical.

It is possible to protect the body against exposure to ambient environmental conditions and so cold is less of a problem than is heat. The temperature in the microclimate next to the skin may be maintained by appropriate choice of clothing and use of more than one layer. Players might respond positively to cold conditions by maintaining a high workrate. Alternatively, they may be spared exposure to the cold by conducting training sessions in indoor training facilities where these are available.

Clothing made with natural fibre (cotton or wool) is preferable to synthetic material in cold and cold-wet conditions. Sweat produced during exercise in these conditions should be able to flow through the garment. The best material will allow sweat to flow out through the cells of the garment whilst preventing water droplets from penetrating the clothing from the outside. Fabric that becomes saturated with water or sweat loses its insulation and the body temperature may drop quickly in cold–wet conditions.

The trunk area of the body should be well protected when training is conducted in the cold. The use of warm undergarments beneath a full tracksuit may be needed. Dressing in layers increases the insulation provided: the outer layers can be discarded as body temperature rises and if ambient temperature gets warmer. In matches, a t-shirt worn underneath the team jersey will help to keep the player warm whereas the goalkeeper may need a full track-suit.

The outer layer of clothing should be capable of resisting both wind and rain, while the inner layer should provide good insulation. The inside layer should also wick moisture from the skin to promote heat loss by evaporation. Polypropylene and cotton fishnet thermal underwear has good insulation and wicking properties and so is suitable to wear next to the skin.

In the period immediately prior to competing in the cold, players should stay as warm as possible. A thorough warm-up regimen (performed indoors if possible) helps in this regard. Cold conditions are thought to increase the risk of muscle injury in sports that involve intense anaerobic efforts and a systematic warm-up may afford some protection in this respect. Players may need to wear more clothing than they normally do during matches.

Aerobic fitness does not offer any direct protection against cold. Nevertheless, it will enable games players to keep more active when not directly involved in play and not increase the level of fatigue. Outfield players with a high level of aerobic fitness will also be able to maintain activity at a satisfactory level to achieve heat balance. In contrast, the individual with poor endurance may be at risk of hypothermia if the pace of activity falls too low. Players who are lean and possess low levels of subcutaneous adipose tissue are poorly insulated and may feel the cold more than others. They may be obliged to stay more active than their better insulated counterparts and generally possess the aerobic fitness to do so. Nevertheless, shivering during activity signals the onset of danger and is a warning of impending hypothermia.

Altitude

Physiological adjustments to altitude

Altitude refers to the elevations above sea level and as altitude increase the barometric pressure falls. At sea level the normal pressure is 760 mmHg, at 1,000 m it is 680 mmHg, at 3,000 m it is about 540 mmHg. High altitude conditions are referred to as hypobaric or low pressure and the main physiological problem associated with this environment is hypoxia or relative lack of oxygen.

Oxygen constitutes 20.93% or normal air, and the partial pressure of the oxygen at sea level is 159 mmHg (20.93% of 760). The partial pressure of oxygen decreases with increasing altitude: this decrease corresponds to the fall in ambient pressure whilst the proportion of oxygen in the air remains constant. The result is that there are fewer oxygen molecules in the air at altitude for a given volume of air. A smaller amount of oxygen is inspired for a given inspired volume which leads to a reduction in the amount of oxygen delivered to the active tissues.

The alveolar oxygen tension (pO_2) is of critical importance in the uptake of oxygen into the body through the lungs. The water vapour pressure in the alveoli is relatively constant at 47 mmHg as is the pCO_2 of 35–40 mmHg. The fall in alveolar tension at altitude results in a less favourable gradient across the pulmonary capillaries for transferring oxygen into the blood. Exercise that depends on oxygen transport mechanisms will be impaired at about 1,200 m once desaturation occurs. This refers to the oxygen dissociation curve of haemoglobin (Hb) which is sigmoid-shaped and is affected by pressure (Figure 9.3). Normally the red blood cells are 97% saturated with O_2 but this figure falls when pO_2 levels drop at a point corresponding to this altitude (1,200 m). The O_2–Hb curve is not affected much for the first 1,000–1,500 m of altitude as suggested by the flatness at its top. As the pressure drops further the curve becomes steeper and the supply of oxygen to the body's tissues in increasingly impaired. At an altitude of 3,000 m the arterial saturation is reduced to about 90%.

An increase in ventilation represents the body's acute physiological compensation for hypoxia. The depth and frequency of breathing both increase.

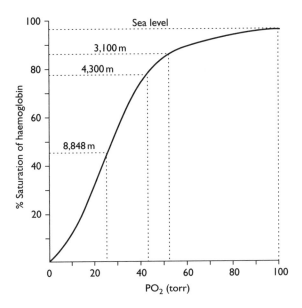

Figure 9.3 The standard oxygen dissociation curve of haemoglobin for a blood pH of 7.4 and body temperature of 37°C. The horizontal lines indicate % haemoglobin saturation of arterial blood at the different altitudes whilst the vertical lines indicate PO_2.

Source: Reprinted from Reilly and Waterhouse, 2005, with permission from Elsevier.

This hyperventilation raises the amount of CO_2 blown off from blood passing through the lungs. As CO_2 is a weak acid when dissolved in body fluid the elimination of CO_2 leaves the blood more alkaline than normal due to an excess of bicarbonate ions. The kidneys compensate by excreting excess bicarbonate, so restoring the normal pH level of the blood over several days. The decrease in the body's alkaline reserve leaves the blood with a poorer buffering capacity for tolerating additional acids (such as lactic acid diffusing from muscle to blood during exercise).

Once at altitude, there is an increased production of the substance 2,3-bisphosphoglycerate (2,3-BPG) by the red blood cells. This effect is beneficial in that it helps the unloading of oxygen from the red blood cells at the tissue level.

An increase in the number of red blood cells enhances the oxygen-carrying capacity of the blood. This process begins within a few days at altitude and is stimulated by the kidney hormone erythropoietin which causes the bone marrow to increase its production of red blood cells. This process requires that the body's iron stores are adequate and may indeed mean supplementation of iron intake prior to and during the stay at altitude (synthetic versions of the hormone have been used for purposes of blood doping, a procedure banned in sport). There is an apparent rise in haemoglobin in the first few days at altitude which is due to haemoconcentration and a transient drop in plasma volume. A true increase in haemoglobin occurs gradually and may take 10–12 weeks to be optimised. After a stay of a year or more at altitude, the increases in total body haemoglobin and red cell count do not match values observed in high altitude natives. Individuals born at sea level will never therefore be able to compete in aerobic events (including soccer) at altitude on equal terms with those native to altitude. Strategies must be devised to allow them to demonstrate their superior skills as well as prepare physiologically by acclimatising to altitude.

Exercise at altitude

Despite the acute physiological adjustments to hypoxia that take pace, soccer players experience difficulty in exercising at altitude compared with sea level. Changes in maximum cardiac output and in the oxygen transport system lead to a fall in maximal oxygen uptake ($\dot{V}O_{2\,max}$). At an altitude of 2,300 m, corresponding roughly to Mexico City, the initial decline in $\dot{V}O_{2\,max}$ averages about 15%. After 4 weeks at this altitude, there is an improvement in $\dot{V}O_{2\,max}$ but it still remains about 9% below its sea level value. For sea level dwellers the initial decline in $\dot{V}O_{2\,max}$ is about 1–2% for every 100 m above 1,500 m (see Reilly, 2003).

For the majority of a game, players operate at sub-maximal intensity with short episodes of maximal anaerobic efforts intervening. Maintaining a fixed sub-maximal exercise intensity is more difficult at altitude than at sea level. The highest level of endurance exercise that can be sustained is determined by the intensity at which lactate begins to accumulate progressively in the blood. This 'lactate threshold' is lowered at altitude although the percentage of $\dot{V}O_{2\,max}$ at which it occurs is unchanged. The active muscles rely more on anaerobic processes to help cope with the relative lack of oxygen, and so soccer players will need longer low-intensity recovery periods during match-play, following from their bouts of all-out high-intensity efforts.

Responses of heart rate, ventilation and perceived exertion are all increased above the normal sea-level values at any given sub-maximal exercise intensity. Therefore the pace of play that can be tolerated is reduced. Players should be prepared to pace their efforts more selectively during soccer matches at altitude. They will also need to accept a lower workrate during training sessions for the same relative physiological stress. These modifications are especially important in the first few days at altitude and differ between individuals according to their level of aerobic fitness, prior acclimatisation, state of health and previous experience of altitude. Physiological factors such as pulmonary diffusing capacity, total body haemoglobin, iron stores and nutritional state are also influential.

With adaptation to altitude, the heart rate response to sub-maximal exercise decreases compared with the heart rate on initial exposure and may approach sea level values after 3–4 weeks of exposure. The skeletal muscles also adapt but improvements in maximum blood flow and oxidative metabolism require a stay of many months at altitude. These long-term adaptations will not benefit anaerobic processes but there are also some changes in enzymes associated with anaerobic metabolism. The buffering capacity of muscle is enhanced with a prolonged stay at altitude. This adaptation, along with changes in activities of enzymes associated with anaerobic glycolysis, complements the adaptations that occur in oxygen transport mechanisms. Altitude conditions may be favourable when training is geared towards improving running speed since faster than normal velocities can be reached due to the reduced air resistance against which the body moves.

The decrease in air density at altitude has other implications for soccer. When speed training is conducted at altitude, the recovery period between sprints should be extended. Furthermore, the ball flies through the air more easily than normal. This phenomenon has implications for playing strategies, including the practice of set-pieces.

Soccer strategies for altitude

Acclimatisation is essential preparation for a soccer team scheduled to compete at altitude. Major international tournaments have taken place at altitude, including two World Cups at Mexico City, the Olympic Games soccer tournament in Mexico in 1968 and the World Student Games in 1979 at Mexico. Other countries play their home matches at altitude, including Bolivia, Colombia, Ethiopia and Kenya. Bolivia plays its home matches at 2,800 m or higher, a factor that bestows a considerable advantage to its players. Indeed, four of its top league clubs play at home at altitudes exceeding 3,000 m and one of its clubs (El Alto) has a home ground at above 4,000 m. Other South American clubs are disadvantaged when playing competitively at these levels. When Copa America was played in Bolivia the home side reached the final, only to be defeated by Brazil – a team renowned for the capability to control the pace of the game.

One option for teams playing at moderate altitude is to redistribute workloads among players so that individuals can selectively take longer recovery periods than normal. They may also need to choose the timing of offensive moves more effectively and concede possession to the opponents for longer than customary. Teams like the Brazilian national side have traditionally had a rhythmic distribution of effort, quickening the pace when fully on the attack. Teams that rely on all-round workrate from players, particularly in putting pressure on opposition players in possession of the ball, will need to modify their usual style of play. The direct style of play in which the ball is transferred quickly from defence to attack with long passes might occasionally prove effective.

The flight characteristics of the ball are altered as a result of the lowered air resistance at altitude. Consequently, kicks for distance will travel further and shots at goal will travel faster. It is good practice for all players to experience these conditions before actually competing in matches at altitude. This recommendation would be especially important for goalkeepers and the strikers. There is no real method of simulating these conditions at sea level and so players have to experience this alteration in the behaviour of the ball at altitude.

Tournaments held in different locations throughout the host country may entail qualifying matches or early rounds at different altitudes. Some teams playing in the 1986 World Cup in Mexico for example, had a number of matches scheduled close to sea level whereas other games were at altitude. In such circumstances, it is difficult for the team management to make plans and generally preparations are made for the worst possible eventualities. One option is to choose living accommodation at a relatively high altitude while the team descends to a lower altitude for specific strenuous training sessions. This strategy is known as the 'live high, train low' approach (Levine, 1997). In this way the players can maintain a high standard of training stimulus and gain a measure of acclimatisation from living at altitude.

Many teams use altitude training camps in the belief that the adaptations that occur will benefit subsequent performance at sea level. There are advantages and disadvantages to the practice. This approach is unlikely to be of much help to soccer players whose competitive season tends to leave little room for such sojourns, apart from the pre-season training period.

Preparing for altitude

Players due to compete at altitude or to stay for a long time at an altitude training camp must consider the physiological consequences of such a visit. Individuals suffering infection or having low iron stores are unlikely to benefit from altitude training camps as their ability to increase red blood cell production is limited.

Strenuous training should not be attempted for at least 2–3 days until the risk of developing acute mountain sickness has passed: this syndrome is characterised by headaches, nausea, vomiting, loss of appetite, sleep disturbances and irritability. These problems can be encountered at altitudes above 2,000–2,500 m but are mostly associated with higher altitudes. After that, prolonged training sessions should be reduced in intensity to the same perceived exertion as at sea level; full workouts are not advisable until 7–10 days after arrival. Recovery periods between intense short-term effort should be lengthened when intermittent exercise is performed: this principle applies both to conditioning work and to game practices.

There is also a need to pay extra attention to hydration. The air at altitude tends to be drier than at sea level and more fluid is lost by means of evaporation from the moist mucous membrane of the respiratory tract. This loss is accentuated by the hyperventilation response to hypoxia. The nose and throat get dry and irritable and this dryness can cause discomfort. It is important to drink more than normal to counteract the fluid loss. Ingjer and Myhre (1992) showed that a rigorous regime of drinking fluids helped to offset the fall in plasma volume that is a characteristic response to altitude (Ingjer and Myhre, 1992).

A greater than normal proportion of carbohydrate should be consumed, especially in the first few days at altitude. This change in diet will compensate for the increased reliance on glycogen as a fuel for exercise and for the fall in the tension of CO_2 in the blood consequent to hyperventilation.

It is thought that about 14 days should be allowed before matches for acclimatisation to altitudes of 1,500–2,000 m and 21 days before matches at 2,000–2,500 m. These periods may be shortened if the players have had previous exposure to altitude in their build-up to the tournament. Individuals without previous exposure to altitude need about 1 month to adapt to locations above 2,500 m and may lose match fitness in the process. Fortunately, soccer play at this altitude is uncommon for sea-level dwellers.

A prolonged stay at altitude before a competition is impractical and so some degree of acclimatisation may be achieved by frequent exposures to simulated altitude in an environmental chamber. Continuous exercise of 60–90 min, 45–60 min of intermittent exercise performed 4–5 times a week at simulated altitude of 2,300 m has produced good results in 3–4 weeks (see Reilly, 2003).

Portable simulators that induce hypoxia are available for wear as a backpack. These devices lower the inspired-oxygen tension and accentuate exercise stress but also increase the resistance to breathing. There is no convincing evidence that they promote the kind of adaptations that are experienced at altitude or that result from sustained exercise in a hypobaric chamber. They may have psychological benefits in allowing players to experience the stress of hypoxia. Portable simulators were used by the Danish soccer team, along with exercise tests in a hypobaric chamber (Bangsbo et al., 1988) in preparation for the 1986 World Cup in Mexico. In more recent years, normobaric hypoxic chambers have become available to professional soccer clubs for training and rehabilitation purposes.

Their main benefit is likely to be during rehabilitation as the relative circulatory strain is greater than a comparable workrate under normal sea-level conditions. They have obvious value also in providing players with an individual experience of exercise under hypoxic conditions.

Circadian rhythms

Soccer matches are played at various times in the day, ranging from morning kick-offs to night-time matches under floodlights. These times may disrupt normal diurnal rhythms as they are out of synchrony with the typical time for training. Competitive performance in soccer is dependent on a host of factors, including physiological and psychomotor variables. The workrate in games is correlated with maximal aerobic power and sprint performance is influenced by anaerobic power (Carling et al., 2005). These performance measures may themselves be affected by diurnal variation, changes that occur within the normal daytime hours.

Circadian rhythms refer to cyclical changes within the body that recur around the 24-h solar day. Core temperature shows a cycle every 24 h and is regarded as a fundamental marker of the body's circadian rhythm. The observations on rectal temperature can be fitted with a cosine function and the time of peak occurrence identified. The time that the peak occurs is referred to as the acrophase and is usually found between 17:00 and 18:00 h. Many measures of human performance follow closely this curve in body temperature (Drust et al., 2005). These measures include components of motor performance (such as muscular strength, reaction time, jumping performance) that are important in soccer play (Figure 9.4). Tasks related to soccer such as dribbling, juggling and chipping a soccer also show a time-of-day effect (Reilly et al., 2005a,b).

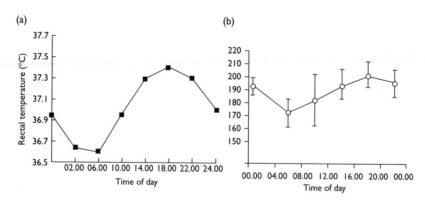

Figure 9.4 The circadian rhythm is shown for body temperature (a) and self-paced exercise intensity expressed in W (b).

Source: (a) Reprinted with permission, from Reilly and Williams, 2003, p. 177. (b) Reprinted from Reilly and Waterhouse, 2005, with permission from Elsevier.

The sleep–wake cycle is another relevant biological rhythm to consider. This cycle is linked with the pattern of habitual activity, that is, sleeping during the hours of darkness and working or staying awake during daylight. Arousal states vary between these times, tending to peak just after midday at the time that circulating levels of adrenaline are at their highest. A team forced to compete at a time of day it would normally be inactive would not be well equipped, biologically or psychologically, to do so.

Circadian rhythms include endogenous and exogenous components, depending on the degree to which they are governed by environmental signals. The exogenous factors include natural and artificial light, temperature, type and timing of meals, social and physical activity. Endogenous rhythms imply internal body clocks, the suprachiasmatic nucleus cells of the hypothalamus being the site of control of circadian rhythms. These cells are linked by neural pathways to the pineal gland and timekeeping functions have been attributed to the pineal, its hormone melatonin and related substances such as serotonin. The most relevant circadian rhythms for sports performance seem to be the body temperature curve and the sleep–wake cycle.

Training and time of day

Physical performance measures usually demonstrate a peak in performance that occurs close to the acrophase of the circadian rhythm in body temperature. On this basis the ideal time for playing soccer would be about 17:00–18:00 h, assuming the environmental temperature is within the comfort zone. There is probably a window of some hours during the day when maximal performance can be achieved. The optimum point can be realised with appropriate warm-up and physical and mental preparation. Consequently, kick-offs at 15:00 and 19:30 hours do not necessarily entail sub-optimal performance, particularly as muscle and core temperatures rise during the course of match-play. Particular consideration to warm-up is needed in late kick-offs, say 20:00 h, in cold conditions.

There is often a mismatch between the time of training and the time at which matches are played. The majority of professional teams train in the morning, starting at 10:00 or 11:00 h. Strenuous physical conditioning exercise is best conducted in the early evening, the time at which many amateur teams train. Joint stiffness is greatest in the morning and so special attention should be given to flexibility exercises in warming-up prior to morning training sessions. When players have to compete at a time of day to which they are unaccustomed, simply training at that time in the few days beforehand seems to be helpful.

Endurance performance is not necessarily hampered by a morning start, provided that exercise is not highly intensive at the start. Reilly and Garrett (1995) allowed subjects to pace themselves over an extended exercise test at two different times of day. Subjects during the morning began slowly but increased the intensity of exercise progressively throughout. In contrast they started at a higher workrate in the evening but by the end of the 90-min period were operating at a lower intensity than they had done in the morning. Sweating takes place at a lower body temperature in the morning than in the evening. In hot conditions the rise in core temperature may reach a critical upper value more quickly in the evening compared to the morning when the environmental temperature is also likely to be cooler. Thus the best time of day for exercise depends on the tasks to be performed, the goals of the session and the environmental conditions.

The circadian variation in skills related to soccer were examined in two separate studies by Reilly *et al.* (2005a,b). Muscle strength and body temperature conformed to the typical circadian rhythm with a peak denoted for about 18:00 h. The soccer-skills tests also demonstrated a diurnal variation. The tasks that required the greater degree of motor control, juggling and chipping tests, tended to peak earlier than those like dribbling speed which involved more gross motor functions. This separation quite likely reflects the existence of more than a single circadian rhythm with functions related to the nervous system tending to reach a peak earlier in the day than those linked with changes in body temperature (Reilly and Waterhouse, 2005). It may also entail a mental fatigue effect associated with the time awake. It seems that skills may be best acquired in mid-day sessions just as the curve in arousal approaches and reaches its high point. Consequently, there is a case for young professionals to have their skills work at light intensity in morning sessions. The more intense exercise can be retained for a later session following lunch and a rest for recovery.

Travel fatigue and jet lag

Soccer players are regularly called upon to travel vast distances to play in international team or inter-club matches. An extreme example is the intercontinental club's championship played in Japan which in 2005 included teams from Liverpool, Sao Paulo, Sydney and Asia, competing within their own domestic seasons. Teams may also participate in closed-season tournaments or friendly games overseas as part of pre-season training. Such engagements are made possible by the speed of contemporary air flight. Although international travel is commonplace nowadays it is not without attendant problems for the travelling soccer player, which should be recognised in advance.

Players have their regular routines disrupted when they travel abroad. They may be particularly excited about the trip or may have had worries associated with planning for the departure. Depending on the country to be visited, visas and vaccinations may be required. Top teams usually have arrangements made for them by their administrative and medical staff, as far as possible, in order to avoid otherwise inevitable embarrassments. These arrangements also extend to coping with formal procedures at departure and disembarkation and avoiding any mix-ups in dealing with ground staff and security controls.

Having arrived safely at the destination, the player may be suffering travel fatigue, loss of sleep (depending on flight times), and symptoms which have

Table 9.3 Symptoms associated with jet lag

- Feeling tired at daytime, yet unable to sleep at night
- Less able to concentrate or motivate oneself
- Decreased mental and physical performance
- Increased incidence of headaches
- Increased irritability and negative moods
- Loss of appetite and general bowel irregularities

come to be known as jet lag. This term refers to the feelings of disorientation, light-headedness, impatience, lack of energy and general discomfort that follow travelling across timezones (Table 9.3). These feelings are not experienced with travelling directly northwards or southwards within the same time zone when the passenger simply becomes tired from the journey or stiff after a long stay in a cramped posture. The feelings associated with jet lag may persist for several days after arrival and can be accompanied by loss of appetite, difficulty in sleeping, constipation and grogginess. Although individuals differ in severity of symptoms they experience, many people may simply fail to recognise how they themselves are affected, especially in tasks requiring concentration and complex co-ordination.

The body's circadian rhythm at first retains the characteristics of the point of departure following a journey across multiple time zones. The new environment soon forces new influences on these cycles, mainly the time of sunrise and onset of darkness. Core body temperature and other circadian rhythms are relatively slow to adjust to this new context. It takes about one day for each time zone crossed for body temperature to adapt completely. Sleep is likely to be difficult for a few days but activity and social contact during the day help to adjust the sleep–wakefulness rhythm. Arousal state adapts more quickly than does body temperature to the new time zone. Until the whole range of biological rhythms adjusts to the new local time and they become re-synchronized, the performance of the soccer player may be below par (Figure 9.5).

The severity of jet lag is affected by a number of factors besides individual differences. The greater the number of time zones travelled, the more difficult it is to cope. A 2-h phase shift may have marginal significance but a 3-h shift (e.g. British or Irish teams travelling to play European soccer matches in Russia or Armenia or teams within the United States travelling coast to coast) will encounter desynchronization to a substantial degree. In such cases the flight times – time of departure and time of arrival – may determine how severe are the symptoms of jet lag that occur. Training times might be altered to take the direction of travel into account. Such an approach was shown to be successful in American soccer teams travelling across time zones within the USA and scheduled to play at different times of day (Jehue *et al.*, 1993).

When journeys entail a 2–3 h time-zone transition and a short stay (2 days), it may be feasible to stay on 'home time'. For example, a strategy used by the

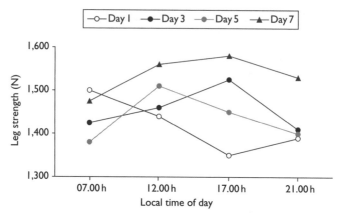

Figure 9.5 The diurnal variation in leg strength after travelling between the United Kingdom and Florida, United States of America (Waterhouse *et al.*, 1997).

Source: Reprinted from Waterhouse *et al.*, 1997, with permission from Elsevier.

national soccer teams of Wales when playing Azerbaijan in a World Cup qualifying match in September, 2004, was to stay on home time for the duration of the short trip. In this instance, the kick-off time of 21:00 hours (17:00 hours on home time) would have suited the strategy. Such an approach is useful if the stay in the new time zone is 3 days or less and adjustment of circadian rhythms is not essential. It also requires the time of competition to coincide with daytime on home time. If this is not the case, then adjustment of the body clock is required. A European team that is to compete in the morning in Japan or in the evening in the United States would require an adjustment of the body clock.

When jet lag is experienced, symptoms recede after the first 2 or 3 days following arrival, but may still be acute at particular times of day for some days. There will be a window of time during the day when time of high arousal associated with the time zone departed from and the new local time overlap. This window may be predicted in advance and should be utilised for timing of training practices in the first few days at the destination.

The severity of jet lag is influenced by the direction of travel. Flying in a westward direction is easier to tolerate than is flying eastward. On flying westward, the first day is lengthened and the body's rhythms can extend in line with their natural free-wheeling period of about 25 h and thus catch up. Travelling to Japan (9 h in advance of British Summer Time) and Malaysia (7 h in advance of British Summer Time) requires more than 9 and 7 days, respectively, for jet lag symptoms to disappear in some individuals. In contrast, re-adaptation is more rapid on returning to Britain (Reilly, 2003). However, when time-zone shifts approach near maximal values (e.g. a 12-h change) there may be little difference between eastward and westward travel and the body clock is likely to adjust as if the latter had occurred (Reilly *et al.*, 2005c).

Sleeping pills have been used by some travelling soccer teams to induce sleep whilst on board flight. Drugs such as benzodiazepines are effective in getting people to sleep but they do not guarantee a prolonged period asleep. They have proved ineffective in accelerating adjustment of the body clock in a group of British Olympic athletes travelling to the United States (Reilly *et al.*, 2001). Besides, they have not been satisfactorily tested for subsequent residual effects on motor performances such as soccer skills. They may in fact be counter-productive if administered at the incorrect time. Melatonin is one substance that can act directly on the body clock as well as being a hypnotic but the timing of administration is critical. Travellers between the United Kingdom and Australia, a journey which can elicit the most severe jet-lag symptoms, were found to have no benefit (Edwards *et al.*, 2000). Melatonin administered in the few hours before the trough of body temperature will have a phase–advance effect whereas if administered in the hours after this trough will delay the circadian rhythm. Ingestion of melatonin at other times will have no chronobiotic effect but will help to induce drowsiness. Since drugs do not provide an easy solution to preventing jet lag, a behavioural approach can be more effective in alleviating symptoms and hastening adjustment (Reilly *et al.*, 2005c).

Fitting in as soon as possible with the phase characteristics of the new environment is important. Focusing on the local time for disembarkation can help in planning the rest of the daily activity. Natural daylight inhibits melatonin and so it is the key signal that helps to re-adjust the body clock to the new environment. There may be other environmental factors to consider such as heat, humidity or even altitude.

Upon travelling westward a phase delay of the circadian rhythm is required and players may be allowed to retire to bed early in the evening. Early onset of sleep will be less likely after an eastward flight. In this case, a light training session on that evening would be helpful in instilling local clues into the rhythms. Exercise may hasten the adaptation to a new time zone and a light training session on the afternoon of arriving in the new country after a flight has proved beneficial (Reilly, 1993). Training in the morning is not recommended after a long-haul flight to the East since it could act to delay the body clock rather than promote the phase adjustment required in this circumstance. This strategy of avoiding morning sessions until it was deemed appropriate was used by British Olympic athletes arriving in Australia for the Sydney Olympics.

For the first few days in the new time zone, the exercise should be light or moderate in intensity as training hard while muscle strength and other measures are impaired will not be very effective (see Figure 9.5). Skills requiring fine co-ordination are also likely to be impaired and this might lead to accidents or injuries if sessions with the ball are conducted too strenuously. Where a series of tournament engagements is scheduled, it is useful to have at least one friendly match during the initial period, that is, before the end of the first week in the overseas country. Naps should be avoided for the first few days since a long nap at the time the individual feels drowsy (presumably at the time he/she would have been asleep in the time zone just departed from) anchors the rhythms at their former phases and so delays the adaptations to the new time zone.

Some precautions are necessary during the period of adaptation to the new time zone. Alcohol taken late in the evening is likely to disrupt sleep and so is not advised. Normal hydration levels may be reduced following the flight due to respiratory water loss in the dry cabin air and so fluid intake should be increased. A diet recommended for commercial travellers in the United States entailed use of protein early in the day to promote alertness and carbohydrate in the evening to induce drowsiness. This practice is unlikely to gain acceptance among soccer players, although they could benefit from avoiding large evening meals. The evening meal might include vegetables with a choice of chipped, roast or baked potatoes, pasta dishes, rice and bread with sufficient fibre to safeguard against constipation.

By preparing for time zone transitions and the disturbances they impose on the body's rhythms, the severity of jet lag symptoms may be reduced. There has been little success in attempting to predict good and poor adaptors to long-haul flights. The fact that an individual feels relatively unaffected on one occasion is no guarantee that the same individual will so again on the next visit. Regular travellers do benefit from their experiences and develop personal strategies for coping with jet lag (Waterhouse et al., 2002). The disturbances in mental performance and cognitive functions have consequences not only for players but also for training and medical staff travelling with the team, who are likely to suffer from jet-lag symptoms. Besides, the long periods inactive during the plane journey may lead to the pooling of blood in the legs and in susceptible individuals cause a deep-vein thrombosis. Moving around the plane periodically during the journey – say every 2 h – and doing light stretching exercises are recommended. Table 9.4 lists key messages which can help deal with jet lag (see Reilly and Waterhouse, 2005).

Air quality

The air that is breathed may contain impurities and may have an effect on the health as well as on the performance of players. At rest air breathed in through the nose is filtered and many pollutants may be prevented from reaching the airways. During exercise there is a shift to oral breathing and the scrubbing action of the nasal passageways is bypassed. When the air is polluted, it is likely that lung function will be adversely affected, depending on factors such as the concentration of the pollutants and the sensitivity of the individual who is exposed.

Soccer players are advised to be careful when playing or training in cities with high levels of air pollution or in pitches close to roadside traffic. Recreational players need to pay attention to the proximity of local smoke sources and industrial processes utilising polluting forms of energy. Since referees postpone

Table 9.4 Key messages to help deal with jet lag

1 Check if the journey is across sufficient time zones for jet lag to be a problem. If it is not, then it is necessary only to refer to advice on overcoming fatigue from the journey.
2 If jet lag is likely, then consider if the stay is too short for adjustment of the body clock to take place (a stay of less than 3 days). If it is too short, then remain on home time and try to arrange sleep and activities to coincide with time at home rather than in the new time zone.
3 If the stay is not too short and adjustment is to be promoted, then consider ways of reducing jet lag. Pay attention to pre-flight aspects, behaviour on-board the plane and after the flight. The most important advice relates to behaviour after arrival.
4 Advice for promoting adjustment is focused on: sleep and melatonin; exposure to and avoidance of bright light; social activity and behaviour; timing of exercise.

Source: Modified from Reilly and Waterhouse, 2005.

matches in foggy conditions due to poor visibility, players should do likewise when training is scheduled. Players suffering from asthma should be especially alert to possible adverse reactions to pulmonary function when pollution levels are high.

Pollutants are described as primary and secondary, according to whether they retain the form in which they were emitted from source or if they are formed through chemical reactions between source and target (Reilly and Waterhouse, 2005). The main primary pollutants are sulphur dioxide (SO_2), carbon monoxide (CO), nitrogen dioxide (NO_2), benzene and particulate matter like dust and smoke. Particulates less than 10 microns in diameter enter the airways relatively easily and are referred to as PM-10s. The secondary pollutants include ozone (O_3) and peroxyacetyl nitrate and are formed as a result of ultraviolet radiation affecting NO_2 and hydrocarbons. Exposure to elevated ozone concentrations gives rise to symptoms such as coughing, chest pain, difficulty in breathing, headache, eye irritation and impaired lung function, all of which are likely to impact on exercise performance (Florida-James *et al.*, 2004).

The World Health Organisation has established standards for health-based air quality in the case of pollutants such as ozone and so their concentrations are monitored regularly in the major cities worldwide. National standards apply in other cases such as PM-10s. There is a suggestion that individuals show some degree of adaptation to ozone, reflected in the reduced sensitivity to ozone of those habitually exposed to it (Florida-James *et al.*, 2004). For those with previous exposure to ozone, performance is only partially recovered when concentrations are high. Antioxidant supplements may ameliorate some adverse effects of ozone by counteracting the oxidative stress caused by the pollutant. Players with asthma may have their symptoms worsened when PM-10 levels are raised, due to inflammation mediated by oxidative-stress (MacNee and Donaldson, 1999).

Many individuals are susceptible to allergic reactions and it is inevitable that some soccer players are in this group. Ragweed and grass pollen act as antigens which stimulate the production of antibodies after penetrating the mucous membrane of the respiratory tract. Some individuals are allergic to antigens, the reactions beginning in the nose where allergens such as pollen are first filtered out. The inflammatory response causes a blocked nose, promotes oral breathing which gives the allergies direct access to the lower respiratory tract. Here the same inflammatory response gives rise to asthma instead (Harries, 1998). Players vulnerable to allergies should seek medical advice for pharmacological therapy.

Overview

There are implications not only for performance but also for health and safety associated with the environment in which the soccer player trains and competes. The quality of the playing surface, for example, forces a choice of appropriate footwear so that performance can be executed without increased risk. Playing conditions sometimes exceed the bounds of safety and the match referee is entitled to declare the pitch unplayable.

A similar decision may be made in cases of air pollution (ozone, CO, SO_2, or Pb). Ozone concentration may exceed acceptable limits in some of the world's large cities (Athens, Mexico City, Seoul, Los Angeles) but generally is not a major problem for European players. The air is impurified in foggy conditions, but in such cases matches and training are usually curtailed for reasons of visibility.

An accurate assessment of environmental variables is needed for calculating the risk of heat injury. The main factors to be considered are the dry bulb temperature, relative humidity, radiant temperature, air velocity and cloud cover. The most widely used index in sports contexts is the wet bulb temperature, which takes both ambient temperature and humidity into account. The wind–chill index is employed in determining risk in cold conditions. Apart from the chilling effect of the wind, blustery conditions make ball flight more difficult to anticipate and skills become more erratic as a consequence.

The novel environmental challenge – hypoxia, temperature, travel, pollution, weather – calls for preparation on behalf of team management. Weather conditions are not always predictable and may even vary widely during the course of a game. An awareness of the dynamic biological adjustments that the body makes means that adverse effects and discomfort associated with environmental variables can be minimised.

References

Anderson, M.J., Cotter, J.D., Garnham, A.P., Casley, D.J. and Febbraio, M.A., 2001, Effect of glycerol-induced hyperhydration on thermoregulation and metabolism during exercise in heat. *International Journal of Sport Nutrition and Exercise Metabolism*, **11**, 315–333.

Armstrong, L.E., 2006, Nutritional strategies for soccer: counteracting heat, cold, high altitude and jet lag. *Journal of Sports Sciences*, **24**, 723–740.

Bangsbo, J., Klausen, K., Bro-Rasmusen, T. and Larson, J., 1988, Physiological responses to acute moderate hypoxia in elite soccer players, *Science and Soccer* (edited by T. Reilly, A. Lees, K. Davids and W.J. Murphy), London: E & FN Spon, pp. 257–264.

Bergh, U. and Ekblom, B., 1979, Effect of muscle temperature on maximal muscle strength and power in human skeletal muscles. *Acta Physiologica Scandinavica*, **107**, 33–37.

Carling, C., Williams, A.M. and Reilly, T., 2005, *A Manual of Soccer Match Analysis*. London: Routledge.

Drust, B., Cable, N.T. and Reilly, T., 2000, Investigation of the effects of precooling on the physiological responses to soccer-specific intermittent exercise. *European Journal of Applied Physiology*, **81**, 11–17.

Drust, B., Waterhouse, J., Atkinson, G., Edwards, B. and Reilly, T., 2005, Circadian rhythms in sports performance – an update. *Chronobiology International*, **22**, 21–44.

Edwards, B.J., Atkinson, G., Waterhouse, J., Reilly, T., Godfrey, R. and Budgett, R., 2000, Use of melatonin in recovery from jet-lag following an eastward flight across 10 time-zones. *Ergonomics*, **43**, 1501–1513.

Ekblom, B., 1986, Applied physiology of soccer. *Sports Medicine*, **3**, 50–60.

Febbraio, M., 2001, Alterations in energy metabolism during exercise and heat stress, *Sports Medicine*, **31**, 47–59.

Florida-James, G., Donaldson, K. and Stone, V., 2004, Athens 2004: the pollution climate and athletic performance. *Journal of Sports Sciences*, **22**, 967–980.

Harries, M., 1998, The lung in sport. In: *Oxford Textbook of Sports Medicine* (edited by M. Harries, C. Williams, W.D. Stanish and L.J. Micheli), Oxford: Oxford University Press, pp. 321–326.

Ingjer, F. and Myhre, K., 1992, Physiological effects of altitude training on elite male cross-country skiers. *Journal of Sports Sciences*, **10**, 37–47.

Jehue, R., Street, D. and Huizengar, R., 1993, Effect of time zone and game time on team performance: National Football League. *Medicine and Science in Sports and Exercise*, **25**, 127–131.

Levine, B., 1997, Training and exercise at high altitudes. In: *Sport, Leisure and Ergonomics* (edited by G. Atkinson and T. Reilly), London: E & FN Spon, pp. 74–92.

MacNee, W. and Donaldson, K., 1999, Particulate air pollution: injurious and protective mechanisms in the lungs. In: *Air Pollution and Health* (edited by T. Holgate, J. Samet, H. Koren and R. Maynard), London: Academic Press, pp. 653–672.

Mustafa, K.Y. and Mahmoud, E.D.A., 1979, Evaporative water loss in African soccer players. *Journal of Sports Medicine and Physical Fitness*, **19**, 181–183.

Nielsen, B., 1994, Heat stress and acclimation. *Ergonomics*, **37**, 49–58.

Pollock, N.W., Godfrey, R.J. and Reilly, T., 1997, Evaluation of field measures of urine concentration. *Medicine and Science in Sports and Exercise*, **29** (Suppl 5), S261.

Reilly, T., 1993, Science and football: an introduction. In: *Science and Football II* (edited by T. Reilly, J. Clarys and A. Stibbe), London: E & FN Spon, pp. 3–11.

Reilly, T., 2000, Temperature and performance: heat. In: *ABC of Sports Medicine* (edited by M. Harries, G. McLatchie, C. Williams and J. King), London: BMJ Books, pp. 68–71.

Reilly, T., 2003, Environmental stress. In: *Science and Soccer (2nd edition)* (edited by T. Reilly and A.M. Williams), London: Routledge, pp. 165–184.

Reilly, T. and Deykin, T., 1983, Effects of partial sleep loss on subjective states, psychomotor and physical, performance tests. *Journal of Human Movement Studies*, **9**, 157–170.

Reilly, T. and Garrett, R., 1995, Effects of time of day on self-paced performance of prolonged exercise. *Journal of Sports Medicine and Physical Fitness*, **35**, 99–102.

Reilly, T. and Lewis, W., 1985, Effects of carbohydrate feeding on mental functions during sustained physical work. In: *Ergonomics International 85* (edited by I.D. Brown, R. Goldsmith, K. Coombes and M.A. Sinclair), London: Taylor and Francis, pp. 700–702.

Reilly, T. and Piercy, M., 1994, The effect of partial sleep deprivation on weight-lifting performance. *Ergonomics*, **37**, 107–115.

Reilly, T. and Walsh, T., 1981, Physiological, psychological and performance measures during an endurance record for 5-a-side soccer play. *British Journal of Sports Medicine*, **15**, 122–128.

Reilly, T. and Waterhouse, J., 2005, *Sport, Exercise and Environmental Physiology*. Edinburgh: Elsevier.

Reilly, T., Maughan, R.J., Budgett, R. and Davies, B., 1997, The acclimatisation of international athletes. In: *Contemporary Ergonomics 1997* (edited by S.A. Robertson), London: Taylor and Francis, 136–140.

Reilly, T., Atkinson, G. and Budgett, R., 2001, Effect of low-dose temazepam on physiological variables and performance tests following a westerly flight across five time zones. *International Journal of Sports Medicine*, **22**, 166–174.

Reilly, T., Fairhurst, E., Edwards, B. and Waterhouse, J., 2005a, Time of day and performance test in male football players. In: *Science and Football V* (edited by T. Reilly, J. Cabri and D. Araujo), London: Routledge, pp. 271–275.

Reilly, T., Farrelly, K., Edwards, B. and Waterhouse, J., 2005b, Effects of time of day on the performance of soccer-specific motor skills. In: *Science and Football V* (edited by T. Reilly, J. Cabri and D. Araujo), London: Routledge, pp. 268–270.

Reilly, T., Waterhouse, J. and Edwards, B., 2005c, Jet lag and air travel: implications for performance. *Clinics in Sports Medicine*, **24**, 367–380.

Shirreffs, S.M., Aragon-Vargas, L.F., Chamorro, M., Maughan, R.J., Serratosa, L. and Zachwieja, J.J., 2005, The sweating response of elite professional soccer players to training in the heat. *International Journal of Sports Medicine*, **26**, 90–95.

Waterhouse, J., Reilly, T. and Atkinson, G., 1997, Jet-lag. *The Lancet*, **350**, 1611–1616.

Waterhouse, J., Edwards, B., Nevill, A., Carvalho, S., Atkinson, G., Buckley, P., Reilly, T., Godfrey, R. and Ramsay, R., 2002, Identifying some determinants of 'jet-lag' and its symptoms: a study of athletes and other travellers. *British Journal of Sports Medicine*, **36**, 54–60.

Webster, J., Holland, E.J., Sleivert, G., Laing, R.M. and Niven, B.E., 2005, A light-weight cooling vest enhances performance of athletes in the heat. *Ergonomics*, **48**, 821–837.

Chapter 10

Evaluation of training

Introduction

An ergonomics model of training signifies that the programme is designed to prepare the individual for the demands of the game. The capabilities of the individual are thereby raised and an enhancement of performance is anticipated. This process is not a singular event but takes place within a highly dynamic and complex soccer context. It is important to know if the training intervention has been effective and whether all players engaged in it have benefited equally. Besides, new players may be entering a team squad, and others returning after a period of injury so it is necessary to establish how their fitness levels differ from the rest of the team.

In individual sports, the effect of a training intervention may be gauged by an improvement in performance. As performance in soccer is not indicated so easily, the impact of training is evaluated by its direct effects on fitness measures. Many soccer teams now regularly assess the fitness of their players so that they can know whether fine adjustments to the training are called for.

The purposes of fitness assessments can be summarised as follows:

1   to establish baselines for each player in the squad;
2   to identify individual strengths and weaknesses;
3   to provide feedback to players on their physical fitness level;
4   to evaluate the effect of specific training interventions.

A test should have discrete characteristics if it is to be adopted and if it is to yield useful information. These characteristics are its reliability, its objectivity and its validity. The test should be highly reproducible if it is to be deemed reliable, that is it should produce the same result if repeated soon after, at the same time of day and under the same conditions of testing. Objectivity means that test performance is free of any subjective bias, usually on the part of the experimenter. For a test to be deemed valid, it must measure the functions that it purports to measure.

Fitness profiling is achieved by means of a battery of tests. The test items may either be part of a comprehensive physiological assessment or be dedicated solely to assessing fitness for performance in soccer. The fitness profiles generated from such batteries have some value in allowing comparisons between individuals and, with the use of normative ranges, individual weaknesses may be identified and remedial training prescribed. Repeated fitness assessment is of further value in that changes in fitness profiles within individuals and throughout the team as a whole can be measured. In this way, the appropriateness and progression of the training regimen applied to the players in the squad can be gauged not only in determining the degree of adaptation, but also any failure to adapt and any maladaptation (overtraining).

Aerobic fitness

Maximal oxygen uptake

The aerobic system is the primary source of *providing* energy for exercise during match-play (Bangsbo, 1994a), as indicated both by measurement of physiological responses during games and by the metabolic characteristics of players' muscles. The maximum oxygen uptake ($\dot{V}O_{2\,max}$) indicates the upper limit of the body's ability to consume oxygen, a function that can be increased with aerobic training. The $\dot{V}O_{2\,max}$ represents an integrated physiological function of the lungs, heart, blood and active muscles. Lung function is not normally a limiting factor in maximal aerobic performance although single-breath spirometry has use in screening for any impairment or pulmonary restriction. The maximal cardiac output and the capacity of the blood to carry oxygen determine the amount of oxygen delivered to the active muscle cells. The oxygen-carrying capacity is determined by the concentration of haemoglobin in the blood, which affects the binding of O_2 in red blood cells, and the blood volume. The total body haemoglobin is therefore highly correlated with the maximal oxygen uptake. Blood volume and total body haemoglobin tend to be about 20% higher in endurance trained athletes than in non-athletes. Haemoglobin concentration and haematocrit (the percentage of blood volume occupied by red blood cells) of soccer players generally lie towards the high end of the normal range. Blood tests have value in screening soccer players for anaemia and in identifying other deficiencies in players whose exercise performances fall below expectations.

The cardiac output determines the amount of blood delivered to the active muscles during strenuous exercise and is a function of the stroke volume and heart rate. The maximal heart rate is not increased as a result of training and is not itself an indicator of fitness. The heart responds to strenuous training by becoming larger and more effective as a pump. The chambers (particularly the left ventricle) increase in volume from a repetitive overload stimulus such as endurance training whilst the walls of the heart thicken and may increase its force development capability as a result of a pressure stimulus provided by weight-training. The adaptation of cardiac muscle to training is reflected in a greater stroke volume and a larger left ventricular size, which allows more blood to fill the chamber before the heart contracts and results in a lowered heart rate at rest. These effects are apparent in well-trained professional soccer players. Resting heart rates of 48 (± 1) beats·min^{-1} and 54–59 beats·min^{-1} have been reported for English League players (Reilly, 1979) and elite Turkish players (Sözen *et al.*, 2000). The slow heart rate allows extended relaxation time during diastole for the pressure to drop below the normal level of 80 mmHg. The pulse pressure, the difference between systolic and diastolic pressures, with an average value of 50 mmHg for the English League players, is larger than the normal 40 mmHg (Reilly, 1979).

The $\dot{V}O_{2\,max}$ is affected by pulmonary ventilation, pulmonary diffusion, the O_2-carrying capacity of the blood and the arteriovenous differences in the O_2 concentrations. Players undergo a progressive exercise test to voluntary exhaustion for its assessment. A motorised treadmill provides the most appropriate mode of exercise for testing soccer players. Expired air is analysed for its O_2 and CO_2 content and the minute ventilation ($\dot{V}E$) is also measured (Figure 10.1). The maximal oxygen uptake ($\dot{V}O_{2\,max}$) is indicated by a plateau in $\dot{V}O_2$ before voluntary exhaustion, a rise in the respiratory exchange ratio ($\dot{V}CO_2/\dot{V}O_2$) above 1.1, an elevation in heart rate to its age-predicted maximum or a rise in blood lactate concentration reflecting anaerobic metabolism.

Since there is a large contribution from aerobic power to playing the game (Bangsbo, 1994b) the average values of $\dot{V}O_{2\,max}$ for top-level soccer players tend

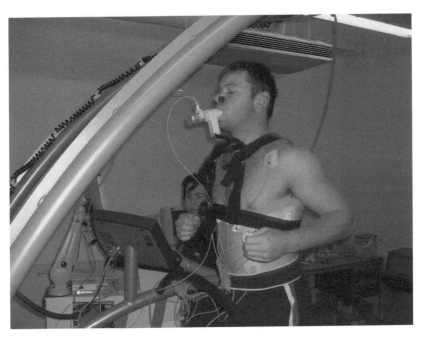

Figure 10.1 The assessment of maximal oxygen uptake on a laboratory treadmill.

to be high. Nevertheless, $\dot{V}O_{2\,max}$ levels do not reach the same figures as in specialist endurance sports such as cross-country running and skiing, distance running or orienteering where values frequently exceed $80\ ml\ kg^{-1}\ min^{-1}$. Values for elite players lie in the region $55\text{--}70\ ml\ kg^{-1}\ min^{-1}$, the higher figures tending to be found at the top level of performance and when players are at peak fitness. The mean value of over 500 professional players reviewed by Reilly and Doran (2003) was $59\ ml\ kg^{-1}\ min^{-1}$. Reilly et al. (2000a) argued that while $\dot{V}O_{2\,max}$ alone does not predispose towards success in soccer, there is a minimum threshold at about $60\ ml\ kg^{-1}\ min^{-1}$ and players falling below it may fail to perform well consistently at the highest level of professional play.

Differences in standard of play and programmes of training can influence $\dot{V}O_{2max}$ values; the stage of the season should also be considered. The $\dot{V}O_{2\,max}$ of professional players improves significantly in the pre-season period when there is strong emphasis on aerobic training (Reilly, 1979; Bangsbo, 1994c; Helgerud et al., 2001). Not all recent reports have demonstrated increased $\dot{V}O_{2\,max}$ during the course of the competitive season (Raastad et al., 1997; Wisløff et al., 1998; Casajús, 2001). An extension of the playing season and the large number of games played make it difficult to employ a progressive and systematic training regimen that causes a continual increase in $\dot{V}O_{2\,max}$. With the introduction of individual conditioning programmes for the 'off-season', there is a reduced time available for detraining to occur prior to the commencement of pre-season training. A thorough pre-season training programme may leave the players aerobically fit, with a need for only marginal further increases in $\dot{V}O_{2\,max}$. Furthermore, some players may have periods off during the season due to injury and their decline in aerobic fitness affects average values of the squad.

The $\dot{V}O_{2\,max}$ varies with positional role and squad-based training may not obscure any specific positional adaptations in aerobic fitness. When English League players were subdivided into positions according to 4-3-3 and 4-4-2 configurations, the midfielders had significantly higher aerobic power values than those in other positions. Central defenders have significantly lower relative values than the other outfield players while the fullbacks and strikers have values that are intermediate (Reilly, 1979; Bangsbo, 1994c; Wisløff et al., 1998; Al-Hazzaa et al., 2001). Positional differences in $\dot{V}O_{2\,max}$ are not always obvious when data are expressed relative to body mass.

Goalkeepers have lower values for $\dot{V}O_{2\,max}$ than centre-backs and the highest values for adiposity are found among goalkeepers. Four goalkeepers in the German national team had values of $56.2\ (\pm1.2)\ ml\ kg^{-1}\ min^{-1}$ compared to $67.0\ (\pm4.5)\ ml\ kg^{-1}\ min^{-1}$ for the squad as a whole (Hollmann et al., 1981). The $\dot{V}O_{2\,max}$ of 19 professional players in the First Division of the Portuguese League was $59.6\ (\pm7.7)\ ml\ kg^{-1}\ min^{-1}$; the average values for goalkeepers and central defenders were below, whilst midfield players and forwards were above $60\ ml\ kg^{-1}\ min^{-1}$ (Puga et al., 1993). Values of $\dot{V}O_{2\,max}$ reported for elite Saudi Arabian players (Al-Hazzaa et al., 2001) of $56.8\ \pm\ 4.8\ ml\ kg^{-1}\ min^{-1}$ were similar to Singaporean national squad's average of $58.2\ \pm\ 3.7\ ml\ kg^{-1}\ min^{-1}$

(Aziz et al., 2000). These values are generally towards the lower end of $\dot{V}O_{2\,max}$ data reported in the literature. In contrast, the maximal oxygen uptake of Spanish First Division players was 66.4 ± 7.6 ml kg^{-1} min^{-1} (Casajús, 2001), while elite Norwegian players demonstrated similar levels of $\dot{V}O_{2\,max}$ at 67.67 ± 4.0 ml kg^{-1} min^{-1} (Wisløff et al., 1998). A sample of players drawn from Norwegian division 1–3 clubs had lower average $\dot{V}O_{2\,max}$ values of 62.8 ± 4.1 (Raastad et al., 1997) and an English Premier League squad had an average $\dot{V}O_{2\,max}$ estimated at 59.4 ± 6.2 ml kg^{-1} min^{-1} (Strudwick et al., 2002). This relatively narrow range of $\dot{V}O_{2\,max}$ values is evident across nationalities and similar competitive levels.

Anaerobic threshold

The $\dot{V}O_{2\,max}$ indicates the maximal ability to consume oxygen in strenuous exercise but it is not possible to sustain exercise for very long at an intensity that elicits $\dot{V}O_{2\,max}$. The upper level at which exercise can be sustained for a prolonged period is thought to be indicated by the so-called 'anaerobic threshold': this variable is usually expressed as the workrate corresponding to a blood lactate concentration of 4 mmol·l^{-1}, the onset of accumulation of lactate in the blood (OBLA) or as a deflection in the relation between ventilation and oxygen consumption with incremental exercise (the ventilatory threshold). The inflection point in blood lactate response to incremental exercise represented 83.9 % $\dot{V}O_{2\,max}$ in top Finnish players studied by Rahkila and Luhtanen (1991). The $\dot{V}O_2$ corresponding to a blood lactate concentration of 3 mmol·l^{-1} was about 80% of $\dot{V}O_{2\,max}$ for both a continuous and an interval test on Danish players running on a treadmill (Bangsbo and Lindquist, 1992). This reference lactate level for the continuous test was significantly correlated with distance covered in a game. The estimated lactate thresholds for elite Norwegian players was between 80 and 86% of $\dot{V}O_{2\,max}$ (Raastad et al., 1997; Helgerud et al., 2001). The ventilatory threshold has been measured at 77, 79 and 76% of $\dot{V}O_{2\,max}$ in English League First Division, Spanish La Liga players and Saudi Arabian national squad members, respectively (White et al., 1988; Al-Hazzaa et al., 2001; Casajús, 2001). Variation in lactate threshold (Tlac) according to positional role has also been reported. Bangsbo (1994a) found that elite Danish midfield players and fullbacks had higher lactate thresholds than goalkeepers and central defenders. Whilst the average fractional utilisation of $\dot{V}O_{2\,max}$ is about 75–80% $\dot{V}O_{2\,max}$ (Bangsbo, 1994a) and is probably close to the 'anaerobic threshold', players operate at or above this intensity frequently during a game.

The lactate threshold is determined from responses to a sub-maximal test. The player runs at 4 different speeds on a treadmill, each for 4 min. A blood sample is drawn from a fingertip or ear lobe during short pauses between the progressive bouts. The relationship between blood lactate and running velocity is plotted and a reference value of 4 mmol·l^{-1} may be selected. The running velocity corresponding to this value can be recorded as V-4 mM. The lactate and ventilatory thresholds (determined by the point at which a disproportionate rise in the

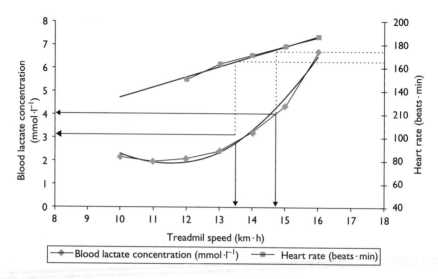

Figure 10.2 The response of the blood-lactate curve to aerobic incremental exercise. The lactate inflection point and V-4mM are indicated by the arrows.

variables occurs relative to $\dot{V}O_2$) also provide a sensitive sub-maximal indicator of physiological adaptation; it represents a means of quantifying a change in performance capability through a season (Al-Hazzaa *et al.*, 2001; Casajús, 2001). With an improvement in training the curve shifts to the right whereas a leftwards shift suggests a loss of endurance fitness (see Figure 10. 2).

Muscle function

Muscle strength

Assessments of muscle strength and power have ranged from use of performance tests such as squats and bench press and measurement of isometric strength to contemporary dynamic measures using computer-linked isokinetic equipment. Tests of anaerobic power output have also evolved to include jumping performance on the force platform. Strength in the lower limbs is clearly important in the game: the quadriceps, hamstrings and triceps surae groups must generate high forces for jumping, kicking, tackling, turning and changing pace. Sustained forceful contractions are also relevant for balance, for example, when being challenged for possession of the ball. Isometric strength is also an important factor in maintaining a player's balance on a slippery pitch and in controlling the ball. Almost all the body's muscle groups are used by the goalkeeper in executing the skills of this positional role. For outfield players the lower part of the trunk, the hip flexors and the plantarflexors and dorsiflexors of the ankle are used most. Upper-body strength is employed in throw-ins and the strength of the neck flexors are important in heading the ball forcefully. Strength in the upper body should help prevent the player from being knocked off the ball. High levels of muscular strength are also important in reducing the risk of injury.

Soccer players are generally found to display only a little above average isometric muscle strength. Static strength may not truly reflect the ability to exert force in dynamic conditions and is also a poor predictor of muscle performance in the game. Nevertheless, isometric activity is important in stabilising the trunk and providing a platform for more dynamic muscular activity of the lower body to take place. The need for 'core stability' training is increasingly recognised; this concept refers to the deep muscles that provide a stable base for the contractions of other muscles directly causing motion of joint segments to occur. Screening and development of isometric muscle activity are integral to most rehabilitation and strength conditioning programmes.

The correlation between leg strength and kick performance (Cabri et al., 1988) suggests that strength training could be effective in improving the kicking abilities of soccer players. Given a certain level of technique, strength training that is added to the normal soccer training seems to improve both muscular strength and kick performance (De Proft et al., 1988). Such positive reports are not always mirrored in recent literature. Aagaard et al. (1996) have shown that a mix of generic and movement-specific resistance training techniques to improve knee flexor strength produced no concomitant change in ball velocity after 12 weeks of training. Helgerud et al. (2001) reported no significant changes in ball velocity after an 8-week programme of training while Cometti et al. (2001) reported that higher levels of isokinetic knee extensor strength between professional and amateur players were not reflected in ball velocity. The angle of approach, the kicking style, the trajectory and other factors in addition to muscle strength all influence the performance of kicking.

The relationship between dynamic muscle strength of the knee extensors and kick performance may also depend on the level of skill already acquired. Trolle et al. (1993) measured isokinetic strength of the leg extensors in skilled soccer players at angular velocities between 0 and 4.18 rad s^{-1}. No relationship was found between these measures and ball velocity recorded during a standardised indoor soccer kick; ball velocity was again unchanged after 12 weeks of strength training. The average angular velocities about the knee during a soccer kick range between 13.5 and 18.5 rad s^{-1} depending on whether kicking is for accuracy or speed (Lees and Nolan, 2002) whereas in isokinetic strength assessment and training, the maximum angular velocity achievable with current technology is about 5.2 rad s^{-1}. Training at these velocities may negate the training specificity required (in terms of the speed of limb movement) to yield measurable changes. Ball velocity is not solely determined by the strength of the knee extensors. Kinematic analysis of kicking actions highlights the complex synergy between the hip and lower limb movement patterns initiated during the striking of the ball (Nunome *et al.*, 2002). Non-specific methods of strength training or assessment disrupt this synergy, and any potential relationship inherent between lower-limb strength development and ball velocity is affected. Where the relationship is maintained, improvements in lower limb strength and ball velocity are observed (Dutta and Subramanium, 2002). Improved rates of force development and improved co-ordination are potential antecedents to improvements in kicking velocity (Almåsbakk and Hoff, 1996) as these neuromotor factors may override muscular strength in well-trained players and obscure potential relationships.

It is common to monitor the muscle strength of soccer players using isokinetic apparatus (Figure 10.3) and such assessment on a regular basis is important. These machines offer facilities for determining torque–velocity curves in isokinetic movements and joint–angle curves in a series of isometric contractions. The more complex systems allow for measurement of muscle actions in eccentric as well as

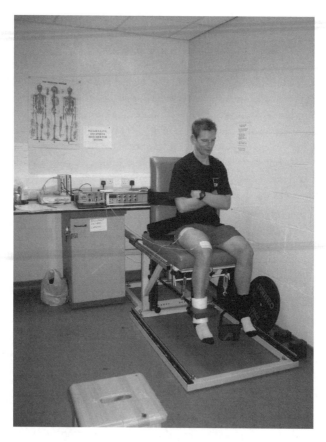

Figure 10.3 Isokinetic assessment of knee extension strength on an isokinetic dynamometer.

concentric and isometric modes. In eccentric actions the limb musculature resists a force exerted by the machine: the muscle is lengthened in the process and hence produces an eccentric contraction. Traditionally, isokinetic assessment of soccer players was concentrated almost exclusively on muscle groups of the lower limb and on concentric contractions. Where knee extension strength in concentric contractions was correlated with kick performance, an even higher correlation was reported for knee flexion strength in eccentric actions (Cabri *et al.*, 1988). Although isokinetic dynamometry is widely used in assessment of muscle strength, some authors view it as not reflecting the specificity of limb movement noted during performance of soccer skills, advocating instead the use of functional tests in performance assessment (Wisløff *et al.*, 1998).

Isokinetic dynamometry is accepted as clinically relevant for assessing deficits and imbalances in muscle strength (Cometti *et al.*, 2001). As approximately 76% of injuries in soccer are to the lower extremities (Morgan and Oberlander, 2001), high levels of muscular strength in the hamstrings relative to quadriceps would seem important in stabilising the knee and reducing the risk of injury (Fried and Lloyd, 1992). The possession of strong hamstrings, particularly in eccentric modes, is an important requirement for playing soccer. Improper balance between hamstrings and quadriceps strength may predispose players towards injury. At slow speeds and under isometric conditions, a knee flexor–extensor ratio of 60–65% has been recommended (Oberg *et al.*, 1986). This ratio is increased at the higher angular velocities of commercially available apparatus, partly because the reliability of measurement is reduced at fast speeds. Graham-Smith and Lees (2002) have applied a model of risk assessment for hamstring injury termed the dynamic control ratio (DCR). Expressed as the eccentric hamstring : concentric quadriceps ratio, it provides a functional assessment of potential injury risk; ideally the DCR ratio should be equivalent to 1.0 although a ratio of less than 0.75 in place kickers has been suggested as a threshold of potential injury risk. Testing of isokinetic strength also allows asymmetries in lower limb muscular strength to be identified; generally where imbalances are present the weaker limb is the one most liable to injury (Fowler and Reilly, 1993). In soccer, where rapid accelerations, decelerations, angled runs and side-stepping manoeuvres can apply substantial mechanical loadings to the knee joint, any inter- or intra-limb asymmetries in knee extensor strength can predispose towards injury particularly where the knee is not adequately stabilised (Besier *et al.*, 2001). Isokinetic test profiles are also important in monitoring muscle strength gains during rehabilitation using the uninjured side as reference. These comparisons to identify asymmetry, weakness or progress within an individual player may be more important than comparison between teams or between team members.

Anaerobic power

During a soccer game, players must often generate high power output and sometimes have to maintain or repeat it with only a brief period for recovery.

The splitting of high-energy intra-muscular phosphagens contributes along with anaerobic glycolysis to the maximal power a player can develop. These substrates (ATP, creatine phosphate and glycogen) are used for combustion by muscle at the onset of exercise and result in a high anaerobic work production. Various approaches have been taken to assess exercise performance at a maximal intensity in soccer players; these estimates are taken to reflect the re-synthesis of ATP via anaerobic energy systems. The maximum power output can be calculated from performance on the stair-run test of Margaria et al. (1966). Measurement is made of the time taken for the player to run between two steps on the stairs, the vertical distance between which is known.

The muscular power produced when jumping on a force platform can also be used as a measure of maximal anaerobic power. The test requires relatively complex equipment, which is not available for routine assessments. The production of power in vertical jumping can be calculated, knowing the player's body mass, the vertical distance through which body mass is moved and the flight time. The vertical distance itself is a good measure of muscular performance, that is, mechanical work done and can be measured using the classical Sargent jump technique. This value can also be recorded using a digital system attached to the subject's waist and based on the extension of a cord, which is pulled from its base on the floor as the individual jumps vertically. The vertical jump is preferable to the standing broad jump which is influenced by leg length and which does not permit calculation of power output. Performance of players in such tests of jumping ability tends to demonstrate positional influences. Generally, goalkeepers, defenders and forwards perform better than midfield players on a counter-movement jump (vertical jump) performance (Reilly and Doran, 2003).

Another means of measuring mechanical power output in jumping was described by Bosco et al. (1983). The player jumps repeatedly for a given period, usually 60 s, the higher time and jumping frequency being recorded. The jumps are performed on a touch-sensitive mat, which is connected to a timer. Power output can be estimated knowing the subject's body mass and the time between contacts on the mat. Performance at various parts of the 1-min test can be compared, the tolerance to fatigue as the test progresses being indicative of the anaerobic glycolytic capacity.

Soccer players are often required to repeat fast bursts of activity supported by anaerobic glycolysis and a high anaerobic capacity is therefore beneficial to performance. The Wingate Anaerobic Test entails a 30-s all-out effort on a cycle ergometer and has been widely adopted as a test of anaerobic capacity. Normative data for the Saudi Arabian national team showed peak power relative to body mass ranging from 11.31 to 13.50 $W\ kg^{-1}$ dependent upon positional role (Al-Hazzaa et al., 2001). The test duration of 30 s is too short to tax anaerobic capacity completely, more correctly it represents an estimate of anaerobic power. A significant aerobic contribution to Wingate test performance of up to 40% has been suggested (Medbø and Tabata, 1986). Besides, low-moderate correlations have been found between $\dot{V}O_{2\ max}$ and anaerobic sprint performance during the Wingate test and repeated sprints in soccer players (Aziz et al., 2000;

Al-Hazzaa *et al.*, 2001), suggesting that the Wingate test is not entirely anaerobic. Measurement of power production and anaerobic capacity on a treadmill is more appropriate for soccer players than using a cycle ergometer for the traditional Wingate test. Power output may be measured whilst the player runs as fast as possible on a 'self-powered' treadmill. The speed of the belt is determined by the effort of the subject. The horizontal forces produced can be recorded using a load cell attached to the individual by means of a harness worn around the waist (Lakomy, 1984). Repeated bouts of exercise, such as 6 s in duration may be performed and power profiles determined with different recovery periods.

The close relationship between the observed oxygen deficit during intense exercise and the anaerobic energy production was used in the measurement of the maximum accumulated oxygen deficit (MAOD) by Medbø *et al.* (1988). Odetoyinbo and Ramsbottom (1995) have utilised a high intensity 20-m shuttle test to estimate MAOD in soccer players using this proposed relationship. The test requires participants to complete as many 20-m shuttles as possible at a speed pre-determined by the final velocity achieved on a previously performed 20-m shuttle test. The test was suggested to be both highly specific to performance in soccer and sensitive to changes in aerobic and anaerobic (MAOD) metabolism with training. It is thought by some authorities that the energy demand during exercise of higher intensities than the maximal aerobic power is underestimated and may not adequately represent anaerobic energy production (Bangsbo *et al.*, 1993). The MAOD test has not been adopted for formal assessment of soccer players although it may remain a convenient laboratory tool.

Performance tests for soccer

Generic tests

Field tests are designed for application in the typical training environment. They are convenient in that they do not require a visit to an institutional laboratory for the assessments to be carried out. Furthermore, the tests can be performed without any complex monitoring equipment. The underlying assumption is that any change in performance of the field test has relevance for performance capability in a competitive context.

The Eurofit test battery (see Table 10.1) offers a range of fitness items for which norms are available to help in interpreting results. The tests utilise performance measures such as runs, jumps, throws and so on, but they are designed to assess motor functions such as strength, power, muscle endurance and aerobic power, albeit indirectly. The main use of the battery may be with recreational teams and underage squads.

The 20-m shuttle run test included in the Eurofit battery was first validated for estimating maximal oxygen uptake (Leger and Lambert, 1982) and represented a progressive step for sports science support programmes. Individuals may be tested as a squad in a gymnasium or open ground such as a soccer pitch or a

Table 10.1 Anthropometry and nine motor tests as employed in the Eurofit Test battery

---

Height, body mass, 4 skinfolds: *(anthropometry)*
Flamingo balance test: *(balance)*
Plate tapping: *(speed of limb movement)*
Sit-and-reach: *(flexibility)*
Standing broad jump: *('explosive strength')*
Grip strength: *(static strength)*
Sit-ups: *(trunk strength)*
Bent-arm hang: *(functional strength)*
Shuttle run: 10 × 5 m: *(running speed/agility)*
Endurance shuttle run (20 m): *(endurance)*

Note
The function measured is indicated in parenthesis.

synthetic sports surface. The velocity of moving between two lines 20 m apart is controlled by instructions given on an audio tape recorder and using an incremental protocol. The pace is increased progressively, as when $\dot{V}O_{2\,max}$ is being determined on a motor-driven treadmill, until the athlete reaches exhaustion. The final stage reached is noted and the $\dot{V}O_{2\,max}$ can be estimated using appropriate tables. Separate prediction tables for children are available and have been validated for estimating $\dot{V}O_{2\,max}$ by Leger *et al.* (1988).

Alternative tests of aerobic fitness have employed runs, either distance run for a given period of time, such as the 12-min run of Cooper (1968). Cooper's test has been used as a field test in soccer players and also for purposes of assessing fitness of referees. Data have been reported for the Brazilian national team and for professional players in the United States (Raven *et al.*, 1976). The test was adopted for assessing the fitness of soccer referees (Reilly and Gregson, 2006) but has not been applied to players in recent years, since tests with specificity to the sport have greater utility value. A number of such tests for field games has been outlined in Eston and Reilly (2001).

Svensson and Drust (2005) described a shuttle-run test with alterations in distance covered before turning and variations in the recovery periods; these changes in activity were designed to suit the intermittent exercise patterns of match-play. The test has a sub-maximal component for assessment of endurance state and a maximal part intended to elicit maximal aerobic power with a large anaerobic contribution to the final effort. The heart rate is monitored throughout the entire test. The sub-maximal stage could be incorporated into the early part of a training session, might be used regularly and has potential for suggesting 'overtraining' by indicating higher than expected heart rate responses. The complete test to the end of the maximal stage might be used less frequently, for example at key stages of the competitive season.

Sprint tests

Performance of high-intensity exercise in training contexts is usually recorded by coaching staff from time trials over short distances. The systematic application of such tests in field settings has proved valuable as both a research and performance evaluation tool (Aziz et al., 2000; Helgerud et al., 2001). Repeated sprint tests over 5, 10 and 20 m are an integral part of the Australian Institute of Sport's protocols for assessment of soccer players (Tumilty, 2000). Where a systematic and careful approach is applied to such tests with adequate familiarisation and preparation of the players, they are a valuable tool in assessing sprinting ability of soccer players.

Sprint tests are usually monitored by means of electronic timing gates. A 30-m sprint could incorporate placing timing lights at the start line, at 10 m and at 30 m. The time at 10 m can indicate the ability to accelerate whilst the 30-m line can suggest running capability during short sprints. The use of timing lights is an improvement in accuracy of timing compared with manual use of a stop-watch. Nevertheless, it is important to standardise the starting posture and the instructions to start for quality control of data collection.

Repeated sprint tests

Soccer incorporates acyclical patterns of movement, the intensity of exercise varying in a relatively unpredictable manner. On average, there is a call for an all-out sprint every 90 s and a run at effort at least every 30 s. The period in between these bouts also varies and may be in some instances too short to permit a full recovery before having to sprint again. The timing of runs is also important in view of the context in which activity takes place. The fitness requirements therefore are for quick movements, high speed, fast recovery and an ability to sustain activity.

The ability to reproduce high-intensity sprints may be examined by means of requiring the athlete to reproduce an all-out sprint after a short recovery period. A distance of 30 m is recommended. Timing gates may be set up at the start, after 10 m, and at 30 m. There is then a 10-m deceleration zone for the athlete to slow down prior to jogging back to the start line. The recovery period is variable, but 25 s has been recommended (Williams et al., 1997). When the interval is reduced to 15 s, test performance is significantly related to the oxygen transport system (Reilly and Doran, 2003).

Seven sprints are recommended for determining peak acceleration (over 10 m) and speed (time over 30 m). A fatigue index can be calculated both for acceleration and speed over 30 m, based on the drop off in performance over the seven sprints. The mean time for the seven sprints is indicative of the ability to perform several short sprints within a short period of time within a game. Generally, the best performances are the first and second sprints, the poorest over the sixth and seventh.

Soccer-specific tests

The Yo-Yo test

The so-called 'yo-yo' tests were designed by Bangsbo (1994c) to determine an individual's capability to tolerate high-intensity activity for a sustained period. In the tests, the player performs repeated 20-m shuttle runs interspersed with short recovery jogs. The time allowed for a shuttle is decreased progressively as dictated by audio bleeps from a tape recorder. The test is terminated when the individual is unable to continue, the recorded score being the number of shuttles completed.

The ability to perform intense exercise repeatedly after prolonged intermittent exercise is evaluated in the 'yo-yo intermittent endurance' test. A 5-s rest period is allowed between each shuttle, and the duration of the test in total is between 10 and 20 min.

The ability to recover from intense exercise is evaluated by means of the 'yo-yo intermittent recovery' test. Running speeds are higher than in the 'yo-yo intermittent endurance test', but a 10-s period of jogging is allowed between each shuttle. Typically the test lasts for between 2 and 15 min.

Each of these tests has two levels, one for elite soccer players and another for recreational players. The tests are conducted on a soccer field, with the players wearing soccer boots and can be completed in a relatively short period of time with a whole squad of up to 30 players tested at the same time. Both tests have been employed by professional teams in various European countries and the 'yo-yo intermittent recovery test' is compulsory for soccer referees in Italy and Denmark.

Soccer-dribbling test

Some of the more skilful movements of the game may be incorporated into so-called field tests. Soccer-dribbling tests, for example, can include a sprint as fast as possible over a zig-zag course whilst dribbling a ball. This procedure incorporates an agility component, calling for an ability to change direction quickly. The tests formed part of a battery designed for monitoring young players by Reilly and Holmes (1983) and have been employed in talent identification programmes (Reilly et al., 2000b).

The slalom dribble designed by Reilly and Holmes (1983) calls for total body movement in which the subject has to dribble a ball around a set obstacle course as quickly as possible. Obstacles comprise plastic conical skittles 91 cm high and with a base diameter of 23 cm. Two parallel lines, 1.57 m apart, are drawn as reference guides. Intervals of 1.83 m are marked along each line, and diagonal connections of alternate marks 4.89 m long are made. Five cones are placed on the course itself, and a sixth is positioned 7.3 m from the final cone, exactly opposite it and 9.14 m from the starting line. On the command, *go*, each subject dribbles the ball from behind the starting line to the right of the first cone and continues to dribble alternately round the remainder in a zig-zag fashion to the sixth, where the ball is left and the subject sprints back to the starting line. The time elapsed between leaving and returning past the start line is recorded to the nearest 0.1 s and indicates the individual's score. Subjects are forced to renegotiate any cones displaced in the course of the test. A demonstration by the experimentor and a practice run by the subject is undertaken before four trials are performed, with a rest of 20 min between trials, the aggregate time representing the subject's score.

An alternative test is the 'straight dribble', which has been used to discriminate between elite young players and their sub-elite counterparts (Reilly et al., 2000b). In the test, five cones are placed in a straight line perpendicular to the start line: the first 2.74 m away, the middle two separated by 91 cm, and the remainder 1.83 m apart. Players dribble around alternate obstacles until the fifth is circled and then must return through the course in similar fashion. The ball has to be dribbled from the final obstacle to the start line, which now constitutes the finish. The aggregate score from four test trials constitutes the overall test score.

Agility and flexibility

Soccer requires players to possess not only speed but also agility. Agility refers to the capability to change the direction of the body abruptly. The ability to turn quickly, dodge and sidestep calls for good motor co-ordination and is reflected in a standardised agility run test. Professional players in the North American Soccer League were found to have times on the Ilinois Agility Run that were on average above the 99.95 percentile for the test norms (Raven et al., 1976). The test distinguished the soccer players as a group from the normal population better than any field test used for strength, power and flexibility. This finding is under-standable, since players have to be capable of weaving easily past opponents. A 40-m sprint fatigue test with an agility component has been incorporated into a battery of fitness assessment tasks for soccer although the speed and agility com-ponents have not been differentiated (Williams et al., 1997). A 20-m soccer-specific agility test which requires participants to sprint a zig-zag course around four cones that deviated to the left by 4 m then to the right by 4 m and is repeated four times was described by Buttifant et al. (2002) (Figure 10.4). An agility test that incorporated dribbling a ball was used by Reilly and Holmes (1983) as part of a skills battery for young soccer players.

Joint flexibility is an important consideration in soccer players. Establishing the range of motion at a joint can be of benefit in screening for injury predisposition. Procedures for determining range of motion at different joints were presented by Borms and Van Roy (1996). Factor analysis of a number of fitness tests on English games players showed that flexibility in a range of movements at the hip joint afforded protection against injury (Reilly and Stirling, 1993). Muscle tightness, particularly in the hamstring and adductor groups, has been linked with increased

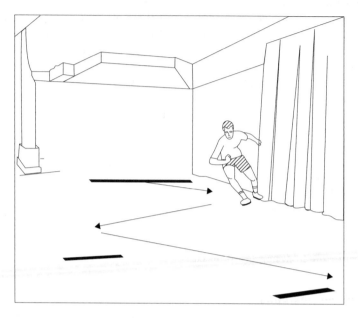

Figure 10.4 A football player performs a zig-zag agility test.

risk of muscle injury in Swedish professionals (Ekstrand, 1982). Graham-Smith and Lees (2002) investigated potential for hamstring injury during place kicking tasks in relation to muscle length and range of motion. They suggested that the dynamic action of place kicking imposes an additional stretch of 10% on the biceps femoris than can be applied during a maximal static stretch. Although this factor may not predispose a player to increased injury risk in itself, a combination of fatigue and imbalances in muscle strength may lead to future injury. Two-thirds of the players monitored had flexibility values poorer than non-players. This inflexibility may be an adaptation to playing soccer, but it may also reflect a lack of attention to flexibility practices in training. Limited range of motion has also been noted at the ankle joint in Japanese (Haltori and Ohta, 1986) and English League (Reilly, 1979) players. The Japanese players were less flexible than a reference group in inversion, eversion, plantarflexion and dorsiflexion of the ankle. These differences may reflect an adaptive response of soft tissue around the ankle, which improves stability at the joint.

Flexibility tests are implemented with a range of devices, as explained in Chapter 6. These include purpose-built flexometers, goniometers and protractors. The most commonly used measure in soccer players is the sit-and-reach test designed to indicate whole-body flexibility. A useful guide is that the player should at least be able to reach the toes with outstretched hands.

Reaction time has also a relevance where fast movements are concerned. The player has to move the entire body quickly, rather than one segment, when playing a game. Whole-body reaction time (WRT) of soccer players was studied by Togari and Takahashi (1977). No differences were found in simple WRT between regular and substitute players but the regular players had the faster 'choice WRTs'. Times did not differ between any of the various playing positions, although goalkeepers were generally faster to react in choice WRT. Fast diving movements are particularly relevant to goal-keeping skills (Suzuki et al., 1988). This superiority in WRT is likely to be a result of training specific to that position. It is unlikely that assessment of reactions has much value in serial assessments of soccer players' responses to training interventions.

Body composition

Body composition reflects the individual's energy balance and is a health-related measure. It is also an important aspect of fitness for soccer as superfluous adipose tissue acts as dead weight in activities where body mass must be lifted repeatedly against gravity. This situation applies to locomotion during play and in jumping for the ball. Whilst the amount of adipose tissue is not necessarily correlated with work-rate across a squad of players, players losing body fat are likely to increase their work-rate and endurance performance as a direct result.

The most commonly used model of body composition divides the body into two compartments – fat and fat-free mass. An alternative is to estimate muscle mass from anthropometric measures using the equation of Martin et al. (1990). This method may overestimate the actual muscle mass, largely because the prediction formula was based on cadavers of non-athletes. Generally, such estimates confirm the tendency towards a muscular make-up among soccer players. The amount of fat in the adult male in his mid-twenties is about 16.5% of body weight. A comparable figure for the adult female is 26%. Figures for soccer players are lower than these values and reports for average male team results have ranged from 9 to 16% (Reilly and Doran, 2003). Higher values are found in goalkeepers than in outfield players, probably because of the higher metabolic loading imposed by match-play and training on outfield players. Soccer players accumulate body fat in the off-season and lose weight more during pre-season training time than in other periods. They may also put on weight as fat when they are recovering from injury and unable to train strenuously, unless they modify their intake of food. They may also lose muscle mass during such periods. Thus, the habitual activity of players at the time of measurement, their diet and the stage of the competitive season should be considered when body composition is evaluated.

The method of estimating or measuring adiposity or percent body fat should also be considered when interpreting observations presented in the literature. Body fat (or body adiposity) is determined indirectly in live subjects. It may be estimated from chemical measures such as total body water or total body potassium. These methods are not accessible for routine use with soccer players and facilities are not generally available to sports science support groups. Similarly, medical imaging techniques are impractical with sports groups and the radiographic dose with computerised tomography makes it unsuitable for repeated application. Magnetic resonance imaging (MRI) overcomes this problem but its expense makes it unrealistic for routine use. Portable devices, such as bio-electric impedance analysis and infrared interactance, have not been sufficiently validated for universal use: the large errors associated with these devices make them unsuitable for use with athletes. The scientifically accepted reference method is underwater (hydrostatic) weighing but it is doubtful whether this is actually true at present for all purposes; the assumptions made with regard to body density are not transferable to all highly trained athletes or between racial groups. Air, rather than water, displacement represents a possible alternative that is used in some professional clubs. Dual energy x-ray absorptiometry (DEXA) is now regarded as the gold standard method and is used in laboratory settings for assessing professional players. The measurement takes less than 5 min to complete and an entire squad may be measured in a single morning. An additional benefit of DEXA is that bone mineral density is also assessed (see Figure 10.5). Its measurement error is low and it is sufficiently sensitive to detect small changes in body composition during the competitive season (Egan *et al.*, 2006).

The most accessible method for obtaining data on body fat is assessment of skinfold thickness by means of calipers. An appropriately trained individual, identifying the correct sites for measurement of skinfolds and using the proper equipment, must make the measurements. Seven anatomical sites are measured

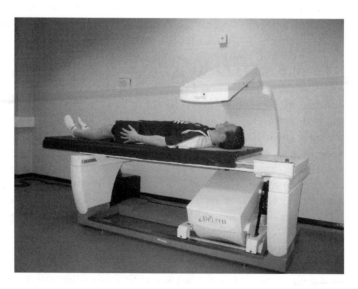

Figure 10.5 Body composition assessed using dual-energy X-ray absorptiometry.

when the recommendations of the International Society for Advancement of Kinanthropometry (ISAK) are adopted (Norton et al., 2000). These sites are – biceps, triceps, sub-scapula and supraspinale, abdominal, front thigh and medial calf. The seven skinfolds should be summed and the resultant value used as an index of subcutaneous adiposity since the skinfold thickness data themselves provide indications of changes in body composition. Guidelines for the British Olympic Association employ the traditional four sites – biceps, triceps, sub-scapula and supra-iliac – plus the anterior thigh (Reilly et al., 1996). A per cent body fat value can be calculated from the first four of these skinfold measures in order to provide a target if weight control is desirable. The expression of percent body fat is widely adopted in literature although more appropriately a combination of the summed skinfolds and estimated body fat percent should be expressed.

Simulations for intervention studies

The analysis of work rates during match-play has also been useful in evaluating training interventions during field games. Exercise protocols are then designed which mimic the exercise patterns observed during match-play and which can be employed for evaluating training or nutritional interventions. The principles involved in designing game-related protocols are, first, to employ an exercise regime in which high-intensity activity is intermittent and, second, that the physiological responses on average bear close correspondence to the stress of competitive play. The overall physiological strain associated with such protocols is greater than physiological responses to continuous exercise at the same average power output.

Drust et al. (2000) designed a soccer-specific protocol consisting of reproducible 15-min cycles of activity in which the intensity is varied at least every 30 s, ranging from walking to sprinting. The protocol as a whole entails 2×45-min period, separated by 15-min rest. It was used to examine the influence of pre-cooling the body on body temperature responses. It could be utilised to examine the physiological consequence of nutritional or other interventions. It has also been employed on a person-driven treadmill to record the power produced during sprinting when all-out short efforts are repeatedly demanded every 90 s, as in a game (Clarke et al., 2005).

An alternative approach to examining the interventions relative to soccer is provided by the Loughborough Intermittent Shuttle test or LIST. The work-rate corresponding to physiological responses to match play is maintained in shuttle running for 75 min. When this time has elapsed, experimental participants continue but alternate between 55% and 95% $\dot{V}O_{2\,max}$ every 20 m up to voluntary exhaustion. The protocol has been used to compare different sports drinks (Nicholas et al., 1995) and to study methods of reducing muscle soreness. A modification of the test has been used to evaluate knee-joint stability after exercise deemed equivalent to playing a full game (Gleeson et al., 1998).

Overview

Sports science laboratories provide a controlled environment in which physiological assessments of physical fitness can be carried out with great precision. These tests are validated and the exercise protocols are standardised. The application of scientific principles to field testing has progressed to a point where existing tests are continually refined and new tests designed. In such instances, one difficulty is that baseline and reference data become obsolete with the use of new versions of a particular test. Applied sports scientists ultimately have to choose between protocols that allow direct physiological interpretations of results or have proven utility for determining game-related performance.

It is inevitable that practitioners will seek to have available tests that have some validity for assessing performance capabilities in their sport. Competitive performance is not a static concept, and performance profiles in soccer games are altered in a progressive upward spiral as intensity of competition increases. Whilst field tests have been used widely due to administrative ease, attention to detail is essential for quality control. Laboratory tests are needed where a physiological interpretation of fitness changes is called for.

References

Aagaard, P., Simonsen, E.B., Trolle, M., Bangsbo, J. and Klausen, K., 1996, Specificity of training velocity and training loads on gains in isokinetic knee joint strength. *Acta Physiologica Scandinavica*, **156**, 123–129.

Al-Hazzaa, H.M., Alumuzaini, K.S., Al-Rafee, A., Sulaiman, M.A., Dafterdar, M.Y., Al-Ghamedi, A. and Khuraji, K.N., 2001, Aerobic and anaerobic power characteristics of Saudi elite soccer players. *Journal of Sports Medicine and Physical Fitness*, **41**, 54–61.

Almåsbakk, B. and Hoff, J., 1996, Co-ordination the determinant of velocity specificity? *Journal of Applied Physiology*, **80**, 2046–2052.

Aziz, A.R., Chia, M. and The, K.C., 2000, The relationship between maximal oxygen uptake and repeated sprint performance indices in field hockey and soccer players. *Journal of Sports Medicine and Physical Fitness*, **40**, 195–200.

Bangsbo, J., 1994a, Energy demands in competitive soccer. *Journal of Sports Sciences*, **12**, S5–12.

Bangsbo, J., 1994b, The physiology of soccer – with special reference to intense intermittent exercise. *Acta Physiologica Scandinavica*, **619** (Suppl.), 1–155.

Bangsbo, J., 1994c, *Fitness Training in Football – A Scientific Approach*, Bagsvaerd. HO & Storm.

Bangsbo, J. and Lindquist, F., 1992, Comparison of various exercise tests with endurance performance during soccer in professional players. *International Journal of Sports Medicine*, **13**, 125–132.

Bangsbo, J., Michalsik, L. and Petersen, A., 1993, Accumulated O_2 deficit during intense exercise and muscle characteristics of elite athletes. *International Journal of Sports Medicine*, **14**, 207–213.

Besier, T.F., Lloyd, D.G., Cochrane, J.L. and Ackland, T.R., 2001, External loading of the knee joint during running and cutting maneuvers. *Medicine and Science in Sports and Exercise*, **33**, 1168–1175.

Borms, J. and Van Roy, P., 1996, Flexibility. In: *Kinanthropometry and Exercise Physiology Laboratory Manual* (edited by R.G. Eston and T. Reilly), London: E & FN Spon, pp. 115–144.

Bosco, C.P., Luhtanen, P. and Komi, P., 1983, A simple method for measurement of mechanical power in jumping. *European Journal of Applied Physiology*, 50, 273–282.

Buttifant, D., Graham, K. and Cross, K., 2002, Agility and speed in soccer players are two different performance parameters. In: *Science and Football IV* (edited by W. Spinks, T. Reilly and A. Murphy), London: Routledge, pp. 329–332.

Cabri, J., De Proft, E., Dufour, W. and Clarys, J.P., 1988, The relation between muscular strength and kick performance. In: *Science and Football* (edited by T. Reilly, A. Lees, K. Davids and W.J. Murphy), London: E & FN Spon, pp. 186–193.

Casajús, J.A., 2001, Seasonal variation in fitness variables in professional soccer players. *Journal of Sports Medicine and Physical Fitness*, 41, 463–467.

Clarke, N.D., Drust, B., MacLaren, D.P.M. and Reilly, T., 2005, Strategies for hydration and energy provision during soccer-specific exercise. *International Journal of Sport Nutrition and Exercise Metabolism*, 15, 625–640.

Cometti, G., Maffiuletti, N.A., Pousson, M., Chatard, J.C. and Maffulli, N., 2001, Isonkinetic strength and anaerobic power of elite sub-elite and amateur French soccer players. *International Journal of Sports Medicine*, 22, 45–51.

Cooper, K.H., 1968, A means of assessing maximal oxygen intake correlating between field and treadmill running. *Journal of the American Medical Association*, 203, 201–204.

De Proft, E., Cabri, J., Dufour, W. and Clarys, J.P., 1988, Strength training and kick performance in soccer players. In: *Science and Football* (edited by T. Reilly, A. Lees, K. Davids and W.J. Murphy), London: E & FN Spon, pp. 108–113.

Drust, B., Cable, N.T. and Reilly, T., 2000, Investigation of the effects of pre-cooling on the physiological responses to soccer-specific intermittent exercise. *European Journal of Applied Physiology*, 81, 11–17.

Dutta, P. and Subramanium, S., 2002, Effects of six weeks of isokinetic strength training combined with skills training on football kicking performance. In: *Science and Football IV* (edited by W. Spinks, T. Reilly and A. Murphy), London: Routledge, pp. 333–339.

Egan, E., Wallace, J., Reilly, T., Chantler, P. and Lawlor, J., 2006, Body composition and bone mineral density during a premier league season as measured by dual-energy X-ray absorptiometry. *International Journal of Body Composition Research*, 4(2), 61–66.

Ekstrand, J., 1982, Soccer injuries and their prevention. Doctoral thesis, Linkoping University.

Eston, R. and Reilly, T., 2001, *Kinanthropometry and Exercise Physiology: A Laboratory Manual 2nd ed. Vol 1 and 2*. London: E & FN Spon.

Fowler, N. and Reilly, T., 1993, Assessment of muscle strength asymmetry in soccer players. In: *Contemporary Ergonomics* (edited by E.J. Lovesey), London: Taylor and Francis, pp. 327–332.

Fried, T. and Lloyd, G.J., 1992, An overview of common soccer injuries. Management and prevention. *Sports Medicine*, 14, 269–275.

Gleeson, N.P., Reilly, T., Mercer, T.H., Rakowski, S. and Rees, D., 1998, Influence of acute endurance activity on leg neuromuscular and musculoskeletal performance. *Medicine and Science in Sport and Exercise*, 30, 596–608.

Graham-Smith, P. and Lees, A., 2002, Risk assessment of hamstring injury in rugby union place kicking. In: *Science and Football IV* (edited by W. Spinks, T. Reilly and A. Murphy), London: Routledge, pp. 183–189.

Haltori, K. and Ohta, S., 1986, Ankle joint flexibility in college soccer players. *Journal of Human Ergology*, **15**, 85–89.

Helgerud, J., Engen, L.C., Wisløff, U. and Hoff, J., 2001, Aerobic training improves soccer performance. *Medicine and Science in Sports and Exercise*, **33**, 1925–1931.

Hollmann, W., Liesen, H., Mader, A. Heck, H., Rost, R. Dufaux, B., Schurch, P., Lagerstrom, D. and Fohrenbach, R. 1981, Zur Hochstund Dauer leistungsfahigkeit der deutschen Fussball-Spitzenspieler. *Deutsch Zeitschrift für Sportmedizin*, **32**, 113–120.

Lakomy, H., 1984, An ergometer for measuring the power generated during sprinting. *Journal of Physiology*, **354**, 33P.

Lees, A. and Nolan, L., 2002, Three-dimensional kinematic analysis of the instep kick under speed and accuracy conditions. In: *Science and Football IV* (edited by W. Spinks, T. Reilly and A. Murphy), London: Routledge, pp. 16–21.

Leger, L.A. and Lambert, J., 1982, A maximal 20-m shuttle run test to predict $\dot{V}O_{2max}$. *European Journal of Applied Physiology*, **49**, 1–12.

Leger, L.A., Mercier, D., Gadoury, C. and Lambert, J., 1988, The multistage 20 metre shuttle run test for aerobic fitness. *Journal of Sports Sciences*, **6**, 93–101.

Margaria, R., Aghemo, P. and Rovelli, E., 1966, Measurement of muscular power (anaerobic) in man. *Journal of Applied Physiology*, **21**, 1661–1664.

Martin, A.D., Spenst, L.F., Drinkwater, D.T. and Clarys, J.P., 1990, Anthropometric estimates of muscle mass in men. *Medicine and Science in Sports and Exercise*, **22**, 729–733.

Medbø, J. and Tabata, I., 1986, Relative importance of aerobic and anaerobic energy release during short-lasting exhausting bicycle exercise. *Journal of Applied Physiology*, **67**, 1881–1886.

Medbø, J., Mohn, A., Tabata, I., Bahr, R. and Sejersted, G., 1988, Anaerobic capacity determined by the maximal accumulated oxygen deficit. *Journal of Applied Physiology*, **64**, 50–60.

Morgan, B.E. and Oberlander, M.A., 2001, An examination of injuries in major league soccer. *American Journal of Sports Medicine*, **29**, 426–430.

Nicholas, C.W., Williams, C., Lakomy, H.K.A., Phillips, L., Nowitz, A., 1995, Influence of ingesting a carbohydrate electrolyte solution on endurance capacity during intermittent, high intensity shuttle running. *Journal of Sports Sciences*, **13**, 283–290.

Norton, K., Marfell-Jones, M., Whittingham, N., Kerr, D., Carter, L., Saddington, K. and Gore, C., 2000, Anthropometric assessment protocols. In: *Physiological Tests for Elite Athletes*, Australian Sports Commission (edited by C. Gore), Human Kinetic Publishers, Champaign, IL, pp. 66–85.

Nunome, H., Ikegami, Y., Asai, T. and Sato, Y., 2002, Three dimensional kinetics analysis of in-side and instep soccer kicks. In: *Science and Football IV* (edited by W. Spinks, T. Reilly and A. Murphy), London: Routledge, pp. 27–31.

Oberg, B., Moller, M., Gillquist, J. and Ekstrand, J., 1986, Isokinetic torque levels in soccer players. *International Journal of Sports Medicine*, **7**, 50–53.

Odetoyinbo, K. and Ramsbottom, R., 1995, Aerobic and anaerobic field testing of soccer players. *Journal of Sports Sciences*, **13**, 506.

Puga, N., Ramos, L., Agostinho, J., Lomba, I., Costa, O. and de Freitas, F., 1993, Physical profile of a First Division Portuguese professional football team. In: *Science and Football II* (edited by T. Reilly, J. Clarys and A. Stibbe), London: E & FN Spon, pp. 40–42.

Raastad, T., Høstmark, A.T. and Strømme, S.B., 1997, Omega-3 fatty acid supplementation does not improve maximal aerobic power, anaerobic threshold and running performance in well-trained soccer players. *Scandinavian Journal of Medicine and Science in Sports*, **7**, 25–31.

Rahkila, P. and Luhtanen, P., 1991, Physical fitness profile of Finnish national soccer teams candidates. *Science and Football*, **5**, 30–33.

Raven, P.R., Geltman, L.R., Pollock, M.L., Cooper, K.H., 1976, A physiological evaluation of professional soccer players. *British Journal of Sports Medicine*, **10**, 209–216.

Reilly, T., 1979, *What Research Tells the Coach about Soccer*, American Alliance for Health, Physical Education, Recreation and Dance, Washington, DC.

Reilly, T. and Doran, D., 2003, Fitness assessment. In: *Science and Soccer, 2nd edition* (edited by T. Reilly and A.M. Williams). London: Routledge, pp. 21–46.

Reilly, T. and Gregson, W., 2006, Nutrition for special populations: the referee. *Journal of Sports Sciences*, **25**, 795–801.

Reilly, T. and Holmes, M., 1983, A preliminary analysis of selected soccer skills. *Physical Education Review*, **6**, 64–71.

Reilly, T. and Stirling, A., 1993, Flexibility, warm-up and injuries in mature games players. In: *Kinanthropometry IV* (edited by W. Duquet and J.A.P. Day), London: E & FN Spon, pp.119–123.

Reilly, T., Maughan, R.J. and Hardy, L., 1996, Body fat consensus statement of the Steering Groups of the British Olympic Association. *Sports Exercise and Injury*, **2**, 46–49.

Reilly, T., Bangsbo, J. and Franks, A., 2000a, Anthropometric and physiological predispositions for elite soccer. *Journal of Sports Sciences*, **18**, 669–683.

Reilly, T., Williams, A.M., Nevill, A. and Franks, A., 2000b, A multidisciplinary approach to talent identification in soccer. *Journal of Sports Sciences*, **18**, 695–702.

Sözen, A.B., Akkaya, V., Demirel, S., Kudat, H., Tükek, T., Ünal, M., Beyaz, M., Güven, Ö. and Korkut, F., 2000, Echocardiographic findings in professional league soccer players. *Journal of Sports Medicine and Physical Fitness*, **40**, 150–155.

Strudwick, A., Reilly, T., Doran, D., 2002, Anthropometric and fitness characteristics of elite players in two football codes. *Journal of Sports Medicine and Physical Fitness*, **42**, 239–242.

Suzuki, S., Togari, H., Lsokawa, M., Ohashi, J. and Ohgushi, T., 1988, Analysis of the goalkeeper's diving motion. In: *Science and Football* (edited by T. Reilly, A. Lees, K. Davids and W.J. Murphy), London: E & FN Spon, pp. 468–475.

Svensson, M. and Drust, B., 2005, Testing soccer players. *Journal of Sports Sciences*, **23**, 601–618.

Togari, M. and Takahashi, K., 1977, Study of 'whole-body reaction' in soccer players. *Proceedings of the Department of Physical Education* (College of General Education, University of Tokyo), **11**, 35–41.

Trolle, M., Aagard, P., Simonsen, P., Bangsbo, J. and Klausen, K., 1993, Effects of strength training on kicking performance in soccer. In: *Science and Football II* (edited by T. Reilly, J. Clarys and A. Stibbe), London: E & FN Spon, pp. 95–97.

Tumilty, D., 2000, Protocols for the physiological assessment of male and female soccer players. In: *Physiological Tests for Elite Athletes* (edited by C.J. Gore), Champaign, IL: Human Kinetics, pp. 356–362.

White, J.E., Emery, T.M., Kane, J.E., Groves, R. and Risman, A.B., 1988, Pre-season fitness profiles of professional soccer players. In: *Science and Football* (edited by T. Reilly, A. Lees, K. Davids and W.J. Murphy), London: E & FN Spon, pp. 164–171.

Williams, A.M., Borrie, A., Cable, T., Gilbourne, D., Lees, A., MacLaren, D. and Reilly, T., 1997, *Umbro: Conditioning for Football*. London: TSL Publishing.

Wisløff, U., Helgerud, J. and Hoff, J., 1998, Strength and endurance of elite soccer players. *Medicine and Science in Sports and Exercise*, **30**, 462–467.

Chapter 11

Lifestyle and long-term development

Introduction

Training is a dynamic process and the means by which the individual attempts to realise potential. Physical training is one part of a holistic process which embraces skills acquisition and enhancement, attitude and motivation to improve and gain tactical acumen and game intelligence. There is a necessity for social skills also for the player to fit into a team and participate in group activities. It should be clear that the ideal training programme is geared to individual needs as well as to team performance and accommodates an overview of the whole person.

Training needs do vary with age and between the sexes. Programmes must be tailored to their requirements and capabilities. These considerations change according to the player's stage of development, fitness level and readiness to progress to the next training step. It has been estimated that recruits to soccer academies in England can expect to have completed 10,000 hours of practice before making their debut in the first team. Over this time formal training will have played an increasing role as part of a long-term development process (see Table 11.1).

It is recognised that a long-term development plan is needed to establish a clear path towards excellence in performance in games. The long-term development model of Balyi and Hamilton (1999) provides a framework in which the young player's training programme can be incorporated. It allows for late developers to catch up on their more advanced colleagues and for those who mature early or are more favourably endowed by nature to make fast progress.

A holistic programme places training in the context of the 'whole person', emphasises the role of education in improving personal skills and the inculcation of a healthy lifestyle. Factors such as nutrition, habitual activity and sleep, lifestyle practices (attitude to alcohol and smoking) are all relevant for consideration in this chapter.

The progression of training

The training environment and the guidance available should be appropriate for the age, sex and capabilities of the individual. The progression of the practical

Table 11.1 Characteristics of Football Academy
recruits in England at age 16

- Players started playing at age 6
- Average 10 h/week for 10 years
- Train for 700 h per year
- Total 7,000 h on aggregate
- Anticipate 1st team debut after 10,000 h

Source: Ward and Williams, 2003.

experiences presented to young players must suit their maturational state. A framework for emphasising training priorities for development purposes was provided by Balyi and Hamilton (1999) and is incorporated in Table 11.2. It may be extended or amended to suit specific groups.

Young players may be introduced to 'academy' pathways for development by ages 6–7 years. Up to the ages of eight the emphasis is firmly placed on fun as the boys and girls acquire game skills in the course of play. Ages 9–12 may be geared towards preparation for a later specialisation. Variations of small-sided games include 4 vs 4 and up to 8 vs 8. Years 13–16 may be seen as the 'age of development', during which more formal elements of training are introduced. Ages 17–19 are treated as the 'age of competition' at which technical and mental skills training are a focus of attention.

Platt *et al.* (2001) showed the advantages of a 3-a-side over 5-a-side games for boys aged 12. In the smaller sided game the participants had more touches on the ball, more successful passes and more tackles than when playing 5-a-side. Furthermore they exhibited a higher mean heart rate throughout a 15-min game. Thus the extra benefit extended to the physiological training stimulus as well as the greater opportunity for skill learning.

Some players have an advantage over their peers by virtue of a greater maturational age. These may be training alongside others of higher chronological age if they are to optimise their improvements. The same can apply to young players precocious in talent. A scheme for harmonising components of training with maturation and chronological age should be sensitive to development periods over the entire period of growth (see Figure 11.1). In basic training, a range of activities may be used for improving techniques and fitness individually and in groups from early to late phases of puberty (Stratton *et al.*, 2004a). In 'build-up' training co-ordination and speed occupy a significant part of the training programme. Resistance exercise using body mass is prioritised over more specialised forms of weight-training and loads should not be increased above 25% over this period, the first to second phases of puberty. The 'correcting' phase of training incorporates individually tailored training plans. Loads are increased progressively by 15–20% and time spent training is extended by 5–10% per annum. After this phase, high performance training includes specialist training for strength, speed, endurance and flexibility.

Table 11.2 The long term player development model may be used as a framework for outlining training priorities

Fundamentals 5–11 years	Training to train 11–14 years	Training to compete 14–16 years	Training to win 16–18 years
• Basic skills	• Players 'learn how to train' during this phase. Monitor and individualise training	• Largest changes occur during this phase	• Specialist support used when required including sport science and medicine professionals
• Short duration activities	• Chronological age may not be the best way to categorise players	• Aerobic and anaerobic systems trained for maximum output	• Advanced physical training techniques utilised
• Endurance developed through game play	• Limb growth may require refinement of skill and technique	• Strength training maximised	• Close monitoring to avoid overtraining
• Body awareness activities	• More structured aerobic training	• Gradual progression in training overload	
• Strength developed through hopping and skipping and other body weight exercises	• Short duration anaerobic work • Develop speed and neurological capacity in the warm-up	• Learning how to compete – technical, tactical etc	

Source: Reprinted with permission, from Stratton *et al.*, 2003, p. 88.

Stratton *et al.* (2004b) provided guidelines for use of resistance training in young players. They recommended that resistance exercise can be positive for this population when part of a balanced activity programme. A principle of good practice was that achievement should take second place to the positive health and welfare of young persons which should be the primary outcome of the resistance training. They concluded that quality resistance exercise programmes support natural growth and maturation.

Nutrition

Good nutritional habits may be developed early in life and players selected for specialist training can be encouraged at 'Academy' level to adopt good dietary

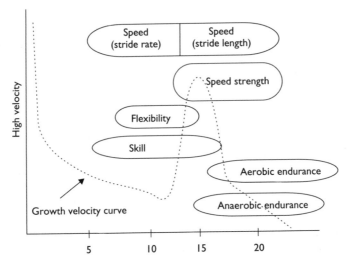

Figure 11.1 The emphasis on different training components of fitness according to chronological age and height velocity.

Source: Reprinted with permission, from Stratton *et al.*, 2004, p. 90.

practices. Nutrition should be part of the 'science support' provided for young players and nowadays there are sports nutritionists linked with most of the major professional soccer clubs. An attention to nutritional preparation is especially important in the build-up to matches, in recovery from matches and in periods of sustained training.

A first principle of nutrition for players is that the energy intake and energy expenditure should be in balance. When weight loss is desired, for example during the early stage of pre-season training, a negative calorie balance must be tolerated. During strenuous training a deficit in the energy–balance equation may occur and the player will not have the energy to perform to his/her capabilities. The training stimulus will therefore be reduced. Besides, low energy levels can cause disturbance to the body's hormonal, metabolic and immune functions (Burke *et al.*, 2006).

The energy in the diet should be distributed in the appropriate amounts of macronutrients – carbohydrate, fat and protein. The diet of soccer players should be rich in carbohydrate, proportionally low in fat and low in protein, typical recommendations being 55–60%, 25–30%, 10–15% respectively for these macronutrients (MacLaren, 2003). Protein intake can be increased during periods of hard training to promote protein synthesis post-exercise and to contribute towards growth processes in young players.

Special attention is directed towards carbohydrate ingestion to promote glycogen storage in preparation for competition. A diet high in carbohydrate can help offset fatigue as muscle glycogen depots are reduced towards the end of the game. Ingestion of carbohydrate soon after exercise is terminated helps in restoring muscle glycogen levels and in countering the immunosuppression that occurs post-exercise. The everyday diet should also reflect a strategic ingestion of carbohydrate and protein prior to and following key training sessions to enhance training adaptations and boost recovery. Nutritional advice is provided in detail for players in a variety of publications, including Williams and Devlin (1994), Burke et al. (2006) and Rosenbloom et al. (2006).

Vitamin and mineral supplements

Many players assume that extra benefits may be derived by adding vitamin and mineral supplements to the normal diet. This view is a result of the content of promotional material from commercial interests. The marketing messages are based on the role of these micronutrients in energy metabolism.

The major physiological functions of vitamins relevant to exercise are shown in Table 11.3. Vitamins act primarily as catalysts for chemical reactions and are either fat soluble or water soluble. Vitamins A, D, E and K are absorbed from the digestive tract bound to fats and stored in the body. Excessive intake of

Table 11.3 The main physiological roles of vitamins in metabolism that are relevant to exercise, with dietary sources of such vitamins listed

Vitamin	Source	Function
A (retinol)	Vegetables, liver, milk, butter	Bone growth, endothelial cells, anti-oxidant
B₁ (thiamine)	Yeast, grains, milk	Carbohydrate and amino acid Metabolism
B₂ (riboflavin)	Green vegetables, wheat germ, milk	Mitochondrial electron transport
B₃ (niacin)	Fish, liver, red meat, peas, beans, nuts	Glycolysis and citric acid cycle
B₆ (pyridoxine)	Fish, liver, yeast, tomatoes	Amino acid synthesis
Folic acid	Liver, green vegetables	Nucleic acid and red blood cell synthesis
B₁₂ (cyanocobalamin)	Liver, red meat, eggs	Red blood cell production, nucleic acid and amino acid metabolism
C (ascorbic acid)	Citrus fruits, tomatoes, green vegetables	Protein metabolism, catecholamine and collagen synthesis, anti-oxidant
D (cholecalciferol)	Fish liver oil, milk, eggs	Calcium homeostasis
E (alpha tocopherol)	Wheat germ, grain, lettuce	Anti-oxidant
H (biotin)	Liver, yeast, eggs	Biosynthetic reactions
K (phylloquinone)	Spinach, vegetable oils, cabbage	Blood clotting mechanisms

these vitamins can lead to toxic accumulations. The B-complex and C vitamins are absorbed from the digestive tract with water and excessive intakes are excreted, largely in urine. Intake of vitamins should be sufficient to achieve the published recommended daily allowances needed for health purposes. Any deficiencies can be identified by means of a standard nutritional analysis such as is conducted by sports nutritionists working with soccer clubs. Typically, a well-balanced diet avoids the need for vitamin and mineral supplementation (Fogelholm, 1994).

Minerals are inorganic substances that are essential for normal cellular functions and account for about 4% of body weight. Mineral compounds that can dissociate into the body as ions are known as electrolytes. Macrominerals are those that are needed in excess of 100 mg per day and include calcium and phosphorous. Microminerals are trace elements needed in smaller amounts, including for example iodine, selenium and zinc. In most cases supplementation is advised by professionals, for example when a deficiency is identified in female players experiencing heavy losses of blood during menses.

Vitamins C and E act as anti-oxidants, countering the effects of reactive oxygen species known as free radicals that are produced during exercise. When the production of free radicals exceeds the capacity of the muscle's own anti-oxidant defence mechanisms, the muscle cell may be damaged. Anti-oxidant substances are marketed for reducing the effects of cellular ageing and include beta-carotene, melatonin, selenium, ubiquinone and other substances. There is no consistent evidence that these anti-oxidant substances add to the body's own defences, notably superoxide dismutase. It seems that anti-oxidant activity may be enhanced as an adaptation to training, especially the stretch–shortening exercises used in plyometric training for soccer.

Ergogenic aids

Supplements are subjectively attractive to players who are constantly in search of means to make them better athletes. A major priority is that their performance is not impaired by a nutritional deficiency and therefore the need for a well balanced diet is essential. The next step is to establish whether there are dietary substances that can enhance performance, over and above the normal levels needed for maintaining health. These substances are regarded as ergogenic aids.

Among the very many supplements available for players to purchase off-the-shelf, a substantial proportion has been found to be contaminated by androgenic prohormones that are banned by the soccer authorities. Three requirements were described by Hespel and co-authors (2006) for a supplement to be recommended for use:

1   the supplement must work in that it has to impact significantly on factors that influence performance;

2   it must not produce any adverse effects on the health of the player;
3   it must not contain any substance that could result in a positive drug test.

Creatine is one substance that has gained in use in field games players since the initial studies demonstrating that ingestion of creatine improved performance in repeated short sprints and is a legal supplement (Hultman *et al.*, 1996). Creatine is a naturally occurring nitrogenous molecule mainly found in skeletal muscles after being metabolised in the liver. It is utilised in anaerobic metabolism in the resynthesis of ATP and is reversibly phosphorylated by the enzyme creatine kinase. Stores tend to be lower in vegetarians than in meat eaters, red meat being the main source of creatine in the diet (Williams, 2000).

The regimen commonly employed for creatine loading is 5 g taken at equally spaced intervals 4 times each day. This loading is maintained for four weeks after which a maintenance load of 2 g per day is used for another month. There is evidence that creatine supplementation can increase power output during maximal sprints with short recovery pauses in between (Terjung *et al.*, 2000). Many of the supportive studies have been conducted using cycle ergometry as the mode of exercise, with body weight supported on the ergometer. Mujika *et al.* (2000) showed that creatine loading improved the performance of soccer players in a series of repeated sprints but 'intermittent endurance' performance was unaffected. Creatine loading causes an increase in body mass, sometimes up to 2 kg, which may be counterproductive in locomotory activities. Besides, the pattern of sprinting during soccer play differs from the repetitive sprints in experimental studies. It is likely therefore that the main benefit of creatine is in a training context where the focus is on developing muscle strength and power. Creatine also has a use in combination with carbohydrate in the resynthesis of glycogen after competition.

Caffeine is another substance that is sometimes used for its ergogenic properties. It has a stimulating effect on the central nervous system, causes a rise in heart rate and an increase in arousal. It can therefore have a use in a training context, particularly where strenuous efforts are involved such as lifting heavy weights. Caffeine also has metabolic effects, more powerful than the other methylxanthines such as aminphyline and theophylline (found in tea). It can promote the mobilisation of fat from adipose tissue stores, spare muscle glycogen and increase endurance. Performance towards the end of a 90-min soccer game would therefore be improved.

The dose of caffeine that has proved effective is 5–6 $mg \cdot kg^{-1}$ body mass, amounting to the equivalent of two large mugs of thick coffee taken before exercise (Costill *et al.*, 1978). Caffeine is now available in the form of a gel for endurance athletes. Frequent intake of such relatively high doses can result in desensitisation so that its ergogenic properties become reduced. Players may need to decrease their normal intake of drinks containing caffeine for 3–4 days before using caffeine for enhancing endurance performances.

The ingestion of caffeine may have no additional metabolic effects when co-ingested with carbohydrate prior to sustained exercise. Jacobson *et al.* (2001) showed that carbohydrate ingestion 1 h before continuous exercise improved subsequent time-trial performance compared with fat ingestion. Combining caffeine (6 mg·kg^{-1}) with either carbohydrate or fat had no *additional* effect on either substrate utilisation or exercise performance. In conditions where players are already carbohydrate loaded, the benefits of caffeine may be limited to its effects on the nervous system.

Alcohol

Alcohol is both a drug and a fuel for providing energy. As a drug it can become addictive and over the years, various high-profile soccer players have developed a dependence on alcohol. It can have adverse effects on health, affecting cardiac and skeletal muscle and the liver in particular. In the past, it has been implicated in shortening the careers of a number of professional players.

Traditionally alcohol in the form of whisky was used to reduce anxiety in players as they left the dressing room to take part in competition. The amount involved is unlikely to have any major adverse effect on physiological responses to exercise. The availability of ethanol in this context was known as 'team spirit'. As the ethanol molecule is relatively small, it penetrates the blood–brain barrier and influences neurotransmitter pathways. Its effect on dopamine release is related to pleasurable sensations whereas the fall-off in noradrenaline after drinking tends to give rise to a transcent depression (see Reilly, 2005). This depressant effect after heavy drinking is most likely to impair motivation in training the morning afterwards.

As a source of energy, alcohol contains 7 kcal·g^{-1} (29.3 kJ·g^{-1}), compared to values of 4 for protein and carbohydrate and 9 for fat. Typically, wine contains about 12% alcohol and so a 1-l bottle will have an energy content of 840 kcal (3516 kJ). The concentrations in beer (~5%) and whisky (~40%) represent variations in the calorific load attributable to drinking. These energy intakes can be influential when weight-control programmes are employed.

The value of alcohol as a fuel source is limited since it is metabolised mainly in the liver and at the fixed rate of about 100 mg·kg^{-1} body weight per hour. For an 80-kg player, this value would amount to 8 g of alcohol hourly. The energy cannot be used by active skeletal muscle so that exercise does not hasten the elimination of alcohol from the blood. Blood alcohol concentrations tend to peak about 45 min after ingestion and the effects are more pronounced if the stomach is empty at the time of ingestion. Performance in skills related to sports are adversely affected when blood alcohol concentrations are 0.05% (mg·100 ml^{-1}), a value below the legal driving limit in the United Kingdom (Reilly, 1997).

Acute effects of alcohol depend on the blood alcohol concentration that is induced (Table 11.4). The adverse effects on performance would apply to training contexts, whether weight-training, endurance sessions or skills practices

Table 11.4 Demonstrable effects of alcohol at different concentrations in blood

Concentration level (mg/100 ml blood)	Effects
30	Enhanced sense of well-being; retarded simple reaction-time; impaired hand–eye co-ordination
60	Mild loss of social inhibition; impaired judgement
90	Marked loss of social inhibition; co-ordination reduced; noticeably under the influence
120	Apparent clumsiness; loss of physical control; tendency towards extreme responses; definite drunkenness is noted
150	Erratic behaviour; slurred speech; staggering gait
180	Loss of control of voluntary activity; impaired vision

Source: Reilly, 1997.

are being conducted. The direct effects on metabolic processes are also likely to cause impairment in endurance performance. Alcohol lowers muscle glycogen at rest, may induce a reduction in glucose output from the spleen, decrease the potential contribution of energy from liver gluconeogenesis and lead to a decline in blood glucose. Its diuretic effect could compromise thermoregulation, for example if playing in hot conditions the day after drinking heavily. It can also inhibit glycogen resynthesis if taken after strenuous training or a match and food ingestion is delayed.

In moderation, alcohol ingestion the night beforehand is unlikely to have a deleterious effect on the performance of players in training and competition. It has a place in social settings, suitably timed so as not to interfere with soccer engagements. Nevertheless, alcohol ingestion is not essential and is shunned in many cultures. Especially in young players, an inculcation of sound dietary practices and a sensible approach to drinking alcohol, are advocated.

Cigarette smoking

Smoking cigarettes is now accepted as a major health hazard. As the tobacco in the cigarette burns, it generates many carcinogenic compounds which implies a link between smoking and cancer. Smoking also has an acute vasoconstrictive effect and heavy smoking leads to chronically poor blood flow to the limbs and hardening of the peripheral arteries. Smoke also paralyses the cilia in the respiratory passages so that their filtering role is ineffective and the individual becomes more susceptible to respiratory tract infections. These adverse consequences of smoking on health underline that tobacco should have no place in the lifestyle of a soccer player. Even passive inhalation from being in the company of smokers has similar effects to those in smokers. About 20% of the smoke exhaled in public places can be recirculated in passive inhalation.

The major substance in cigarette smoke that alters physiological capacity is carbon monoxide (CO). Carbon monoxide reduces the oxygen transport capacity of the blood by combining preferentially with haemoglobin (Hb), taking the place of O_2 in the bloodstream and impairing aerobic exercise performance. The affinity of Hb for CO is more than two hundred times that of O_2. There is about 4% CO in tobacco smoke, so 10–20 cigarettes per day results in a blood COHb concentration of 4.9%. Smoking 15–25 cigarettes a day increases this figure to 6.3% and 30–40 each day brings the level to 9.3%. Adverse effects only become obvious during exercise when the need for O_2 by the active muscles is increased. After smoking, it may take 24 h or more for blood CO levels to return to normal.

The addictive ingredient in cigarette smoke is nicotine. It is a cholinergic agonist and acts as a brain stimulant. Its secondary effects include a rise in plasma corticosteroids and an increase in the central release of noradrenaline. These responses are also associated with stress and arousal, reactions that the soccer player should have no need to rely upon.

Sleep

Sleep is essential for maintaining normal homeostasis. One school of thought relates the need for sleep to the restitution of the body's tissues. An alternative view is that the need for sleep is specific to nerve cells – the so-called brain restitution theory of sleep. Sleep also seems to be important in maintaining immune status intact. The need is most apparent when sleep is deprived or disturbed as may occur after travelling across time zones, staying in conditions that are too hot or noisy.

Whilst the average sleep of the 20–30 year old is about 7–8 h each night, there is a large variation between individuals both in the need for sleep and in the amount taken. Some individuals feel uneasy unless they sleep soundly for 8–9 h and place a priority on their sleeping arrangements, others take much less sleep nightly but may have a persistent 'sleep debt'. The existence of a 'sleep debt' can be quantified by how easily the individual falls asleep in controlled conditions during the day.

Brain states can be monitored during sleep by electroencephalography (EEG). Traces from EEGs demonstrate cycles of about 90 min, each cycle containing stages known as rapid eye movement (REM) and non-REM sleep. Non-REM sleep is further classified into stages 1–4. It is easy to awaken individuals from REM sleep but more difficult during non-REM sleep. Consequently, players who doze in the morning rather than arise from bed may slip into a further 90-min cycle of sleep which may in fact do them little extra good.

Professional soccer players tend to get adequate sleep when the whole week is considered. The timing is often inconsistent, players staying up late especially after an evening match away from home. In such events it is difficult to get to sleep since arousal levels are elevated above normal after a game and players still mentally recall details from the match completed earlier. A conscious mental effort to relax following a game may be needed and this facility differs from individual to individual.

Pre-match anxiety can disrupt sleep the night before playing. Players man complain that they were unable to sleep but may have spent short periods asleep during the nights, which do provide a restorative function. In such cases a short nap during the day for restorative purposes could be encouraged. A brief afternoon nap prior to an evening kick-off can promote a release from pre-match anxiety and function as a 'power nap'. There is a natural tendency to drowse in the mid-afternoon which is generally referred to as a 'post-lunch dip' (Reilly et al., 1997).

Muscle performance may be unaffected by sleep loss, at least as shown in experiments of partial sleep deprivation where subjects are permitted only 2.5–3 h in sleep a night (Reilly and Deykin, 1983). The performance tasks in these studies have tended to be maximum efforts over short duration. Complex tasks and decision-making, especially if demanded over a prolonged period such as 90 min, deteriorate with the duration of the task. Thus, concentration during a match following nights of disrupted sleep requires a distinct motivational drive from the player concerned. It is most likely that lapses of concentration will occur more frequently during a game than if sleep quality had been normal.

Effects of partial sleep loss accumulate and become increasingly evident with consecutive nights of progressive sleep disruption. Effects on training performance are more pronounced as the training session progresses in duration as it becomes difficult for the player to maintain motivation (Reilly and Piercy, 1994). A decline in the ability to concentrate is likely to promote errors in long training sessions with the consequence also of increased injury risk. Players with a 'nightclub' lifestyle are therefore unlikely to gain optimal benefits from training.

It has been possible to play soccer for days without sleep, although this feat was achieved indoors and at a low intensity. For over 91 h the level of play showed a cyclic change that corresponded to the circadian rhythm in core temperature of the players (Reilly and Walsh, 1981). The appearance of psychotic-like symptoms, particularly following the second night without sleep, makes meaningful play difficult under such circumstances. Clearly such a regime is not conducive towards serious soccer performance and is more closely associated with events organised for purposes of charity.

Overview

A personal commitment to training and competition is required of players for a soccer team to be successful as a playing unit. Regard for others in the social context of the team and personal discipline in one's own lifestyle are espoused by the mentors of young players as part of their development. Positive attitudes are advocated towards avoidance of excesses such as use of alcohol or recreational drugs and erratic sleeping patterns. The adoption of appropriate dietary practices and use of high-performance nutrition are necessary aspects of the commitment to training and preparing for matches.

References

Balyi, I. and Hamilton, A.E., 1999, Planning of training and performance. *British Columbia's Coaching Perspective*, **3**, 6–11.

Burke, L.M., Loucks, A.B. and Broad, N., 2006, Energy and carbohydrate for training and recovery. *Journal of Sports Sciences*, **24**, 675–685.

Costill, D.L., Dalsky, G.P. and Fink, W.J., 1978, Effects of caffeine ingestion on metabolism and exercise performance. *Medicine and Science in Sports and Exercise*, **10**, 155–158.

Fogelholm, M., 1994, Vitamins, minerals and supplementation in soccer. *Journal of Sports Sciences*, **12** (Special Issue), Summer, S23–S27.

Hespel, P., Maughan, R.J. and Greenhaff, P., 2006, Dietary supplements for soccer. *Journal of Sports Sciences*, **24**, 749–761.

Hultman, E., Soderland, K., Timmons, J.A., Cederblad, G. and Greenhaff, P.L., 1996, Muscle creatine loading in men. *Journal of Applied Physiology*, **81**, 232–237.

Jacobson, T.L., Febbraio, M.A., Arkinstall, M.J. and Hawley, J.A., 2001, Effect of caffeine co-ingested with carbohydrate or fat on metabolism and performance in endurance-trained men. *Experimental Physiology*, **86**, 137–144.

MacLaren, D., 2003, Nutrition. In: *Science and Soccer* (edited by T. Reilly and A.M. Williams), London: Routledge, pp. 73–95.

Mujika, I., Padilla, S., Ibanez, J., Izquierdo, M. and Gorostiaga, E., 2000, Creative supplementation and sprint performance in soccer players. *Medicine and Science in Sports and Exercise*, **32**, 518–525.

Platt, D., Maxwell, A., Horn, R., Williams, M. and Reilly, T., 2001, Physiological and technical analysis of 3 v 3 and 5 v 5 youth football matches. *Insight: the FA Coaches Association Journal*, **4**(4), 23–24.

Reilly, T., 1997, Alcohol: its influence in sport and exercise. In: *The Clinical Pharmacology of Sport and Exercise* (edited by T. Reilly and M. Orme), Amsterdam: Elsevier, pp. 281–292.

Reilly, T., 2005, Alcohol, anti-anxiety drugs and alcohol. In: *Drugs in Sport, 4th Edition* (edited by D.R. Mottram), London: Routledge, pp. 258–287.

Reilly, T. and Deykin, T., 1983, Effect of partial sleep loss on subjective states, psychomotor and physical performance tests. *Journal of Human Movement Studies*, **9**, 157–170.

Reilly, T. and Piercy, M., 1994, The effect of partial sleep deprivation on weight-lifting performance. *Ergonomics*, **37**, 106–115.

Reilly, T. and Walsh, T.J., 1981, Physiological, psychological and performance measures during an endurance record for 5-a-side soccer play. *British Journal of Sports Medicine*, **15**, 122–128.

Reilly, T., Atkinson, G. and Waterhouse, J., 1997, *Biological Rhythms and Exercise*. Oxford: Oxford University Press.

Rosenbloom, C.A., Loucks, A.B. and Ekblom, B., 2006, Nutrition and football's special populations: the female player and the youth player. *Journal of Sports Sciences*, **24**, 783–793.

Stratton, G., Reilly, T., Williams, A.M. and Richardson, D., 2004a, *Youth Soccer: From Science to Performance*. London: Routledge.

Stratton, G., Jones, M., Fox, K.R., Tolfrey, K., Harris, J., Maffulli, N., Lee, M. and Frostick, S.P., 2004b, BASES Position Statement on Guidelines for Resistance Exercise in Young People. *Journal of Sports Sciences*, **22**, 383–390.

Terjung, R.L., Clarkson, P.M., Eichner, E.R., Greenhaff, P.L., Hespel, P., Israel, R.G., Kraemer, W.T., Meyer, R.A., Sprett, L.L., Tarnopolsky, M.A., Wagenmakers, A.J. and Williams, M.H., 2000, American College of Sports Medicine roundtable. The physiological and health effects of oral creatine supplementation. *Medicine and Science in Sports and Exercise*, **32**(3), 706–717.

Ward, P. and Williams, A.M., 2003, Perceptual and cognitive skill development in soccer: the multidimensional nature of expert performance. *Journal of Sport and Exercise Psychology*, **25**, 93–111.

Williams, C. and Devlin, J., 1994, *Foods, Nutrition and Sports Performance*. London: E. & F.N. Spon.

Williams, M.H., 2000, The physiological and health effects of oral creatine supplementation. *Medicine and Science in Sports and Exercise*, **32**, 706–717.

Index